Great Desserts of the South

Great Desserts of the South

By Mary Leigh Furrh
and Jo Barksdale

Calligraphy by DORIS ANN SPELL

PELICAN PUBLISHING COMPANY
GRETNA 1988

Library of Congress Cataloging-in-Publication Data

Furrh, Mary Leigh.
   Great desserts of the South.

   Includes index.
   1. Desserts.   2. Cookery, American — Southern style.
I. Barksdale, Jo.   II. Title.
TX773.F87   1988   641.8′6′0975   88-9825
ISBN 0-88289-682-2

Manufactured in the United States of America
Published by Pelican Publishing Company, Inc.
1101 Monroe Street, Gretna, Louisiana 70053

To our grandchildren — James Brooke Furrh IV and Jimmie Lauren Wilson — who were born during the writing of this book and to Jo's grandson and favorite cookie tester, Rocky Clark.

Contents

Preface

The Southern sweet tooth is a powerful force. It prods a Southerner's memory, making him recall nostalgically that childhood desserts were the best food he ever tasted. It dominates Southern cookbooks to the point that desserts often comprise half the recipes. It inspires Southern hosts and hostesses to serve Northern visitors their most mouth-watering confections, sending them home proclaiming the wonders of Pecan Pie and Floating Island.

Some say we inherited our love of sweets from English ancestors. Whatever the reason, Southern cooks learned long ago that a sumptuous dessert can lift an ordinary meal to celestial heights, whether it is Strawberry Shortcake after Sunday dinner, tea cakes to top off a tailgate picnic, or Bananas Foster to celebrate a festive brunch.

In writing *Great Desserts of the South*, our goal was to assemble the very best regional sweets in a single volume. If you long to recreate your grandmother's Hummingbird Cake but have misplaced her recipe, look in our cake chapter. If you are curious about the origins of chess pie, investigate our section on pies. If you need a new company dish, Ann Fournet's Chocolate Terrine will please your guests. So will Jeff Davis Pie and Cabinet Pudding—marvelous old desserts that are unfamiliar to most.

We collected recipes from many sources: family files, famous Southern restaurants, generous friends, and cherished, out-of-print cookbooks. Most, however, are our own versions of Southern classics. When testing, we were amazed by the delicious flavors of the older, often neglected desserts—Hot Caramel Dumplings, Shrewsberry Cakes, Blackberry Roly-Poly, and Date Loaf Candy. We hope you will join us in resurrecting them. But don't overlook the old favorites—Coconut Cake, Ambrosia, Charlotte Russe—all are priceless friends.

We researched the origins of many well-known favorites and were amused by their history. Who would have thought Lady Baltimore Cake played a role in a novel or that fudge making once flourished in a girls' dormitory? Before trying our recipes, we give you a warning: Southern desserts are highly addictive. Expect to have a sweet tooth for the rest of your life.

MARY LEIGH FURRH
and JO BARKSDALE

Acknowledgments

We want to thank Shirley Tate for her invaluable help in typing mountains of material, Doris Ann Spell for contributing the calligraphy for our chapter dividers, and Mary Leigh's husband, Jim Furrh, for his counsel and encouragement. We appreciatively acknowledge Craig Claiborne, Joe Middleton, Winifred Cheney, and the chefs of Southern restaurants and inns who graciously contributed recipes.

Our special gratitude goes to our friends who generously shared research material and treasured family recipes. And to Emily Barksdale and Allen Moore, whose wedding was the occasion for testing our White Chocolate Coeur à la Crème. Thanks also to the rest of our children who were our tasters: Brooke, Shelley, Roy, and Leigh Furrh, Jayne and Katherine Barksdale, Bethany Clark, and Mary Wilson.

Great Desserts of the South

Dining room of Mary Washington House, home of Mary Ball Washington, mother of George Washington, in Fredericksburg, Virginia.

Introduction

$\mathcal{D}$esserts have been popular in the South since the first settlers arrived in Virginia with visions of English puddings and double-crusted pies. By the early 1700s, the colonies were on the brink of establishing a civilized society in which the proper preparation and serving of food were important. Native fruits, nuts, dairy products, imported seasonings, and extracts were used to create desserts which were made by European rules but had a distinctly American flavor.

For many years, sugar was impractical and costly to use. It was sold in hard cones sometimes weighing ten pounds and requiring tedious chipping to produce usable crystals. It was so expensive that only the wealthy could afford it. Consequently, molasses was the usual sweetener.

Williamsburg was the first center of festive entertaining in the South. The seat of the state's government, it was the scene of numerous balls and parties when the Assembly was in session. The hosts' English heritage was obvious at these affairs, which featured lavish assortments of creams, jellies, molds, and puddings, placed side by side on a separate table from the entrées.

The French influence appeared when Thomas Jefferson returned from serving as minister to France with recipes for Charlotte Russe, meringues, and other French sweets. Virginia hostesses welcomed these pretty delicacies and added them to the spectacular displays on their dessert tables. Indeed, looks were so important to colonial cooks that they often tinted desserts with spinach or beet juice, oblivious to the strange tastes that resulted.

Further south, Charleston soon became another important center of fine cuisine. The French Huguenot influence united with the English to popularize soufflés, boiled custards, and whipped cream creations. The city's humidity prevented pie crusts from turning out well, so recipes using lady fingers came into vogue. During the slavery period and later, when servants were plentiful, it was customary in Charleston for the lady of the house to make the dessert. This was particularly true of cake making — a time-consuming job requiring spices to be hand-ground, flour to be dried, and butter to be washed free of salt. A reputation for making good cakes was a source of pride.

Famous Charleston benne wafers owe their origins to black cooks who brought benne seeds (sesame seeds) from Africa, but the black influence is more evident in New Orleans desserts than in those of Virginia and South Carolina. Creative slaves used their talents for combining spices to flavor Creole sweets as well as other Louisiana foods.

Before the Civil War, New Orleans was a sophisticated city where luxury-loving Creoles enjoyed a fashionable social life highlighted by elaborate masked balls and stylish dinners. Planters from River Road plantations often owned town houses in the Vieux Carré, where they spent the winter attending operas and plays and revelling in the city's fast-paced social scene. Space was at a premium and houses were joined together directly on the sidewalks. Street vendors were a familiar sight on French Quarter streets, especially the pralinières who sold Pralines and the Calas women who hawked their spicy breakfast cakes on cool mornings.

The Mississippi River was the great thoroughfare of the middle South. Imported foods were shipped upstream with French furniture and Italian mantels to the mansions of the planter aristocracy along the River Road and in Natchez. Before 1830, cotton was king and Natchez boasted more millionaires than any other city in the United States except New York. Setting a fine table was a top priority with wealthy Natchezians, and elegant parties featuring sumptuous desserts took place.

In rural areas on the Mississippi, plantation life was similar to that throughout the South. A tremendous amount of cooking was necessary to feed the owners' families and slaves plus a constant flow of visitors. Distances between towns were great and inns were scarce; travelers stopped at plantations unannounced to spend the night and often lingered for weeks. The strain on household budgets could be severe: George Washington and Thomas Jefferson suffered financial difficulties brought on by the continual influx of visitors to Mount Vernon and Monticello.

Dinner was served in mid-afternoon on most plantations and the variety and amount of food was staggering. Diners had several choices of pies, puddings, and custards, and they consumed as many servings as they pleased. In early evening, a light meal similar to English tea was presented with cookies, cakes, and tea breads. The constant cooking kept mistress and slave in the kitchen for hours.

Because plantations were self-sufficient entities, the planter's wife was usually an excellent manager, who was unlike the frivolous creature portrayed in popular novels. She found it necessary to practice strict economy and make do with food raised on the land. Her mentor was her black cook — a genius at improvisation. The women became adept at turning plantation-grown sweet potatoes, fruit, nuts, and dairy products into tasty desserts, using recipes from the few available cookbooks or creating them as they went along.

Resourcefulness was also evident in the pioneer states of Kentucky, Tennessee, and Texas. Old cookbooks reveal that pies were the most popular desserts on the frontier. They were made with whatever the hardy settlers had on hand: vinegar, jam, raisins, and fruit. Inventive cooks worked wonders with puddings, seasoning them with spices and creating sauces flavored with spirits.

The Shakers, a religious group named for the dance they performed as part of their ritual, made an outstanding contribution to Kentucky cuisine. In the nineteenth century, the Shakers formed a community near Harrodsburg where men and women lived on separate sides of the same buildings and practiced celibacy. In spite of their strict religious beliefs, they ate well. The sect is particularly remembered for the lemon pie recipe which appears at the beginning of our pie section.

The Civil War brought the South to its knees and the harsh realities of Reconstruction dismissed entertaining as a trivial concern. Even in such dire circumstances, Southerners found comfort in getting together with friends for simple parties where the only refreshments were inexpensive sweets. When prosperity finally returned, Southern hospitality was evident on a less elaborate scale. The glory years of the antebellum South were gone forever.

The dawn of the twentieth century brought enormous improvements in labor-saving tools and packaged ingredients. Mechanical eggbeaters and flour sifters were early inventions that facilitated cake making, but, today, mixers and food processors make fast work of a job that formerly took all day. Baking powder, canned coconut, and condensed milk were greeted with joy by early twentieth century cooks who would be amazed by the number of ingredients that come in cans today. Perhaps the greatest boon to dessert makers was the invention of the modern refrigerator. Now, pies and molds can finish "cooking" without the cook's constant attention.

The great desserts of the South will always be vital elements of Southern hospitality. They are the logical endings to family dinners and the anticipated climax of elegant parties. They are as old-fashioned as ambrosia at Christmas and as up-to-date as America's current interest in back-to-basics cooking. No matter how homogeneous our society becomes, they will remain symbolic of the South.

Cakes

The family dining room at Mount Vernon, home of
President George Washington, near Washington, D.C.

Wedding Cake

1 pound of sweet butter
1 pound of sugar
Allspice, cloves, and cinnamon
1 coffeecupful of molasses
3 pounds of dry flour
1 pound of almonds, blanched
12 eggs
1 wine glass of wine
1 wine glass of brandy
2 pounds of stoned raisins
3 pounds of currants
1 pound of citron

Stir the butter and sugar to a cream. Add the spices to the molasses and steep gently twenty minutes. Mix all ingredients together (except citron), adding the fruit last; it should be well floured. Butter a sheet of paper and lay it in the pan. Lay in some slices of citron, then a layer of the mixture, then of citron, etc., till the pan is nearly full. Bake for three to four hours in a tolerably hot oven, and with a steady heat. Let it cool in the oven and ice when cold.

*C*akes are the ultimate Southern dessert. The elegant creations are especially in evidence at Thanksgiving and Christmas when tables groan beneath platters of delicate Coconut Cake, crunchy Texas Toasted Pecan Cake, and rich Fruitcake. Cakes are important to other celebrations such as Mardi Gras when the colorful Kings' Cake plays an essential role in the festivities. The yeasty, ring-shaped dessert is decorated with sugar crystals tinted with brilliant carnival colors — purple, green, and gold. Traditionally, a bean or pecan half is tucked inside and the finder is named king of the next party.

Cakes appear frequently throughout Southern history. George Washington's mother, Mary Ball Washington, was among our first cakemakers. She served fresh-baked gingerbread, accompanied by a glass of Madeira, to General Lafayette when he visited her at Fredericksburg. Showy Lord and Lady Baltimore Cakes are thought to have been named for the third Lord Baltimore and his Lady, who arrived in 1661 from England to govern the land which later became Maryland. Writer Owen Wister became so enamored with the taste of Lady Baltimore Cake that he named his novel *Lady Baltimore* in 1906. The moist, fruit-and-nut-filled Lane Cake, named for Emma Rylander Lane of Clayton, Alabama, became a sensation in 1898. Mrs. Lane published the recipe in her cookbook, *Some Good Things to Eat*. It has been called the "Southern Belle" of cakes.

Southerners are prone to associate cake making with love and friendly concern. We appear at our new neighbor's door with welcoming squares of Mississippi Mud, applaud a baby's arrival with slices of Hummingbird, cheer sick friends with soothing Lemon Cheese, and comfort grieving families with consoling Caramel. Whether the occasion is happy or sad, making someone a cake is a Southerner's way of saying, "I care."

ALICE REILLY'S SECRET CARAMEL ICING

A friend shares this fabulous frosting for the first time

½ **pint heavy cream**
2 **cups sugar**
⅛ **teaspoon salt**
½ **cup sugar, caramelized**
⅔ **stick margarine**
1 **teaspoon vanilla**

Combine cream, 2 cups sugar, and salt in a saucepan. Bring to a boil; turn heat to low. Meanwhile, caramelize ½ cup sugar in a heavy skillet over low heat. When sugar mixture is light brown and transparent, slowly add to cream mixture, stirring constantly with a spoon or wire whisk. Cook until 236° (soft ball stage) on candy thermometer. Remove from stove; add margarine; return to heat and cook again to 236°. Remove from heat and cool 5 to 10 minutes. Add vanilla. It probably will be spreadable, but if not, let stand a few more minutes. Icing will not be stiff but becomes harder after spreading. Ice top and sides of Golden Cake below. Serves 15 to 18.

For many years, Alice Reilly of Jackson, Mississippi, has used this recipe to make grooms' cakes for her family and friends. She bakes four 9 x 13 inch cakes and makes two batches of caramel icing, doubling each icing recipe. After spreading two cakes with icing, and topping each with another cake to form layers, she places them side by side and frosts them as if they were one cake. They may be frozen. On the wedding day, she decorates them with fruit or fresh flowers.

GOLDEN CAKE

1 **cup butter**
2 **cups sugar**
4 **eggs, separated**
3 **cups cake flour, sifted**
1 **tablespoon baking powder**
½ **teaspoon salt**
1 **cup milk**
1½ **teaspoons vanilla**

Cream butter and sugar until light. Beat egg yolks well and add to mixture, creaming thoroughly. Sift together cake flour, baking powder, and salt. Add to batter alternately with milk, scraping sides of bowl frequently. Add vanilla. Beat egg whites until stiff and fold into batter. Grease and flour a 9 x 13 inch pan and fill two-thirds full with mixture. Bake at 350° for 35 to 40 minutes.

𝒰se large eggs in all recipes unless otherwise specified.

CRIS BURNS' CARAMEL CAKE

The ultimate caramel cake with caramel icing

CARAMEL SYRUP

1 cup sugar
1 cup hot water

Melt sugar over medium heat in an iron skillet. Slowly add hot water and simmer 5 to 10 minutes, stirring occasionally with a wooden spoon.

1 cup butter (no substitute)
1½ cups sugar
5 eggs, separated
2½ cups flour
¾ cup milk
1 teaspoon vanilla
6 tablespoons caramel syrup
3 teaspoons baking powder

Cream butter and sugar, saving 5 tablespoons of sugar for later use. Add beaten egg yolks. Mix in 2 cups flour alternately with milk. Beat well. Add vanilla and 6 tablespoons caramel syrup. Then add remaining ½ cup flour and baking powder. Fold in egg whites, beaten with remaining 5 tablespoons of sugar. Bake in buttered tube pan 40 to 45 minutes in 325° oven until done.

ICING

2½ cups sugar
1 stick butter
1 cup milk
½ teaspoon vanilla

Combine sugar, butter, and milk in a saucepan. Place candy thermometer on pan. Cook over medium heat until it comes to a boil. Add remainder of caramel syrup and cook to the soft ball stage on candy thermometer. Remove from heat; cool; add vanilla. Beat with a hand mixer or wooden spoon until spreading consistency. If it gets too thick, add a little cream. Ice the cooled cake.

To grease pans, put butter in a small saucepan and place on the back of a warm stove. When melted, salt will settle to the bottom; butter is then clarified. Just before putting in batter, brush with butter, dredge pans thoroughly with flour, invert, and shake pan to remove all excess flour.

CHOCOLATE-CHOCOLATE-CHOCOLATE CAKE

From the Pirate's House restaurant in Savannah, Georgia

¾ cup butter
5 eggs, separated
2½ cups sugar
4 ounces unsweetened baking chocolate, melted
2½ cups sifted flour
1 teaspoon baking soda
1 cup buttermilk
1 teaspoon vanilla

Have butter and eggs at room temperature. Line bottoms of 3 8-inch round cake pans with wax paper; grease paper and flour. Preheat oven to 350°. Cream butter and sugar until light and fluffy. Beat in egg yolks one at a time; beat in melted chocolate. Sift flour and baking soda together. Beat in alternately with buttermilk, starting and ending with flour. Beat in vanilla. Beat egg whites until stiff but not dry. Beat one-fourth of the egg whites into chocolate mixture to lighten it, then fold chocolate mixture into egg whites gently but thoroughly. The chocolate batter will be very heavy and won't want to cooperate, but be firm. Divide batter among pans; smooth tops and bake for 30 to 35 minutes, until tops spring back when lightly touched and cakes shrink from sides of pans. Cool on wire racks and turn out. You may have to slip a finger under the wax paper to get it started. Fill and ice. Serves 12 or more.

FILLING

½ cup sugar
3 tablespoons flour
Pinch of salt
1 egg
2 ounces unsweetened chocolate, melted
1 cup milk
1 tablespoon butter
½ teaspoon vanilla extract

Mix dry ingredients. Whisk in egg until smooth. Melt chocolate in milk in a heavy saucepan, stirring constantly. Gradually pour milk into egg mixture, whisking rapidly and constantly. Return mixture to saucepan and cook, stirring constantly with a wooden spoon, until mixture thickens and comes to a boil. Remove from heat; beat in butter and vanilla. Pour into a bowl, place a piece of plastic wrap directly on the surface of the filling, and refrigerate until cool. Use between layers of cake.

ICING

2 ounces unsweetened baking chocolate
⅓ cup butter
1 teaspoon flour
1 cup milk
2 cups sugar
1 teaspoon vanilla extract

Melt chocolate and butter in a large, heavy saucepan over low heat, stirring constantly. Dissolve flour in part of the milk; add milk, flour and sugar to chocolate, bring to a boil, stirring frequently, and boil until mixture reaches soft ball stage on a candy thermometer (234°). Remove from heat, stir in vanilla, and beat with an electric mixer until icing becomes just thick enough to spread. Do not let it harden too much. If icing does become too hard, beat in a little milk. Ice entire outside of cake. Dip spatula or knife in hot water to smooth icing.

Note: Don't let the length of this recipe intimidate you. For true chocolate lovers, it is well worth the effort.

This recipe is from the Pirate's House in Savannah, Georgia. The restaurant is located in a building which was originally an inn for visiting seamen, and was built in the mid-1700s. It is recognized by the American Museum Society as an authentic house museum.

RED VELVET CAKE

From Shirley McConnell — a food specialist from Pensacola, Florida

1½ cups sugar
½ cup shortening
2 eggs
2 cups flour
1 tablespoon cocoa
1 teaspoon salt
1 cup buttermilk
1 teaspoon vanilla
2 ounces red food coloring
1 teaspoon soda
1 tablespoon vinegar

Cream sugar and shortening. Add eggs and beat well. Sift flour, cocoa, and salt three times and add alternately to creamed mixture with buttermilk. Add vanilla and food coloring. Dissolve soda in vinegar; fold it into the cake (do not beat). Bake in 2 greased and floured 9-inch cake pans at 350° for 25 or 30 minutes or until a cake-tester comes out clean. Turn cake out on a rack; cool and frost. Will serve 12.

FROSTING

¼ cup flour
1 cup milk
¼ teaspoon salt
1 cup butter
1 cup confectioners' sugar
2 teaspoons vanilla
1 cup chopped pecans

Mix flour, milk, and salt in a blender until smooth. Cook slowly until very thick. Cool completely. Cream butter and sugar until fluffy. Beat in vanilla. Add to cooled mixture and beat well. Frost the cake and garnish with pecans.

During the late 1920s or early 1930s a Southern lady is said to have eaten at the Waldorf Astoria. She especially enjoyed this cake and requested the recipe. At the end of the meal she was presented with the recipe and a bill for a large sum of money. She paid it and graciously shared the recipe along with the joke on herself with friends. Now it is one of the South's favorite desserts.

WHITE CHOCOLATE CAKE

A sumptuous cake with White Chocolate Icing

¾ cup white chocolate, coarsely
   chopped
½ cup hot water
1 cup (2 sticks) butter, room
   temperature
1½ cups sugar
3 eggs
2½ cups flour
1 teaspoon baking soda
½ teaspoon baking powder
½ teaspoon salt
1 cup buttermilk
1 teaspoon vanilla
½ cup pecans, chopped
½ cup flaked coconut

WHITE CHOCOLATE ICING

¾ cup white chocolate, coarsely
   chopped
2½ teaspoons flour
1 cup milk
1 cup (2 sticks) butter, room
   temperature
1 cup sugar
1½ teaspoons vanilla
½ cup flaked coconut

Melt white chocolate in hot water in top of a double boiler. Mix butter and sugar until a light lemon color. Add eggs one at a time and beat well after each addition. Sift flour, baking soda, baking powder, and salt. Add the dry ingredients to the butter-sugar-egg mixture, adding buttermilk alternately with dry ingredients. Add chocolate and vanilla. Beat 3 to 5 minutes at medium setting. Stir in pecans and coconut. Pour batter into 2 greased and floured 9-inch pans. Bake for 30 to 35 minutes at 350°, or until top springs back when touched with fingers. Remove from oven. Cool 30 minutes. Run a knife around the edges of the pan and carefully remove layer cakes from pans. Allow to cool completely.

In a saucepan set in hot water, melt white chocolate and add flour. Blend. Add milk and blend. Stir constantly until mixture thickens. Cool. Cream butter, sugar, and vanilla. Beat 2 to 3 minutes and gradually add cooled chocolate mixture. Beat at high speed with an electric mixer. Icing should be of the consistency of whipped cream. Stack cake layers with bottoms toward each other. Ice bottom layer and sides and top of the cake. Sprinkle coconut over icing. Serves 12 to 14.

To cream, use a wooden spoon, working mixture with a gliding motion between the back of the spoon and the side of the bowl, in short strokes. It should become light in color and even, smooth, and creamy in texture. If it becomes curdled and frothy, you have worked it too long and it will result in a coarsely grained cake.

LONE STAR SHEET CAKE

Cut into squares for a pick-up dessert

1½ cups sugar
2 cups flour
½ teaspoon baking soda
4 tablespoons cocoa
2 sticks margarine
1 cup water
½ cup buttermilk
2 eggs
1 teaspoon vanilla

Sift together sugar, flour, baking soda, and cocoa. Set aside. Bring margarine and water to a boil. Pour over dry ingredients, combining well. Stir in buttermilk, eggs, and vanilla. Pour into a greased and floured 12 x 15 inch pan. Bake at 350° for 30 to 45 minutes. Cool 10 minutes. Remove from pan. Cool well on racks.

ICING

1 stick margarine, softened
½ stick butter, softened
4 tablespoons cocoa
6 tablespoons buttermilk
1 pound confectioners' sugar
1 teaspoon vanilla
2 cups nuts, chopped

Beat margarine and butter; add cocoa; gradually add sugar, alternately with buttermilk. Mix in vanilla and nuts. Spread on top and sides of cake. Makes 15 to 18 dessert-size squares or 30 to 36 party pick-ups.

TEXAS CANDY CAKE

People who do not like fruitcake love this cake

½ pound chopped candied red
   cherries
½ pound chopped candied
   pineapple
½ pound chopped dates
1 tablespoon flour
4⅓ cups chopped pecans
4 ounces flaked coconut
1 14-ounce can sweetened
   condensed milk

Mix the chopped fruit with the tablespoon of flour. Stir in the chopped pecans, flaked coconut, and the can of condensed milk. Preheat the oven to 250°. Grease and flour a tube pan. Press mixture into pan and bake 1½ hours. Allow the cake to cool and wrap tightly in cheesecloth. Refrigerate at least 2 weeks. Makes about 24 thin slices.

Dip small pieces or squares of angel food cake into Seven-Minute Frosting and roll in coconut for party snowballs.

NATCHEZ CHRISTMAS CAKE

From Bobby J. Porter at the Post House Restaurant in Natchez, Mississippi

1 15-ounce package golden
  raisins
1 15-ounce package currants
1 fifth bourbon
1½ (3 sticks) cups butter
2 cups sugar
1 dozen eggs
1 cup wild plum jelly
2 pints preserves, cut and drained
  (strawberry, fig, pear, or
  blackberry)
1 teaspoon soda
1 cup Louisiana molasses
4 cups whole wheat flour
1 teaspoon allspice
1 teaspoon mace
1 teaspoon black pepper
2 teaspoons cloves
2 teaspoons cinnamon
3 cups pecans, chopped
½ pound lemon peel, chopped
½ pound orange peel, chopped
4 ounces candied ginger
1 pound chopped candied dates
  or figs
1 pound chopped candied
  pineapple
1 pound chopped candied
  apricots

Cake should be made 4 to 6 weeks in advance. Reduce ginger by half if you use it earlier. Three hours before starting, empty raisins and currants into a saucepan and pour all but 1 cup bourbon over. Simmer over low heat until they are puffed, stirring every 20 minutes. Cream butter and sugar, adding eggs one at a time, beating well. Add jelly and preserves. Mix soda into the molasses. When doubled in size and light brown in color, add to batter. Using reserved bourbon, rinse out molasses jar and add to batter. To the flour, in a separate bowl, add seasonings and thoroughly dredge all nuts and fruits (except raisins and currants). When thoroughly dredged, and using all flour from dredging process, add fruit and nuts to the batter. It is best to put the dredged fruit and nuts in a large preserving kettle and add batter to it. Stir thoroughly. Then add puffed raisins and currants and any bourbon residue that may be left. Prepare 2 tube pans or 4 loaf pans. Line with greased brown paper. Pour in batter and bake at 275° for 2 hours. Remove from oven and soak cakes with bourbon—all they will hold. When cool, wrap and store 4 to 6 weeks before cutting. Makes 2 tube cakes or 4 loaf cakes.

When a cake is done it should be cooled in the pan on a rack, for about 5 minutes, and then cooled out of the pan, on a rack, until all heat has left. There are a few exceptions which a recipe will point out.

AUNT JESSIE'S LIGHT FRUITCAKE

From Katherine Killelea of Natchez, Mississippi

1 pound pecan halves
¾ pound chopped candied
   pineapple
¾ pound whole candied cherries
1 pound seedless white raisins
½ pound butter, softened
2½ cups sugar
6 eggs
1 ounce brandy flavoring
4 cups flour, sifted
1 teaspoon salt
1 teaspoon nutmeg
1½ teaspoons cinnamon
Honey or light corn syrup

Line a baking pan with foil, or grease and flour 2 9 x 5 x 3 inch loaf pans. You may also use a 10 x 4 inch tube pan. Save some nuts and fruit to decorate the top. Mix butter and sugar; add eggs one at a time, beating well. Stir in brandy flavoring. Sift together remaining dry ingredients. Mix thoroughly with butter, sugar, and egg mixture. Work the nuts and fruit into the batter with a heavy spoon or with hands. Fill pans two-thirds full of batter and bake in a slow oven at 275°. Bake tube cake approximately 3 hours; small ones about 2 hours. One-half hour before the cake is done, brush the top of it with honey or light corn syrup. Decorate with nuts and fruit, pressing down firmly to make them stick. Return the cake to the oven to finish baking. When completely cool, lift from the pan and wrap cake with wine-dampened cloth. Store in an airtight container in a cool place for at least several weeks.

FLAMING LEMON SAUCE

To be served with fruitcake

½ cup sugar
1 tablespoon cornstarch
¼ teaspoon salt
½ teaspoon nutmeg
1 cup boiling water
2 tablespoons butter
1½ tablespoons lemon juice
1 thin lemon slice
3 sugar cubes
Brandy

Combine sugar, cornstarch, salt, and nutmeg; mix well. Add boiling water and cook until mixture is clear and coats the back of a spoon, about 5 minutes. Add butter and stir until melted. Add lemon juice. Cut thin lemon slice into thirds. Place Lemon Sauce in a small shallow bowl that will hold 1 cup sauce. Float sections of lemon slices on the hot sauce. Dip sugar cubes in brandy and place one on each section of lemon. Arrange slices of fruitcake on tray or platter around the bowl of sauce. When ready to serve, ignite the sugar cubes and bring to the table flaming. Makes 1 cup.

ELLEN HENDEE'S BLUEBERRY CAKE

Serve plain or top with whipped cream

1 pint blueberries
½ cup margarine
1 cup sugar
3 eggs, well beaten
2 cups flour
2 teaspoons baking powder
Confectioners' sugar
Whipped cream (optional)

Wash blueberries and dry on paper towels. Cream margarine with sugar. Add beaten eggs. Blend in flour sifted with baking powder. Fold in the berries gently. Bake in greased, floured 9 x 12 inch metal pan at 375° for approximately 30 minutes. Dust with confectioners' sugar. Cut into squares and serve from the pan. Top with whipped cream if you wish. Makes 16 squares.

CANDY BAR CAKE

Candy is not one of the ingredients — the cake is similar to a famous candy bar

2 cups sugar
1 cup margarine
5 eggs
1 cup all-purpose flour
1 cup self-rising flour
1 cup milk
1 teaspoon vanilla

Cream sugar and margarine together. Beat eggs into the mixture one at a time. Sift the two flours together, add alternately with the milk. Stir the vanilla in the mixture and pour batter into 3 greased and floured 8-inch pans. Bake at 350° for 30 minutes.

FILLING

1 cup sugar
1 cup evaporated milk
16 ounces coconut
12 large marshmallows
1 teaspoon vanilla

It is important to prepare the filling while the cake is baking. The cake should be stacked while it is still warm and the filling is still hot. The heat holds the layers together. Put sugar and milk in a saucepan and bring to a boil. Add coconut and marshmallows. Stir and cook for 5 minutes. Add vanilla. Spread between cake layers as you remove layers from the pans. Do not put any on the top layer; it will be frosted.

FROSTING

2 cups sugar
½ cup cocoa
½ cup butter
½ cup milk

Combine ingredients and, stirring constantly, bring to a boil. Boil hard for 2 minutes. Remove from heat and beat until thick enough to spread. Frost cake. Serves 16.

JUDY BLACKBURN'S WALNUT CREAM CAKE

Grand prize winner in a recipe contest

5 extra-large eggs, separated
2 cups sugar, divided
½ cup butter
½ cup margarine
½ teaspoon salt
1½ teaspoons vanilla
1 teaspoon baking soda
1 cup buttermilk
2 cups flour
1 cup walnuts, finely chopped
1 can (3½ ounces) flaked coconut

Have all ingredients at room temperature. Beat egg whites until they form soft peaks. Add ½ cup sugar slowly; beat until like meringue. Cream butter, margarine, remaining sugar, salt, and vanilla. Add egg yolks one at a time. Stir baking soda into buttermilk. Alternately add the buttermilk and flour to the butter mixture. Start and finish with flour. Fold in egg white mixture, then walnuts, then coconut. Bake in 3 9-inch greased and floured pans at 325° for about 40 minutes. Cool. Ice layers and sides with icing. Keeps well in refrigerator. Serves 12 or more.

ICING

1½ sticks butter
1½ 8-ounce packages cream cheese
1½ boxes confectioners' sugar
1½ teaspoons vanilla

Beat all ingredients until consistency of whipped cream. Ice cake; decorate top with a ring of chopped nuts.

Judy Blackburn won a Grand Prize in the 1984 Clarion-Ledger/Jackson Daily News (Jackson, Mississippi) Cookbook Contest for her Walnut Cream Cake.

MONNY'S VIRGINIA POUND CAKE

An heirloom from Mary Leigh's mother-in-law

1 stick butter, softened
1 stick margarine, softened
1½ cups sugar
5 eggs
2 cups cake flour, sifted
1 teaspoon vanilla
½ teaspoon almond extract

Beat butter and margarine until fluffy. Gradually add sugar. Beat slowly for 5 minutes. Add eggs, one at a time. Gradually beat in cake flour and add flavorings. Bake at 300° for 1 hour.

GLAZE

1 tablespoon butter
1 cups confectioners' sugar
2 tablespoons lemon juice

Melt butter, stir in sugar, and add lemon juice. Bring to a boil and pour over warm cake. Serves 12 or more.

GERMAN CHOCOLATE CAKE

A delicately rich chocolate cake with a buttery coconut pecan frosting

4 squares (4 ounces) semisweet
   chocolate
½ cup boiling water
1 cup butter
2 cups sugar
4 egg yolks
1 teaspoon vanilla
2½ cups self-rising flour, sifted
1 teaspoon soda
½ teaspoon salt
1 cup buttermilk
¼ cup coconut, finely chopped
¼ cup pecans, finely chopped
4 egg whites, beaten

Melt chocolate in boiling water. Cool. Cream butter and sugar until fluffy. Add yolks, one at a time, beating well after each addition. Blend in chocolate and vanilla. Sift flour with soda and salt; add alternately with buttermilk to chocolate mixture, beating after each addition until smooth. Add coconut and pecans. Fold in beaten egg whites. Pour into 3 9-inch layer pans that have been lined on the bottoms with brown paper. Bake in a 350° oven for 30 to 35 minutes. Cool. Frost between the layers and the top and sides of cake. Serves 16.

COCONUT-PECAN FROSTING

1 12-ounce can evaporated milk
1½ cups sugar
¾ cup butter
3 egg yolks, slightly beaten
1 tablespoon vanilla
2 cups moist, sweetened coconut
1½ cups pecans, chopped

Combine milk, sugar, butter, and slightly beaten egg yolks; cook over low heat stirring constantly until it starts to thicken, about 10 minutes. Add vanilla, coconut, and pecans. Cool until thick enough to spread. Punch holes in the layers and allow it to run down in the cake. Ice the top and sides of cake.

   German Chocolate Cake was created in 1852 to celebrate Samuel German's perfecting a sweet baking chocolate. Southerners have adopted it as their own, creating many variations of the original which used a sweet baking chocolate instead of the semisweet. Faye Swales of Jackson, Mississippi, has worked on her interpretation over the years and has given us permission to use the recipe for the best German Chocolate Cake that we have ever tasted.

To make coconut milk without a blender, mix 2 cups shredded coconut (fresh or packaged) with 2 cups light cream. Heat just below simmering point, then remove from heat and steep 30 minutes. Pour through a wire strainer or cheesecloth, pressing or squeezing out all liquid. Makes 2 cups.

KINGS' CAKE

Celebrate Mardi Gras with the purple, green, and gold Gâteau des Rois or "Kings' Cake"

1 package yeast
¼ cup warm water
6 tablespoons milk
4 cups flour
1 cup (2 sticks) butter
¾ cup sugar
¼ teaspoon salt
4 eggs
Melted butter
1 dried bean
3 cups granulated sugar
2 to 3 drops purple food coloring
2 to 3 drops green food coloring
2 to 3 drops yellow food coloring
White corn syrup

Dissolve yeast in warm water. Add milk that has been scalded and cooled. Mix in ½ cup of the flour to make a soft dough. In a separate bowl, combine butter, ¾ cup sugar, salt, and eggs. Mix well and add soft ball of yeast dough. Mix thoroughly. Gradually blend in 2½ cups of flour to make a medium dough. Place in a greased bowl and brush top of dough with the melted butter. Cover with a damp cloth and let it rise until doubled in bulk, about 3 hours. Use remaining 1 cup flour to knead dough and to roll into a "rope" of dough. Place on a large greased cookie sheet and shape "rope" into a circle, connecting ends of dough by dampening with water. Cover with a damp cloth and let rise until doubled in bulk, about 1 hour. A bean may be placed in the cake at this point, if desired. Bake in a preheated 325° oven for 35 to 45 minutes, or until lightly browned. Decorate by coloring the sugar, 2 to 3 drops of each color to 1 cup of sugar. To achieve a gold color you may add a tiny drop of red to the yellow food color. Brush the top of the cake with corn syrup and alternate 3-inch bands of purple, green, and gold colored sugar. Serves 16 to 24.

Note: If you wish to mail the cake, place it in a large plastic zip-lock bag. Place the bag in a box filled with unsalted popped pop corn.

The Gâteau des Rois or "Kings' Cake" is inseparably connected with Mardi Gras — New Orleans and carnival season. The most famous of the Creole desserts, the "Kings' Cake" evolved from the Creole custom of choosing a king and queen on the Twelfth Night (January 6), the feast day that commemorates the visit of the three Wise Men of the East to the Christ Child in Bethlehem. The method of choosing a king was cutting the Kings' Cake and serving each person present a piece of the cake with a glass of champagne. Cleverly hidden within the cake was a bean. If the finder of the bean was a lady, she chose her king by presenting to him a bunch of violets. If the finder was a gentleman, he would choose his queen by offering her the flower in his lapel and would then escort her around the parlor in le tour de salon. *Ever since those early days, during the period between January 6 and Mardi Gras, a king and queen were chosen for the occasion in this manner, and a new royal pair was chosen every week thereafter until Mardi Gras.*

BARBARA'S KING CAKE

This version is a real winner!

1 cup milk
½ cup butter or margarine
½ cup sugar plus 1 tablespoon
1 teaspoon salt
4 large eggs, beaten
Grated rind of 1 lemon or orange
¼ cup warm water
2 packages dry yeast
4½ cups bread flour
¼ cup oil

Scald milk (microwave about 5 minutes on high or you may use a pot on top of stove). To scalded milk add butter or margarine and ½ cup of sugar. The hot milk will melt the butter and dissolve the sugar. Add salt, beaten eggs, and grated rind. Stir gently. To ¼ cup warm water add the extra tablespoon of sugar and the yeast. The sugar will cause the yeast mixture to foam; this proves the yeast is active. After yeast is thoroughly dissolved, add to cooled milk mixture. Add flour 1 cup at a time, mixing thoroughly after each addition. The dough will be very sticky and soft. The soft dough makes for a light texture of the cake. Drizzle the oil around the side of your mixing bowl. At this point you may have to use your hands to mix the dough. Roll the dough around the bowl, greasing the sides of the bowl with the oil. Cover the bowl with a damp towel. Allow to rise until dough has doubled in volume, approximately 3 hours. After rising, punch dough down and knead on a floured board gently for about 2 minutes. This amount of dough will make 1 large King Cake or may be split to make 2 smaller cakes.

FILLING

1 stick butter or margarine,
  softened
½ cup brown sugar
½ cup granulated sugar
2 tablespoons cinnamon
  (or to taste)

Roll dough on a well-floured board into a large rectangle, rolling the dough as thin as possible without tearing it. Spread dough rectangle with softened butter. Mix brown and granulated sugar and cinnamon together. Sprinkle over entire rectangle, spreading it evenly. Cut rectangle into thirds (a pizza cutter gives you a nice clean cut). Roll each third of dough like a jelly roll. Stretch rolls to give you 3 equal lengths. Braid the 3 strips and shape into a ring on a greased baking sheet. If you cover your baking sheet with a heavy duty foil and then grease, it makes the cake easier to handle after baking. Let braided ring rise 1½ to 2 hours. Bake at 375° in a preheated oven for about 20 minutes, or until brown.

ICING

3 cups confectioners' sugar
½ stick butter or margarine, softened
½ teaspoon vanilla extract
¼ cup milk
Juice from the grated fruit
Colored sugar (dye sugar with food coloring: purple, gold, and green)
1 plastic baby (if baby unavailable you may use a pinto bean)

After baking, hide the baby or bean in baked cake, inserting from underneath. Make icing while cake cools. Mix icing ingredients together, except for colored sugar. The icing should be the consistency of pancake batter. After cake is cooled ice cake and decorate with colored sugar. Slice, serve, and enjoy. As the tradition goes, the person who gets the slice with the baby must provide the next King Cake.

This recipe comes from Barbara Schwegmann, a nurse in Marrero, Louisiana.

DUNLEITH CAKE

A flavorful gem from an antebellum home in Natchez

Cooking oil spray
Shortening
Flour
3 cups sugar
1 stick butter
1 stick margarine
5 eggs
3 cups all-purpose flour
1 heaping teaspoon baking powder
1 cup milk
1 tablespoon rum flavoring
1 tablespoon coconut flavoring

Preheat oven to 350°. Coat bundt pan with cooking oil spray, then grease with shortening and flour. Cream sugar, butter, and margarine. Add eggs, flour, baking powder, milk, and flavorings. Mix until smooth. Bake 1 hour.

SYRUP

1 cup sugar
1 cup water
1 tablespoon almond flavoring

Combine in saucepan the sugar, water, and almond flavoring. Cook for 10 to 15 minutes until it boils. Punch holes in cake with ice pick. Pour syrup over warm cake, then turn upside down onto cake plate. Serves 12 or more.

Ella Mae Green, who is the cook at Dunleith, makes this tasty cake often. She warns that one should not bake Dunleith Cake on a cloudy day or open the oven door until the one hour baking period is complete for fear the cake will fall.

OLD-FASHIONED COCONUT CAKE

A classic

2¼ cups sifted flour
1½ teaspoons baking powder
½ teaspoon baking soda
¾ teaspoon salt
½ cup unsalted butter
1¼ cups sugar
3 eggs
½ cup angel flake coconut
1¼ cups buttermilk
1½ teaspoons vanilla
Seven-Minute Frosting (see index
    for recipe)
Coconut

Sift together the dry ingredients. Cream butter and sugar. Add the eggs one at a time to the creamed mixture. Beat well after each addition. Combine the ½ cup coconut and the buttermilk. Add alternately with flour mixture to sugar mixture (on slow speed if using mixer). Add vanilla. Pour into 2 greased and floured 9-inch cake pans. Bake at 375° for 25 to 30 minutes. This can be made in 3 layers with the cooking time shortened. Serves 12 or more.

FILLING

2 egg whites
½ cup nonalcoholic pina colada
    mix
1½ cups angel flake coconut
4 tablespoons confectioners'
    sugar

Beat egg whites until stiff. Add other ingredients to egg whites. Mix gently with spoon. Do not cook. Spread between cake layers. Ice cake with Seven-Minute Frosting. Sprinkle cake with coconut.

This wonderful recipe was contributed by Nancy Calhoun, vice-president of Pelican Publishing Company in Gretna, Louisiana.

To crack a coconut, puncture the eyes at the end of the coconut and drain off liquid. Place in a 350° oven for 30 minutes. Place hot coconut on a hard surface and hit hard with a hammer; pry out meat with an old table knife, remove brown skin with a potato peeler, rinse, and dry on paper towels. One coconut will provide 3 to 4 cups meat. To grate in a blender or food processor, cut into ½-inch cubes and drop in 1 cup at a time.

COCONUT CAKE (BASIC 1-2-3-4 CAKE)

Tall and showy with lemon and raspberry filling

3 cups cake flour, sifted
2 teaspoons baking powder
½ teaspoon salt
1 cup butter or margarine,
    softened
2 cups sugar
4 eggs
1 teaspoon vanilla
1 cup milk
1 cup raspberry jam
1 recipe Lemon Cheese Cake
    filling (see index)
1 recipe Seven-Minute Frosting
    (see index)
1 cup flaked coconut (freshly
    grated, if possible)

Sift together cake flour, baking powder, and salt. Set aside. Cream butter and sugar; add eggs and vanilla; beat at high speed for 3 minutes. Add flour mixture alternately with milk, at low speed on mixer. Scrape sides of bowl with rubber spatula after each addition. Pour batter into 3 greased and floured 8-inch cake pans. Bake at 350° for 30 minutes or until the centers spring back when lightly pressed with fingertip. Cool layers in the pans on wire racks 10 minutes. Turn out onto racks. Cool thoroughly. Spread raspberry jam thinly over two layers. Spoon and smooth lemon cheese filling over jam. Stack, ending with plain layer. Frost sides and top with Seven-Minute Frosting. Sprinkle with coconut. Serves 12 or more.

BECKY'S PUMPKIN ROLL

Serve it on an autumn day

3 eggs
1 cup sugar
⅔ cup pumpkin
1 teaspoon vanilla
¾ cup flour
1 teaspoon baking powder
2 teaspoons cinnamon
1 teaspoon ginger
½ teaspoon nutmeg
¼ teaspoon salt
1 cup pecans, finely chopped

Beat eggs on high speed of mixer for 5 minutes; gradually add sugar. Stir in pumpkin and vanilla. Combine flour, baking powder, cinnamon, ginger, nutmeg, and salt and fold into pumpkin mixture. Spread in greased and floured 15 x 10 x 1 inch jelly-roll pan. Top with pecans. Bake at 375° for 15 minutes. Turn out on towel sprinkled with confectioners' sugar. Starting at narrow end, roll towel and cake together. Cool, unroll, and spread on filling. Reroll and chill. To make filling, beat cream cheese and butter. Add sugar and vanilla. Spread over cake, roll, and chill. Serves 8.

FILLING

6 ounces cream cheese
4 tablespoons butter
1 cup confectioners' sugar
½ teaspoon vanilla

GINGERBREAD WITH HOT BUTTERED RUM SAUCE

From Diane Griffin, a caterer in East Texas

1½ sticks margarine
2 cups brown sugar
2 cups flour
1 teaspoon soda
1 tablespoon ginger
2 teaspoons cinnamon
1 teaspoon nutmeg
2 eggs
1 cup buttermilk
½ cup pecans, chopped

Cream margarine and brown sugar. Add flour gradually. Set aside one cup of this mixture. To remainder, mix in soda and spices. Add eggs and combine well. Stir in buttermilk. Pour into an ungreased 12 x 8½ inch pan. Sprinkle reserved mixture over top, then pecans. Bake for 30 to 40 minutes at 350°. Serves about 12.

HOT BUTTERED RUM SAUCE

1 cup sugar
½ cup evaporated milk
½ cup melted margarine
3 tablespoons rum

Heat sugar and milk to boiling point. Beat in melted margarine with mixer. Add rum. Cook until slightly thick. Top squares of gingerbread with sauce.

LEMON CHEESE CAKE

Not a cheesecake, but an old-fashioned recipe that is hard to find

½ cup shortening
1 cup sugar
3 eggs
½ cup milk
½ teaspoon vanilla
2 cups flour
3 teaspoons baking powder
½ teaspoon salt

Cream shortening and sugar together; add eggs, one at a time. Slowly mix in milk and vanilla. Sift together the flour, baking powder, and salt. Add gradually to shortening mixture, beating well after each addition. Turn into 2 greased and floured 8-inch cake pans. Bake at 350° for 30 to 35 minutes. Cool in pans 10 minutes; turn onto cake racks to cool 30 minutes more.

FILLING

4 tablespoons butter
¾ cup sugar
⅛ teaspoon salt
2½ teaspoons grated lemon rind
½ cup lemon juice
3 eggs, well beaten

Melt butter in the top of a double boiler. Stir in sugar and salt. Add lemon rind and juice. Stir in beaten eggs slowly. Cook over moderate heat, stirring constantly until thick. Cool before spreading between layers and on sides and top of cake. The filling is not thick and will not completely cover cake, but it is truly wonderful. Serves about 10.

SALLY LUNN

Delightful as a tea bread or with the main course

1 stick butter
1 cup milk, scalded
2 eggs, beaten
1 teaspoon salt
⅓ cup sugar
4 cups flour
1 package yeast, dissolved in ½
   cup warm water
Melted butter

Melt butter in scalded milk. Beat eggs. Mix dry ingredients and add alternately with milk and butter mixture. Add dissolved yeast. Cover and let rise in a warm place approximately 1 hour, or until doubled. Punch down and place in a buttered bundt pan. Let rise to top of pan. Brush melted butter on top. Bake at 350° for 45 minutes to an hour. Serves 10.

Sally Lunn probably originated in Bath, England, where a woman named Sally Lunn reportedly sold the tea bread on the streets. Other sources claim the name is derived from the French "sol et lune" or "sun and moon cake," because of its golden color. Sally Lunn may be served as a bread with entrées as well as a tasy snack with coffee or tea.

UNCLE JOHN MORGAN STEVENS' BOURBON NUT CAKE

Almost every Southern family has a version of this famous cake that is thought to have originated in Kentucky

2 cups sugar
½ pound (2 sticks) butter
6 eggs, separated
3 heaping cups flour
2 tablespoons baking powder
¼ teaspoon salt
2 quarts pecans
1 pound golden raisins
1⅓ cups bourbon

With electric mixer, cream sugar and butter until light and fluffy. Beat in egg yolks, one at a time. Measure the flour without sifting, then sift with baking powder and salt. Dredge the nuts and raisins with ½ cup of the flour mixture. Stir remaining flour into creamed mixture alternately with the bourbon. Stir in raisins and pecans. Beat egg whites until stiff but not dry and fold into the cake batter, which will be rather heavy to handle at first. Bake in a large greased and floured tube pan at 275° for about 2 hours or until a cake-tester comes out clean. The top should be brown with small cracks when it is ready to be tested. Cool on a rack for 20 minutes before inverting. Cure (ripen) the cake for 3 weeks, basting occasionally with bourbon. Serves 16.

The cookie jar was always filled and open at Jo's Great-Uncle Morgan's house, but this special cake was reserved for the grown-ups.

WINIFRED CHENEY'S BLACKBERRY JAM CAKE

Winifred Green Cheney is one of the South's most noted food writers

1 cup butter, softened
2 cups sugar, sifted
4 large eggs, room temperature
3 cups cake flour, measured after
  sifting
3 teaspoons baking powder
1 teaspoon ground cinnamon
⅛ teaspoon salt
1 teaspoon ground cloves
1 cup milk
1 teaspoon lemon extract
1 teaspoon grated lemon rind
1 cup fairly firm blackberry jam,
  preferably seedless

In a large bowl, cream butter and sugar until light and fluffy. Add eggs one at a time; beat well. If using an electric mixer, place butter, sugar, and 2 eggs in a large, deep bowl and beat 4 minutes at high speed. Add remaining 2 eggs, one at a time, and beat well. Sift flour, baking powder, cinnamon, salt, and cloves together three times. Add flour mixture to creamed mixture alternately with milk, a small amount each time, ending with flour mixture. Beat well. Add lemon extract and rind, then jam. Spoon batter into 3 greased and floured layer pans. Bake in a preheated 350° oven for 20 to 25 minutes until cake tests done. Cool on wire rack for 15 minutes. If making cake for a party, use two batches of icing—one for putting between the layers, the other for top and sides of cake. Makes 3 9-inch layers (serves 14 to 16).

NEVER FAIL WHITE ICING

3 medium-size or large eggs,
  whites only
¼ teaspoon cream of tartar
1½ cups sifted sugar
5 tablespoons cold water
1½ teaspoons light corn syrup
1 teaspoon vanilla extract

Place all ingredients with exception of vanilla in top of a double boiler over rapidly boiling water. Beat mixture with electric mixer at high speed. You may use a rotary beater or wire whisk, but the electric mixer makes it easier. Cut down mixture from sides of pan with spatula as it cooks. Beat constantly about 7 minutes or until icing will stand in peaks and has attained a high gloss. Remove icing from heat and add vanilla. Center a layer of cake on cake plate and put 5 heaping tablespoons of icing in a circle on top and gently spread toward the sides. Use a dinner knife or a 1-inch wide spatula for spreading. Position top cake layer and repeat icing method. To ice the sides apply a tablespoon of icing at top of side, working it down as you go around the cake. Repeat until cake is completely covered. Makes icing for sides and tops of 2 (8-inch) layers.

Winifred Green Cheney, noted Southern food writer and hostess, has authored two cookbooks, Cooking for Company *and* The Southern Hospitality Cookbook. *The latter was selected by the American Book Publishing Association as one of 250 best books in America and as a result is included in the White House Library. The Jam Cake is from* The Southern Hospitality Cookbook *and is reprinted with the permission of Oxmoor House, Inc.*

TEXAS TOASTED PECAN CAKE

The Deep South's favorite nut in an unforgettable cake

4 tablespoons butter
1½ cups pecans, chopped
¾ cup butter
1⅓ cups sugar
1½ teaspoons vanilla
2 eggs
2 cups flour
2 teaspoons baking powder
¼ teaspoon salt
⅔ cup milk

Melt 4 tablespoons butter in a baking pan in the oven at 350°. Add pecans and toast 10 to 15 minutes. Cream ¾ cup butter; gradually add sugar; beat until fluffy. Add vanilla. Beat in eggs, one at a time. Sift together flour, baking powder, and salt. Add to creamed mixture alternately with milk. Beat after each addition. Fold in 1 cup pecans. Set aside remaining ½ cup pecans for top of cake. Bake at 350° in greased and floured pans for 30 to 35 minutes. Cool completely before icing.

FROSTING

6 tablespoons butter
3 cups powdered sugar
1 teaspoon vanilla
3–4 tablespoons light cream

Cream butter. Add powdered sugar gradually. Add vanilla and cream. Beat until smooth. Spread frosting between layers and on cake. Sprinkle remaining pecans atop cake. Serves 12.

HUMMINGBIRD CAKE

Cinnamon, fruit, and nuts create a spicy flavor

3 cups all-purpose flour
2 cups sugar
1 teaspoon salt
1 teaspoon cinnamon
1 teaspoon soda
3 eggs, beaten
1 cup salad oil
1½ teaspoons vanilla
1 can (8-ounce) crushed
   pineapple, undrained
1 cup pecans, chopped
2 bananas, mashed with fork

Combine the dry ingredients in a bowl. Stir in eggs and salad oil until dry ingredients are moistened, but do not overbeat. Add vanilla, crushed pineapple, pecans, and bananas and stir well. Pour batter into 3 well-greased and floured 8-inch cake pans. Bake at 350° for 25 to 30 minutes or until cake tests done. Cool cake in pans for 10 minutes, remove from pans to racks, and cool thoroughly before icing.

FROSTING

8 ounces cream cheese, softened
1 cup butter or margarine,
   softened
1¾ pounds confectioners' sugar
2 teaspoons vanilla
1 cup pecans, chopped

Mix cream cheese and butter together and cream until smooth. Add powdered sugar slowly and beat until light and fluffy. Add vanilla. Spread between layers and on top and sides of cake. Sprinkle with pecans. Serves 12.

DOUBLE-FROSTED ANGEL FOOD CAKE

Iced with Seven-Minute Frosting; glazed with chocolate sauce

1¼ cups egg whites, room
    temperature
¼ teaspoon salt
1¼ teaspoons cream of tartar
1½ cups sugar, sifted
¾ teaspoon vanilla
¾ teaspoon almond flavoring
1 cup flour, sifted

Beat egg whites until they begin to foam. Add salt and cream of tartar. Beat until egg whites form peaks. Gradually add ¾ cup sugar until well blended. Mix in flavorings. Sift remaining sugar with flour and fold into whites. Pour into ungreased stem pan. Cut through batter with a knife to eliminate air holes. Bake for one hour in 300° oven. Invert and cool in pan. Serves 12 or more. When cool, ice with Seven-Minute Frosting, substituting 1 teaspoon almond extract for vanilla.

SEVEN-MINUTE FROSTING

1½ cups sugar
¼ cup water
2 egg whites
2 tablespoons light corn syrup
1 teaspoon vanilla
¼ teaspoon salt

Combine ingredients in top of double boiler. Beat well. Place over simmering water. Cook, beating constantly at high speed with an electric hand mixer about 7 minutes or until it is triple in volume and holds firm peaks. Remove from heat and ice cake.

CHOCOLATE GLAZE

1 4-ounce bar sweet chocolate
1 tablespoon margarine
¼ cup water
1 cup confectioners' sugar, sifted
⅛ teaspoon salt
½ teaspoon almond extract

Melt chocolate and margarine in water in a double boiler over low heat. Whisk in sugar, salt, and almond extract. Pour carefully over frosted cake.

When making angel food cakes, eggs should be at least 3 days old, at room temperature (60° to 70°), and separated just before use.

JELLY ROLL

The old-fashioned kind with jelly or jam in it

4 eggs, separated
1 cup sugar
3 tablespoons cold water
1 teaspoon vanilla
1 cup cake flour, sifted
1¼ teaspoons baking powder
¼ teaspoon salt
1 cup strawberry or raspberry jam
Confectioners' sugar

Beat egg whites until stiff but not dry. Gradually beat in ½ cup sugar. Beat egg yolks, water, and vanilla together until thick. Slowly blend in the remaining ½ cup sugar. Sift the flour, baking powder, and salt together, and fold into the batter. Carefully fold yellow mixture into whites. Pour into a 10 x 15 inch jelly-roll pan that has been lined with greased wax paper. Bake at 425° for 12 to 15 minutes, or until cake springs back when lightly pressed with finger. Slightly dampen a tea towel with warm water and immediately turn hot cake onto towel. Remove paper and cut off crusty edges of cake. Spread with jelly or jam. Roll lengthwise, cover with towel, and let stand a few minutes. Remove towel and sift confectioners' sugar lightly over top. Serves 12.

In the South, the jelly roll is often used for trifles or other custard desserts in place of lady fingers or vanilla wafers.

PRALINE CAKE

Take on your next picnic — it is easy to make

1 cup butter or margarine
2 cups sugar
4 eggs, separated
3 cups cake flour, sifted
1 teaspoon cream of tartar
1 teaspoon soda
1 cup buttermilk

Cream butter or margarine with sugar until light. Add egg yolks, one at a time, and beat until fluffy. Combine sifted cake flour with cream of tartar and soda; sift again. Add to the batter alternately with the buttermilk. Fold in stiffly beaten egg whites. Bake in a 9 x 13 inch greased, floured pan at 350° for 50 minutes. Remove from oven and spread with topping.

TOPPING

½ cup brown sugar
1 cup chopped nuts
¼ cup melted butter
3 tablespoons cream

Mix and spread on hot cake straight from the oven. Place under broiler 3 inches from heat for 1 to 2 minutes. Serves 12 to 16.

SWEET POTATO PUDDING CAKE WITH BOURBON-PECAN TOPPING

This Deep-South pudding cake may also be served with Bourbon Caramel Sauce

1½ cups flour, sifted
¼ teaspoon salt
2 teaspoons baking powder
½ cup margarine
2 eggs, beaten
¾ cup sugar
1 teaspoon nutmeg
1 teaspoon cinnamon
2 cups hot sweet potatoes, mashed
½ cup milk
1 tablespoon lemon juice
⅛ cup bourbon, warmed

Combine flour, salt, and baking powder; sift. Add margarine, eggs, sugar, nutmeg, and cinnamon to hot mashed sweet potatoes. Beat thoroughly. Add flour and milk alternately. Beat well after each addition. Add lemon juice. Grease a loaf pan and pour mixture into it. Bake in a 350° oven for 1 hour to 1 hour and 20 minutes or until a knife inserted in the center comes out clean. Remove from the oven and immediately punch holes in the top of the cake with toothpick or ice pick. Brush top with the warmed bourbon. Make the topping and spoon over the pudding cake while still in the pan. To serve, cut cake down the middle and then slice crosswise. Pudding cake may be served with Bourbon Caramel Sauce (see index for recipe), if desired.

BOURBON PECAN TOPPING

½ cup (1 stick) butter
½ cup brown sugar, packed
¼ cup cream
¼ cup bourbon
1 cup coconut
1 cup pecans, chopped

Melt butter. Add sugar and cream. Stir in the bourbon. Bring to a boil and boil 3 minutes. Cool and beat until it thickens. Add coconut and pecans. Pour over cake and run under the broiler until it bubbles. Serves 16.

CARROT CAKE

Ice with pineapple or coconut pecan icing

1½ cups salad oil
2 cups sugar
4 eggs, well beaten
2 cups cake flour
2 teaspoons cinnamon
2 teaspoons soda
2 teaspoons baking powder
1 cup pecans, finely chopped
3 cups grated carrots

Mix salad oil and sugar. Beat well. Add eggs to the mixture. Sift dry ingredients together twice and add pecans. Mix into egg mixture. Add carrots in small amounts and mix well. Grease and flour 2 9-inch cake pans. Fill pans and bake at 350° for about 30 minutes. Cool and remove from pans. Ice with either one of the following icings. Serves 12.

PINEAPPLE ICING

1 8-ounce package cream cheese
1 stick butter
1 pound box confectioners' sugar
1 teaspoon vanilla
½ cup crushed pineapple, well
   drained

Have ingredients at room temperature; blend together the butter and cream cheese. Slowly blend in confectioners' sugar. Add vanilla and crushed pineapple. Frost cake.

COCONUT-PECAN ICING

4 tablespoons butter
1 8-ounce package cream cheese
2 cups confectioners' sugar
1 teaspoon vanilla extract
½ cup cocnut
½ cup pecans, chopped

Have ingredients at room temperature; blend together the butter and cream cheese. Slowly blend in confectioners' sugar. Add vanilla, coconut, and pecans, mixing well. Frost cake.

VICKSBURG PRUNE CAKE

Moist and flavorful—this recipe is one of the best

3 eggs
1 cup vegetable oil
1½ cups sugar
2 cups flour
1 teaspoon soda
1 teaspoon cinnamon
1 teaspoon allspice
1 teaspoon nutmeg
1 teaspoon salt
1 cup buttermilk
1 cup cooked pitted prunes,
   cut up
1 cup chopped nuts (optional)

Mix all cake ingredients in order given. It is best to sift all dry ingredients together before adding to mixture. Grease and flour a large baking pan 10 x 14 inches or larger. Pour in cake batter and bake at 350° about 40 minutes. Remove from oven and immediately prick all over top with a knife or fork before pouring icing over cake. Serves 12.

ICING

1 cup sugar
½ cup buttermilk
1 teaspoon soda
1 tablespoon dark corn syrup
½ cup butter or margarine
Whipped cream (optional)

Mix all ingredients, except whipped cream, in a boiler and bring to a rolling boil. Remove from heat and beat slightly. While still very warm, pour over hot cake which has been pricked. Serve with whipped cream if desired.

This recipe is from Mrs. George Jabour, Sr., and is used with the permission of the Vintage Vicksburg Cookbook committee.

CRAIG CLAIBORNE'S WALNUT AND GINGER CAKE

From the famous New York Times *food writer*

½ pound candied ginger, cut into
  ¼-inch cubes (about 1 cup)
½ pound golden raisins
1 pound black walnuts or
  walnuts, broken into pieces
3 cups sifted all-purpose flour
1 teaspoon baking powder
½ teaspoon salt (optional)
1 pound butter, cut into 1-inch
  cubes, softened
2 cups sugar
6 egg yolks
⅓ cup Madeira or dry sherry
6 egg whites
Madeira, dry sherry, cognac, or
  rum

Preheat oven to 275°. Lightly grease a 10-inch, 12-cup bundt pan. Sprinkle with flour and shake out excess. In large bowl, combine ginger, raisins, and walnuts. Sift together flour, baking powder, and salt. Sift again over fruit-nut mixture. In another large bowl with mixer at medium speed, beat butter, gradually adding sugar. Cream mixture well. Gradually beat in egg yolks. Beat in Madeira. Pour and scrape butter mixture over nut-flour mixture, mixing together thoroughly with hands. In large bowl with clean beaters, beat egg whites until stiff peaks form. Fold into batter thoroughly, until whites do not show. Pour batter into prepared pan and smooth top with spatula. Place pan on baking sheet and bake about 2½ hours, or until cake is puffed above pan and nicely browned on top. While still hot, invert cake onto wire rack and remove pan. If cake sticks, tap bottom with back of heavy knife. Cool. Wrap snugly in cheesecloth and foil and store in the refrigerator at least 10 days. Unwrap it occasionally and douse with spirits. Rewrap tightly. Serves about 10. It is important to mix the butter mixture and the nut-flour mixture by hand rather than with a spatula or machine. It will be a very stiff batter. Wrapped in cheesecloth and foil, the cake keeps well for at least a year.

Craig Claiborne was born and raised in the heart of the Mississippi Delta. He has always had a special fondness for Southern cuisine, which he learned to appreciate from an exceptional cook—his mother. He claims that black walnuts remind him of his boyhood in Mississippi. "I can still remember shelling black walnuts and the resulting greenish stain on my hands."

To beat or whip a batter, use a long, free-swinging, lifting motion, which brings the bottom mass constantly to the top, trapping as much air as possible in the mixture.

GENERAL ROBERT E. LEE ORANGE-LEMON CAKE

Mouth-watering cake from Kentucky's Beaumont Inn

2 cups cake flour (sift twice
   before measuring)
1½ teaspoons baking powder
½ teaspoon cream of tartar
2 cups sugar (sift six times)
½ cup salad oil
1 lemon (juice and grated yellow
   of rind)
9 eggs, separated
A few grains of salt

Sift cake flour, baking powder, and cream of tartar together six times. Stir in sugar. Pour salad oil over these ingredients and mix well. Stir in lemon juice and rind. Beat egg yolks in electric mixer, add salad oil mixture, and blend well. Add salt to egg whites and beat until stiff. Combine with egg yolk mixture. Grease 4 9-inch cake pans; divide batter among them equally and bake at 325° for 20 minutes. Turn cake upside down on rack until cool. There will be 4 thin layers. Serves 12 or more.

ORANGE-LEMON FROSTING

2 pounds confectioners' sugar
½ cup butter, softened
4 tablespoons lemon juice
6–8 tablespoons orange juice
   (enough to make frosting easy
   to spread)
3 egg yolks
Rind of 2 lemons (yellow only),
   grated
Rind of 4 oranges, grated

Cream sugar and butter. Gradually beat in juices, then egg yolks. Mix in rinds. Ice cake. This cake should be refrigerated in a tight container due to icing being uncooked.

The Beaumont Inn in Harrodsburg, deep in the heart of Bluegrass country, is a former girls' school which has been converted into a lovely inn. Famous for the delicious Southern food served in its dining room, the inn is over one hundred years old.

For separating eggs, paper cups are handy to have on hand. Separate the eggs into them and store what is not needed with a plastic covering.

SCRIPTURE CAKE

Great for church bazaars — include the recipe with the cake

½ cup Judges 5:25, last clause
2 cups Jeremiah 6:20
2 tablespoons I Samuel 14:25
6 Jeremiah 17:11
1½ cups I Kings 4:22
2 teaspoons Amos 4:5
II Chronicles 9:9, to taste
Pinch of Leviticus 2:13
½ cup Judges 4:19, last clause
2 cups Nahum 3:12
2 cups Numbers 17:8
2 cups I Samuel 30:12

Whip the Judges 5:25, Jeremiah 6:20, and Samuel 14:25 until light. Beat the 6 Jeremiah 17:11 yolks and add. Add Kings, Amos, Chronicles, and Leviticus alternately with Judges 4:19. Fold in Nahum, Numbers, and Samuel 30:12, then also the 6 Jeremiah 17:11 whites, beaten stiff. Bake 2 hours in a greased 10-inch tube pan at 300°.

TRANSLATION OF SCRIPTURE CAKE

Beat together until light and fluffy ½ cup butter, 2 cups sugar, and 2 tablespoons honey. Beat 6 egg yolks until light and add. Add sifted mixture of 1½ cups sifted flour, 2 teaspoons baking powder, 2 teaspoons cinnamon, ½ teaspoon ginger, 1 teaspoon nutmeg, ½ teaspoon cloves, and a pinch of salt, in alternate portions with ½ cup milk. Stir in 2 cups chopped figs, 2 cups raisins, and 2 cups chopped almonds. Fold in 6 egg whites, beaten stiff. Bake the cake in well-greased 10-inch tube pan (lined with greased brown paper) 2 hours at 300°. Serves 12 to 16.

To make coconut milk from fresh coconut, drain and crack a coconut. Cut meat in ½-inch cubes. To each cup of meat, add ¾ cup hot liquid (hot water added to milk drained from coconut) in the blender. Whirl for 20 to 30 seconds, then steep for 30 minutes. Strain through a double thickness of cheesecloth, squeezing out liquid. Makes about 2 cups.

LANE CAKE

Tall and showy with a rich nut and fruit filling

1 cup butter, softened
2 cups sugar
4 cups cake flour, sifted
2 teaspoons baking powder
½ teaspoon salt
1 cup milk
8 egg whites, stiffly beaten
1 teaspoon vanilla

FILLING

8 egg yolks
1 cup sugar
1 stick butter, softened
1 cup pecans, chopped
1 cup maraschino cherries,
    chopped
1 cup raisins
1 cup grated coconut
2 tablespoons bourbon

Cream butter, add sugar slowly, and mix well. Sift dry ingredients and add alternately with milk. Fold in egg whites and add vanilla. Bake in 3 8-inch greased and floured cake pans at 350° for 30 minutes, or until a wooden pick inserted in center comes out clean. Cool in pans 10 minutes; remove from pans, and cool completely. Serves 10 or more.

Beat egg yolks until light. Beat in sugar and butter. Cook in a double boiler over medium heat until thick. Stir in remaining ingredients. Cool. Spread between layers. Frost sides and top with Seven-Minute Frosting (see index for recipe).

Lane Cake was named for Emma Rylander Lane of Clayton, Alabama, who published it in her cookbook Some Good Things to Eat *(1898). Mrs. Lane thought the flavor improved if it were made several days before serving — giving the fruit and nuts time to mellow with the bourbon.*

PINEAPPLE UPSIDE-DOWN CAKE

A one-layer beauty with pineapple rings and cherries baked on the top

½ cup butter or margarine
1 cup sugar
2 large eggs, well beaten
2 cups flour, sifted
2 teaspoons baking powder
¼ teaspoon salt
1 No. 2 can pineapple slices
4 tablespoons butter
1 cup brown sugar
Maraschino cherries

Cream butter or margarine and sugar; stir in eggs. Sift flour, baking powder, and salt. Add to creamed mixture alternately with pineapple juice. Reserve pineapple slices for top. Mix well. Place 4 tablespoons butter and the brown sugar in a 9-inch cast-iron skillet, heating until sugar is melted. Arrange pineapple slices in the skillet over butter and sugar mixture, placing a cherry in the center of each slice. Pour batter on top. Bake at 350° about 50 minutes. When a cake-tester comes out clean remove from oven and turn out on a plate at once. The pineapple and cherries will be on top. Serves 8 to 10.

LADY BALTIMORE CAKE

A novel was named for this cake

1 cup butter
2 cups sifted sugar
3½ cups sifted cake flour
4 teaspoons baking powder
¼ teaspoon salt
1 cup milk
2 teaspoons vanilla
½ teaspoon almond extract
8 egg whites

Cream butter and sugar until light. Add flour, sifted with baking powder and salt, alternately with milk. Beat well after each addition. Add extracts. Beat egg whites until stiff and fold into the mixture. Bake in 3 8-inch, well-greased layer pans at 350° for about 30 minutes. Cool in pans on racks for 10 minutes. Invert layers onto racks to finish cooling.

LADY BALTIMORE ICING

3 egg whites, unbeaten
2¼ cups sugar
½ cup cold water
2 teaspoons light corn syrup
1 teaspoon vanilla
½ cup raisins, finely chopped
1 cup pecans, finely chopped
6 dried figs, finely chopped

Place egg whites, sugar, water, and corn syrup in top of a double boiler. Cook over boiling water, beating constantly for 7 minutes. Remove from heat, add vanilla, and blend well. Reserve one-half of icing for top and sides of cake. To the remainder add finely chopped raisins, pecans, and figs. Spread the two bottom layers with this filling and cover the top and sides with plain icing. Serves about 10.

Lady Baltimore Cake was immortalized by novelist Owen Wister, who was served a piece by a Charleston lady named Alicia Rhett Mayberry. The writer was so taken with the cake that he not only described it in his next novel, but named the book — published in 1906 — Lady Baltimore.

LORD BALTIMORE CAKE

This companion to Lady Baltimore features egg yolks

¾ cup butter, softened
1¼ cups sugar
8 egg yolks
2½ cups cake flour, sifted
¼ teaspoon salt
1 tablespoon baking powder
¾ cup milk
½ teaspoon almond extract
½ teaspoon vanilla
½ teaspoon lemon extract

Cream butter; gradually add sugar; beat until fluffy. Beat egg yolks until thick and slowly add to mixture. Mix together the cake flour, salt, and baking powder and add alternately with milk. Add extracts. Pour mixture into 3 greased and floured 9-inch layer pans. Bake at 350° for 25 to 30 minutes. Cool in pans on racks for 10 minutes. Invert pans and continue cooling. Frost with Lord Baltimore Frosting. Serves 12 or more.

LORD BALTIMORE FROSTING

3 cups sugar
¾ cup water
¼ teaspoon cream of tartar
4 egg whites
2 teaspoons vanilla
¼ teaspoon lemon extract
2 teaspoons orange juice
¼ cup chopped mixed candied
    fruits
¼ cup sliced toasted almonds
¼ cup pecans, chopped
¼ cup macaroon crumbs

Cook sugar, water, and cream of tartar in a heavy saucepan to soft ball stage (238°) on candy thermometer. Beat egg whites until stiff peaks form. Slowly add sugar mixture to egg whites in a steady stream, beating constantly. Mix in vanilla, lemon extract, and orange juice. Divide mixture in half. Add mixed candied fruits, toasted almonds, pecans, and macaroons to one half. Spread between the layers. Use remaining icing to cover top and sides of cake.

MISSISSIPPI MUD CAKE WITH BAYOU ICING

Cut into small squares for a party pick-up

1 cup butter
2 cups sugar
4 eggs
1½ cups flour
⅛ teaspoon salt
½ cup cocoa
1 teaspoon vanilla
1 cup pecans, chopped

Grease a 9 x 13 inch pan. Preheat oven to 350°. Cream butter and sugar. Add one egg at a time, mixing well after each addition. Stir together flour, salt, and cocoa and blend in gradually. Add vanilla and pecans. Bake for 30 to 35 minutes.

BAYOU ICING

½ cup butter, softened
1 box (16 ounces) confectioners'
    sugar
⅓ cup cocoa
⅓ cup milk
1 teaspoon vanilla
1 7-ounce jar marshmallow creme

Cream butter, sugar, and cocoa. Add milk and vanilla. Leave cake in the pan. Smooth marshmallow creme over hot cake. Immediately spread on icing. Cool. Cut into 3 x 3 inch squares for dessert or 1½ x 1½ for party pick-ups. Makes 15 large squares or 30 small squares.

If pans are lined with paper, paper is cut to fit the bottom of the pan. The sides of pan and the paper are then buttered.

SAM LITZENBERG'S WORLD FAMOUS CHEESECAKE

The Hungry Potter Restaurant in Marshall, Texas ships this cheesecake all over the world

½ cup graham cracker crumbs
½ teaspoon nutmeg
½ teaspoon cinnamon
40 ounces (5 8-ounce bricks)
   cream cheese, room
   temperature
1½ cups sugar
1 cup sour cream
1 teaspoon vanilla extract
6 large whole eggs, plus 3 egg
   yolks
1 tablespoon lemon zest

Coat the inside of a 10-inch springform pan with a food release product. Mix the graham cracker crumbs with nutmeg and cinnamon. Cover bottom of pan with the mixture. Pat it smooth with a spoon, covering bottom evenly. The seam where the side meets the bottom should be covered. Place cream cheese in a mixing bowl, one stick at a time, and blend until smooth. Add sugar and blend again. Add sour cream, mixing well. Scrape sides and bottom of the bowl with a spatula. Add vanilla, eggs, and lemon zest. Mix a few minutes to remove any lumps. To prevent batter from splattering and ruining the crust, place spatula in the bowl and lean it against the side. Pour batter onto the blade. Fill pan until you have ½ inch of pan left showing. Using a toothpick, pop any bubbles in the batter. Preheat oven to 350°. Place cake in the center on middle rack. Remove top rack from oven. Close oven door and turn heat down to 325°. Bake 1 hour or until a light crust has formed on top of cake. Cake will rise and be over edge of pan. Reduce heat to 200° and bake 1 more hour. Turn oven off and allow the cake to stay in the oven until cool enough to touch. The center of cake should be firm and should have come back into pan. Chill overnight before serving. Serves 16.

VARIATIONS

Other flavors: To add any of the many spirits that are so much fun to work with, pour them into the batter and mix. Start off with ½ cup and taste. Add more if you wish but do not add more than 1 cup (8 ounces) or the cake will be too moist.

Amaretto Cheesecake: It will take more than 1 cup of Amaretto to get the proper flavor. Therefore, mix 2 tablespoons almond extract, 1 tablespoon vanilla extract, and 2 teaspoons chocolate extract to your cheesecake batter in place of the vanilla. This will give you that wonderful amaretto flavor without all of the extra liquid.

Lemon Cheesecake: Add ½ cup fresh lemon juice and 1 tablespoon of lemon zest. Bake as directed.

Pumpkin Cheesecake: Make batter as for plain cheesecake. Before placing on the crust remove 1¼ cups of batter and add 10 ounces pumpkin and 1 tablespoon of pumpkin pie spices to remaining batter. Blend together and bake as directed.

Chocolate Swirl Cheesecake: In a small mixing bowl pour 2 cups of the cheesecake batter. Whisk in ½ can of your favorite chocolate syrup. Mix until it is a dark brown. To pour batter use the spatula as you did for plain cheesecake. Stop at about halfway. Pour half of the chocolate mixture into the pan and pour in a circle around the side of the pan. With a fork swirl the chocolate batter around. Do no go too deep and disturb the crust. Pour in the rest of the plain batter leaving enough room in the pan for the rest of the chocolate mix. Pour in the chocolate mixture and swirl it with a fork again. Swirl in circles and make little designs in it. Don't overdo. Bake as you would the plain cheesecake.

PRALINE CHEESECAKE

5 8-ounce bricks cream cheese
1 ¾ cups brown sugar, packed
2 cups sour cream
2 tablespoons vanilla extract
6 whole eggs, plus 3 yolks
1 cup pecans

Use the same crust as the original recipe. Proceed with cream cheese. Add sugar and sour cream. Add vanilla.

Break your eggs into your blender or food processor. Add pecans and turn it on. Process or blend until the pecans are dust in the fluid. Pour into the bowl with the cream cheese. The rest of the directions are the same. The batter will be a bit thinner because of the added water in the brown sugar. If you add enough pecans it will make up for this. Bake as instructed. Serve the cake with a spoonful of pecan praline sauce over it.

PECAN PRALINE SAUCE

1 cup heavy cream
1 cup pecans, chopped
½ cup butter (1 stick)
2½ cups brown sugar
¼ teaspoon salt
2 tablespoons vanilla

Pour cream into a blender and run on low. Slowly add the pecans into the blender to grind them. Set aside. In a large pot, melt butter over high heat. Add brown sugar and salt. Whisk with wire whisk. When it starts to bubble well, add cream and pecan mixture. Keep whisking until well mixed and uniform in color. Reduce heat to medium, stirring constantly. Cook for 5 more minutes, stirring. Remove from heat, add vanilla, and allow to cool. Place in a container and refrigerate. To serve, place a spoonful in a skillet and heat. You may adjust flavor a bit by adding an ounce of bourbon along with the vanilla. The sauce is excellent over praline cheesecake, bread pudding, or ice cream. Makes about 2½ cups.

To test a cake for doneness, insert a wire cake-tester or a toothpick (broom straws may also be used). It will emerge clean when the cake is done. Cake should be lightly browned and beginning to shrink from the sides of the pan.

Candy and Confections

The dining room at the Two Meeting Street Inn, built in 1890, in Charleston, South Carolina.

Peach Leather

4 quarts peach pulp
4 cups brown sugar
Granulated or powdered sugar

Take a peck or two of soft, free-stone peaches; peel and mash them. Press the pulp through a coarse sieve and to four quarts of pulp add one quart of good brown sugar. Mix well together and boil for about two minutes.

Spread the paste on plates and put them in the sun every day until the cakes look dry and will leave the plates readily when a knife is passed around the edges of the cakes. Sprinkle some white sugar over the rough side and roll them up like sweet wafers. If the weather is fine, three days will be enough to dry them.

Apple leather is made in the same manner.

*T*he art of candy making is nearly as old as recorded history; references were found in Egyptian papyri dating hundreds of years before Christ. The universally popular sweet appeared early in the colonies of the Southern United States.

Sugar plums, made from boiled sugar, were eaten in colonial Virginia as well as candy called "marchpane," which was a form of marzipan. In Louisiana, pralines were prepared in New Orleans over two hundred years ago. Inspired by the French version using almonds, the Creoles created their own interpretation by substituting from Louisiana's abundant supply of pecans.

During antebellum times, a confection called "peach leather" was made on hot summer days on South Carolina and Georgia plantations. Puréed peaches were placed in the sun and covered with netting; at night, they were brought inside. After several days of this treatment, the mixture cooked down until it looked like leather.

Candy played an important role in Christmas celebrations on antebellum plantations just as it does today. Trees were decorated with handmade sugarplum baskets and stockings bulged with assorted confections. The laughter of children pulling taffy rang from great house and slaves' quarters alike for "taffy pulls" were a favorite social activity in both parts of the plantation.

Fudge was unknown until the late 1800s, when students began making it at Eastern girls' schools such as Vassar and Wellesley. Later, fudge making was adopted at Southern female colleges like Wesleyan in Macon, Georgia. There are many Southern variations of traditional chocolate fudge: buttermilk, peanut butter, caramel, and divinity.

Several Southern candies, such as Date Loaf Candy, are based on pecans; others, like Peanut Brittle, rely on peanuts. Florida and Texas grapefruit are spotlighted in Candied Citrus Peel and Kentucky bourbon flavors Walnut Bourbon Balls. Thus, candies become uniquely Southern when spiced from our market basket of local produce.

Two Hundred Years of Charleston Cooking
Blanche S. Rhett, Lettie Gay, Helen Woodward, Elizabeth Hamilton
Copyright University of South Carolina, 1976

BUTTER RUM MINTS

An old West Virginia recipe written in rhyme

It's creamy, pillowy, minty, and rummy —
Man-o-man, this candy is yummy!

2 cups sugar
⅔ cup hot water
1 teaspoon vinegar
¼ teaspoon cream of tartar
1 tablespoon cold butter
1 tablespoon rum
½ teaspoon spearmint flavor

Take sugar and water for a starter;
to it, add vinegar and cream of tartar.
Boil it rapidly and do not stir,
Till 260 degrees is the temperature.
Remove the syrup after it's boiled
And pour it over a surface you've oiled
With broken cold butter; then you dot it
And a full 3 minutes you allot it.
Fold over the edges when it is cool
With a candy scraper or a kitchen tool;
Now sprinkle in rum and flavor of mint,
And you're ready for the pulling stint.
Then make a rope from there to here,
And cut into pillows with a kitchen shear.
Drop them in sugar for a couple of days
In a seal-tight jar for the ripening phase.
Serve it with nectar, for this is ambrosia,
And you'll be the envy of all who knowsia!

This recipe written in rhyme has been handed down for generations in the family of Mrs. Robert Austin of Bluefield, West Virginia.

SHELLEY'S PARTY BALLS

Roll in coconut and chopped nuts

4 ounces cream cheese
2½ cups confectioners' sugar
¾ teaspoon almond extract
¾ teaspoon peppermint extract
1 or 2 drops red and green food colorings
Grated coconut
Pecans or other nuts, finely chopped

Cream cheese and sugar until stiff. Divide dough in half. Flavor one half with almond extract and tint with red food coloring. Flavor the other half with peppermint extract and tint with green food coloring. Chill 2 hours. Roll dough into marble-size balls. Roll pink balls in coconut and green balls in ground nuts. Chill until serving time. Makes 2½ dozen.

OLD-FASHIONED TAFFY

Children love to pull the taffy

2½ cups sugar
½ cup water
¼ cup vinegar
⅛ teaspoon salt
1 tablespoon butter or margarine
1 teaspoon vanilla extract

Combine the sugar, water, vinegar, salt, and butter or margarine in a large, heavy saucepan. Cook, without stirring, over medium heat just until mixture reaches the soft crack stage (270°). Remove from heat. Stir in vanilla. Pour candy onto a well-buttered jelly-roll pan or slab of marble. Let cool to the touch. Butter hands and pull candy until light in color and difficult to pull. Divide candy in half, and pull into a rope, 1 inch in diameter. Cut taffy into 1-inch pieces; wrap each piece individually in wax paper. Makes about 40 pieces.

Molasses was used for making taffy on many Southern plantations instead of sugar. Children would wrap the candy in collard green leaves to separate it and keep it from getting sticky. At times, taffy is still referred to as collard candy.

SHIRLEY'S PARTY MINTS

Pastel and pretty—perfect for a wedding

4 ounces cream cheese
1 pound box confectioners' sugar
1 teaspoon peppermint extract
1 or 2 drops each of two desired
    food colorings

Soften cream cheese. Combine with sugar and peppermint extract in food processor, using steel blade. Batter will be very stiff. Divide batter and beat the desired color into each half. Pinch off enough dough to make marble-size balls. Roll in your hand and place balls in a single layer on a tray. Air dry 30 minutes. Press each dough ball into a small mint mold (leaf, rose, or other design). Immediately pop from mold and place in single layer to air dry overnight. Makes about 5 or 6 dozen. May be frozen, but will keep in refrigerator several weeks. May be served chilled, but are better at room temperature.

Always choose a pan with about four times as great a volume as that of the ingredients used, to avoid candy boiling over.

ENGLISH TOFFEE

From Helen Conwell of Daphne, Alabama

2 cups sugar
¾ cup white corn syrup
¼ cup water
¼ cup (½ stick) butter
½ teaspoon salt
1 teaspoon soda
½ cup almonds, toasted and
    coarsely chopped
6 ounces semisweet chocolate
½ cup almonds, toasted and
    finely chopped

Bring sugar, corn syrup, and water to boil. Cook over medium-high heat until syrup reaches the hard crack stage (290°). Remove from fire, add butter, salt, soda, and coarse almonds. Stir quickly to distribute nuts and pour out on a well-buttered cookie sheet. With two table knives, stretch candy out into rectangle as it cools, lifting with one knife under the candy while pulling with both. Mark off into squares with the knife before completely hard. When cool, melt chocolate and spread over brittle. Sprinkle with finely chopped nuts. Break into squares when completely cool. Makes about 30 pieces.

Helen Conwell was winner in five categories and overall winner at the National Seafood Contest in Gulfshores, Alabama in 1985. Jo was one of the judges.

PEANUT BRITTLE

Great for gift giving

1½ cups sugar
⅔ cup white karo
⅔ cup hot water
3 tablespoons butter
1 to 1½ cups raw peanuts
½ teaspoon salt
1½ teaspoons baking soda
1 teaspoon vanilla
1½ teaspoons cold water

Butter a 3-quart heavy saucepan. Place sugar, white karo, and hot water in the pan and stir with a slotted spoon until boiling and the sugar is dissolved. Cook to the hard ball stage (254°). Add butter and raw peanuts. Cook and stir 10 minutes at medium-high heat. (Peanuts should turn a nice brown and may pop!) Remove from the heat. Mix together the salt, soda, vanilla, and cold water. Add to the peanut mixture. Stir until mixture is evenly colored. Working quickly, turn onto a large buttered cookie sheet and spread with a buttered fork and knife until thin. Break into pieces when cool and store in tightly covered tins. Makes about 30 pieces.

If you do not have a marble slab, a stoneware platter is a good substitute.

AUNT ESTHER'S PRALINES

A crisp version of the Creole specialty

1 cup sugar
1 cup boiling water
2 cups sugar
2 cups chopped pecans
1 tablespoon butter or margarine
1 tablespoon vinegar
1 teaspoon vanilla

Caramelize 1 cup sugar. Add boiling water, stirring until all lumps are dissolved. Stir in 2 cups sugar, pecans, butter, and vinegar. Bring to a boil and cook until the syrup forms a soft ball in a cup of water. Remove from stove and stir in vanilla. Continue stirring until mixture starts to glaze over. If it should get too hard, add a few drops of hot water and continue stirring. Drop by the tablespoon onto wax paper. Cool well. Makes 4 to 5 dozen.

PEANUT BUTTER ROLLS

Peanut butter encased in divinity

3 cups sugar
1 cup white corn syrup
1 cup cold water

Bring to a boil, stirring until sugar has dissolved. Don't stir anymore or scrape the pan. Cook until 260° on candy thermometer.

1 cup sugar
½ cup water
3 egg whites
1 teaspoon vanilla
Confectioners' sugar
2½ cups smooth peanut butter

In another pan, bring sugar and water to a boil and cook until 238°, stirring only until sugar has dissolved. Combine the two sugar syrups. Beat the egg whites until stiff and pour the sugar mixture into them in a slow, steady stream, beating constantly. Add vanilla. Continue beating until mixture holds a peak. Pour out onto a bread board which has been sprinkled with confectioners' sugar. Knead lightly. Break off one-fourth of mixture and roll into a square. Spread with peanut butter, stopping one inch from the sides, and roll into a jelly roll. Repeat the process with the rest. Chill until cool; slice. Makes 100 to 120 pieces.

This recipe is from Annie Ruth Johnson of Troy, North Carolina. Mrs. Johnson, a talented cook, presents her friends with boxes of assorted candies every Christmas.

LYNDIA'S DIVINITY

No Southern Christmas is complete without it

4 cups sugar
1 cup white karo
1 cup water
Dash salt
4 egg whites
2 teaspoons vanilla
2 cups chopped nuts

Mix sugar, karo, water, and salt. Cook over medium heat until syrup will form a hard ball when dropped in cold water or until a "hard ball" measurement on candy thermometer. While syrup is cooking, beat egg whites with mixer until very stiff. When syrup has reached hard ball stage, remove from heat and pour over stiffly beaten egg whites, *very slowly*, beating constantly while pouring. When all syrup has been mixed with egg whites and batter is thick, add vanilla and nuts and continue beating with wooden spoon until mixture loses its glaze. Drop by teaspoonsful onto wax paper. (If mixture becomes too hard to drop, place bowl in hot water and continue dipping.) Makes about 36 pieces.

KENTUCKY COLONELS

Bourbon balls dipped in chocolate

1 pound confectioners' sugar
½ cup butter, softened
4 tablespoons bourbon
1 cup pecans, finely chopped
   (optional)
6 squares (1 ounce each)
   unsweetened chocolate
6 squares (1 ounce each)
   semisweet chocolate
¼ of a 3-ounce bar of paraffin,
   grated

Cream sugar and butter. Add bourbon and the finely chopped pecans, if desired. Roll into very small balls and place on wax paper in the refrigerator. Melt the chocolate in the top of a double boiler over simmering water. Add the grated paraffin, stirring. Dip the balls into the melted chocolate with a toothpick. Place on wax paper and refrigerate. When dry store in a covered container. (Some Kentucky Colonel fans prefer to place the balls between two pecan halves.) Makes about 50 balls.

When using paraffin to dip candy, use the least amount called for and add more until you get the desired amount.

HEAVENLY HASH

Easy-to-make, fudgelike texture

1 12-ounce package semisweet
   chocolate chips
1 14-ounce can condensed milk
1½ cups pecans, chopped
1 10-ounce package miniature
   marshmallows
½ teaspoon vanilla

Melt chocolate chips in a double boiler over low heat. Mix in condensed milk. Stir in pecans, marshmallows, and vanilla. Pour into 9 x 13 inch buttered glass dish. When firm, cut into 2-inch pieces. Makes 3½ dozen.

EASTER EGGS

Fun to make — children and grown-ups enjoy these

¼ cup butter
1 14-ounce can sweetened
   condensed milk
1 pound box confectioners' sugar
1 14-ounce package coconut
1 teaspoon vanilla
12 ounces sweet baking chocolate
1 2-inch square paraffin

Melt butter and add sweetened condensed milk. Work in the confectioners' sugar, coconut, and vanilla. Chill and form into eggs. Chill again for several hours or overnight. Over hot but not boiling water, melt chocolate and paraffin which has been grated or processed. Dip eggs into chocolate (spear eggs with a toothpick). Cool on wax paper. Makes 2 to 3 dozen depending on size. Peanut Butter Balls or Martha Washington Creams may also be used to make Easter Eggs.

EASTER BASKETS

A very old recipe for shredded wheat caramel baskets

1½ cups brown sugar
2 teaspoons corn syrup
½ cup milk
¼ cup butter or margarine
6 large shredded wheat biscuits

Combine sugar, syrup, milk, and butter or margarine. Cook in a heavily buttered saucepan, stirring occasionally, to the soft ball stage (238°–240°). Pour hot syrup over shredded wheat biscuits that have been crumbled into a buttered bowl. Mix well and pack into well-buttered muffin pans, shaping to form cups for baskets. Chill until firm. To serve, unmold and fill centers with candy Easter eggs. Peaches or berries are good served with whipped cream in the baskets, also. Makes 6 to 8 baskets.

BUTTERMILK FUDGE

As it cooks it turns a caramel color

1 teaspoon soda
1 cup buttermilk
2 cups sugar
2½ tablespoons light corn syrup
3 tablespoons butter
1 cup pecans, chopped
1 teaspoon vanilla

Stir soda into buttermilk; add sugar and combine well. Add corn syrup and butter. Cook in a large pan over medium heat until it comes to a boil. Reduce heat and cook until it forms a soft ball in cold water (234° on your candy thermometer). Remove from heat; stir in pecans and vanilla. Cool for approximately 10 minutes. Beat until thick. Pour into a buttered 1 ½-quart dish. Cut when cool. Makes 3 dozen squares.

ROY HENDEE'S PEANUT BUTTER FUDGE

A treasure from Mary Leigh's brother in Atlanta

1 5-ounce can evaporated milk
2 cups sugar
3 tablespoons peanut butter
½ teaspoon vanilla

Bring milk and sugar to a boil over medium heat. Reduce heat to low. Cook to soft ball stage or 234° on candy thermometer. Add peanut butter and stir well. Cool 5 minutes. Add vanilla. Beat until it creams and pour into greased 1 ½-quart dish. Cool until firm. Cut into squares. Makes 2½ dozen.

GRANNY'S CARAMEL FUDGE

Jo's mother's recipe

3¼ cups sugar, divided
½ cup butter or margarine
1 cup evaporated milk
1 teaspoon vanilla
1 cup pecans or walnuts

Caramelize ¼ cup sugar in a heavy 3-quart sauce-pan. Let sugar turn to a light brown. Add butter or margarine, mixing well. Stir in the rest of the sugar and the milk. Cook over medium heat to soft ball stage or 240°, stirring constantly. Remove from heat and add vanilla. Let it cool for about 25 minutes, then beat until thick, smooth, and glossy. Add nuts. Pour into a buttered 9 x 13 inch baking dish. Cut into squares while still warm. Makes about 30 pieces.

Jo's mother makes her caramel icing for cakes by letting it boil to 238°. This amount will ice three layers of the 1-2-3-4 cake. Granny also pours the candy over marshmallows for Caramel-Covered Marshmallows.

AUNT SARA'S WHITE FUDGE

Perfect for gift giving

2¼ cups sugar
½ cup sour cream
¼ cup milk
2 tablespoons butter
1 tablespoon light corn syrup
¼ teaspoon salt
2 teaspoons vanilla
1 cup pecans or walnuts, chopped
⅓ cup candied cherries, chopped

Combine sugar, sour cream, milk, butter, corn syrup, and salt in a heavy 2-quart saucepan. Stir over medium heat until sugar is dissolved and mixture reaches a boil. Boil over medium heat 9 to 10 minutes to 238° (soft ball stage). Remove from heat and allow to stand until lukewarm (110°), about 1 hour. Add vanilla and heat until mixture just begins to lose its gloss and hold its shape, which does not take long. Quickly stir in nuts and cherries. Turn into an oiled pan. Let stand until firm before cutting. Makes 1½ pounds.

Jo's Aunt Sara, who lives in Pensacola, Florida, is a descendant of Newt Vick's brother. Newt Vick was the founder of Vicksburg.

EGGNOG FUDGE

Pretty with melted chocolate drizzled over the tops

2 cups sugar
1 cup eggnog, homemade or
    commercial
1 tablespoon light corn syrup
2 tablespoons butter or margarine
1 teaspoon vanilla
½ cup walnuts or pecans,
    chopped
2 tablespoons semisweet
    chocolate pieces
2 tablespoons butter or margarine

Butter sides of a heavy 3-quart saucepan. Combine sugar, eggnog, and corn syrup. Cook over medium heat stirring constantly, until sugar dissolves and mixture boils. Cook to the soft boil stage (238°), stirring as necessary. Immediately remove from heat and cool to lukewarm (110°) without stirring. Add 2 tablespoons butter and the vanilla. Beat vigorously until it is thick and loses its gloss. Quickly stir in the nuts. Spread in a buttered 8 x 4 x 2 inch pan. In a glass measuring cup combine chocolate and remaining butter. Set cup in a pan with 1 inch of hot water. Melt chocolate and drizzle over the top of fudge. Makes 1 pound.

A candy thermometer is invaluable in candy making.

MISS NINA'S CHOCOLATE FUDGE

Smooth, creamy, perfect texture

2½ cups sugar
1 5-ounce can evaporated milk
¼ cup cocoa
2 tablespoons light corn syrup
1 teaspoon vanilla
1 tablespoon butter
1 cup pecans, chopped

Bring sugar, milk, cocoa, and corn syrup to a boil over medium heat. Reduce heat to low and cook slowly until it forms a soft ball in cold water or to 234° on the candy thermometer. Add vanilla and butter. Cool for 10 minutes (approximately). Beat until creamy but not too thick. Stir in pecans. Pour into a buttered 1½-quart dish. When firm, cut into squares. Makes 2½ dozen.

WALNUT BOURBON BALLS

A staple during the Christmas holidays

2½ cups vanilla wafers, crushed
1 pound box confectioners' sugar
2 tablespoons cocoa powder
1 cup walnuts, finely chopped
    (pecans may be substituted)
3 tablespoons white corn syrup
¼ cup bourbon

Mix crushed vanilla wafers, 1 cup of the confectioners' sugar, cocoa powder, and finely chopped walnuts until well blended. Mix the syrup and the bourbon. Stir into the dry mixture. Roll into 1-inch balls, then coat with the remaining confectioners' sugar by placing sugar in a brown paper bag. Add the balls and shake to coat evenly. Chill the balls in the refrigerator overnight or store for several weeks in tins in the refrigerator. Makes about 40 to 50 bourbon balls.

PEANUT BUTTER BALLS

An easy-to-make confection that is good any time of the year

1 cup confectioners' sugar, sifted
½ cup peanut butter
¼ teaspoon salt
1 cup pecans or walnuts
1 teaspoon vanilla
3 tablespoons water
    (approximately)
½ cup peanuts, finely chopped

Place sugar, peanut butter, and salt in a bowl; blend with a fork until evenly mixed and like coarse meal. Add nuts, then vanilla and 2 tablespoons of the water, a small amount at a time. Knead until consistency of fudge, adding more of the water if necessary. Shape into small balls or 1-inch rolls. Roll in crushed peanuts or confectioners' sugar. Peanut Butter Balls may be coated in melted chocolate with paraffin, if desired. (See index for Martha Washington Creams.) Makes about 30 to 40.

MARTHA WASHINGTON CREAMS

A Southern classic

2 pounds (2 boxes) confectioners'
  sugar
1 8-ounce can sweetened
  condensed milk
1 cup (2 sticks) butter, softened
1 teaspoon vanilla
1 cup pecans, finely chopped
1 16-ounce package semisweet
  chocolate
A 2- to 3-inch square paraffin,
  grated

Mix sugar with condensed milk and butter. Add vanilla and pecans. Roll into small balls about ¾-inch in diameter and place on wax paper. Refrigerate covered until ready to dip. Melt chocolate squares in the top of a double boiler over hot, not boiling, water. Stir in grated paraffin, testing until you get the desired consistency. Spear balls with toothpicks and dip in the melted chocolate. Allow excess to drip off balls and place them on wax paper. When chocolate is set store in airtight container lined with wax paper. The creams keep, chilled, for up to 2 weeks. Makes 200 balls.

This recipe is from Molly Thompson of Florence, Mississippi. The whole family gathers around to make Martha Washington Creams at Christmas.

COCONUT CANDY

Always made with fresh coconut

3 cups sugar
1 cup coconut milk
½ teaspoon salt
3 cups grated fresh coconut
1 teaspoon vanilla

Combine sugar, coconut milk, and salt. (If you do not get enough milk from coconut, add a little plain milk to the juice to measure 1 cup.) Boil until it forms a hard ball in cold water or registers 250° on a candy thermometer. Remove from heat and beat until thick. Add coconut and vanilla. Drop by teaspoonful onto a greased cookie sheet or wax paper. Makes about 50 pieces.

BRANDI'S HOT DATES

Sweet dates wrapped in spicy cheese blankets

2 sticks butter
½ pound sharp cheddar cheese,
  grated
2 cups flour
¼ teaspoon cayenne pepper (or
  more, to taste)
1 8-ounce package pitted dates

Cream butter and cheese. Slowly beat in flour; add cayenne. Pinch off pieces of mixture to wrap each date. Bake at 425° on ungreased cookie sheet for 10 to 15 minutes. Makes 35.

CANDIED CITRUS PEEL

So pretty and good, you may never throw away another fruit peel

3 grapefruit, preferably pink
6 oranges, with thick skins
6 large limes
6 lemons
3 cups sugar, plus enough to roll
    peel in
4 quarts water

Reserve a plastic bag in the freezer to place peel in as you use the fruit. When peeling the fruit keep in mind that you will be using it for this purpose and section fruit attractively. With a knife, make incisions through the skin of each piece of fruit to separate it into six or eight sections from stem end to bottom of fruit. Separate the skin from fruit and place in bags in refrigerator or freezer. It will keep for 3 days in the refrigerator and 3 months in the freezer. Do *not* remove the white pith from the peel. Place peel in a large, heavy pot and cover with cold water. Bring to a boil and let boil for 30 seconds. Pour into a colander, rinse under cold water, and rinse the pot. Return the peels to the pot and repeat the procedure. Return the peels to the clean pot again and add 3 cups and 4 quarts water. Bring to a boil and boil gently, uncovered, until the skins are transparent. This will take 1½ to 2 hours. Cover a cookie sheet with granulated sugar and roll peels in the sugar until well coated. Let them cool and dry for at least 1 hour. Store in glass jars in the refrigerator.

Fruit peels have decorated Southern desserts for many years. They are not only indispensible for fruitcakes but are often used to decorate the many pudding and poached fruit desserts Southerners are fond of. Chocolate-coated, they make welcome gifts and are often used to decorate the tea tray.

CHOCOLATE COATING FOR CANDIED CITRUS PEEL

Dark chocolate is elegant on one end of the peel

4 ounces semisweet chocolate
2 ounces unsweetened chocolate
1 teaspoon butter
Candied citrus peel

Melt chocolate in the top of a double boiler and stir in the butter. Do not let the chocolate get too hot. Dip half the peel in the chocolate. Remove peel and let the excess chocolate drip off for a few seconds. Place peel onto wax paper. You may store in a jar in the refrigerator. Should coat at least 50 pieces.

WHITE CHOCOLATE COATING

2 tablespoons thick cream
6 ounces white chocolate, shaved
 or broken into very small
 pieces
Candied citrus peel

Heat the cream in the top of a double boiler over hot but not boiling water. Stir in the shaved white chocolate. Remove from heat and cool slightly. Dip half of peel in the mixture and let excess drip off for a few seconds. Place peel onto wax paper. Store in a jar in the refrigerator. Should coat at least 50 pieces.

KUMQUAT BASKETS

Beautiful on a tray of chocolate-dipped candied citrus peel

1 12½-ounce jar preserved
 kumquats or crystalize fresh
 ones (see index for Candied
 Citrus Peel)
4 cups sugar
½ cup crystalized ginger

Drain kumquats and cut in half. Carefully remove the inside pulp. Arrange on sugar in a small pan and sprinkle sugar very thickly over them. Allow them to dry for about 24 to 36 hours. Shake off excess sugar and fill each half with chopped crystalized ginger. Makes about 48 filled kumquat halves.

SUGAR PLUMS

Small balls of dried fruit, nuts, and candied orange peel

1 cup figs
1 cup raisins
1 cup pitted dates
1 cup walnuts
1 tablespoon candied orange peel
2 to 4 tablespoons orange juice
½ pound confectioners' sugar

Put through food chopper or process with the steel blade of a food processor the figs, raisins, dates, walnuts, and candied orange peel. Moisten with the orange juice until the right consistency to make into small balls. Roll in confectioners' sugar. Store in tightly covered tins in the refrigerator. Makes about 80 small balls.

𝒫runes stuffed with almond paste and soaked in sherry make nice sugarplums.

CHRISTMAS BERRIES

Pretty candies — similar to marzipan

1 can sweetened condensed milk
4 3½-oz. cans flaked coconut
1 6-oz. package strawberry
  gelatin
1 cup ground blanched almonds
1 teaspoon almond extract
Red food coloring as needed

Combine milk, coconut, and ⅓ cup gelatin. Add almonds, almond extract, and food coloring to tint mixture. Chill until firm enough to handle. Form by ½ tablespoons into strawberry shapes and roll in the remaining gelatin to coat. Place on wax paper lined baking sheets and refrigerate. Makes about 60 berries. These will keep up to 2 weeks in the refrigerator.

STEMS FOR BERRIES

2 cups sifted confectioners' sugar
¼ cup heavy cream
Green food coloring

Combine ingredients and put into a pastry bag with a large open star tip. Pipe stem onto top of berry.

Christmas Berries are served at the annual Victorian Christmas Luncheon at Magnolia Hall in Natchez, Mississippi.

APRICOT STICKS

Appropriate anytime, they are a delight to serve

1 large orange
1 12-ounce package dried apricots
1 cup sugar
1 cup pecans, coarsely ground
Very fine granulated sugar

Squeeze orange, reserve juice. Force peel and apricots through a food chopper twice, grinding peel at fine and apricots at medium. Add 1 cup sugar and ¼ cup juice; cook over very low heat about 30 minutes. Add more juice if necessary. Mixture should be quite stiff. Cool; add pecans and mix well. With damp hands shape into small sticks. Roll in sugar. Store in airtight container and refrigerate or freeze. Sticks may be rolled in sugar again just before serving. Makes about 12 dozen.

Apricots plumped and one-half dipped in melted white chocolate make a nice addition to confection tray.

DATE LOAF CANDY

Pack in "goody boxes" for Christmas gifts

3 cups sugar
1 cup milk
¼ teaspoon baking soda
2 cups pitted dates, chopped
1 tablespoon butter
1 cup pecans, chopped
½ teaspoon vanilla

Bring sugar and milk to a boil. Add soda, dates, and butter. Cook to soft ball stage (234° on candy thermometer). Add pecans and vanilla. Cook about 5 more minutes. Remove from heat. Beat until it holds its shape. Soak a dish towel in cold water. Wring dry. Spread the towel on a tray. Spoon the candy mixture onto the center of the cloth in a long line. Roll the cloth around the mixture to form a loaf. Place tray with rolled candy in refrigerator. Chill overnight. Slice into thin slices. Makes 5 dozen.

ORANGE PECANS

A holiday tradition

1½ cups sugar
½ cup fresh orange juice
½ teaspoon salt
1 tablespoon grated orange peel
2½ cups pecan halves

Boil sugar, orange juice, and salt together to the soft ball stage (240°). Remove from the fire and add orange peel. Stir in the pecans. Keep stirring until syrup begins to look cloudy. Pour out on a lightly buttered surface. Separate at once into small clusters or halves. Store in an airtight container. Makes 75 to 100 pieces.

Orange Pecans have been a holiday tradition in Kate Box's family in Jackson, Mississippi for generations.

STUFFED DATES

Heavenly, laced with bourbon

1 box pitted dates
15 marshmallows
15 pecan halves
1 cup bourbon
2 cups confectioners' sugar

Open dates and stuff with a half of a marshmallow and a half of a pecan. Press closed. Dip stuffed dates in a bowl of bourbon. Leave long enough to get the flavor desired (from 1 hour to overnight). Roll in confectioners' sugar. Set on wax paper to dry slightly. Store in tins in the refrigerator. Makes about 30 stuffed dates.

CHOCOLATE STUFFED FIGS

Stuffed and coated with chocolate, these are heavenly

1 pound dried whole figs
½ cup heavy cream
4 ounces (squares) sweet
   chocolate, cut into pieces
¼ cup pecans, finely chopped
½ teaspoon vanilla
2 ounces (squares) sweet
   chocolate, melted

Soften figs in a little warm water if they appear to be too hard. Dry thoroughly. Remove stems and slit the figs almost to the bottom (do not cut all of the way). Gently pull sides apart. Heat heavy cream in the top of a double boiler and add chocolate pieces. Bring water to a boil and let chocolate mixture come to a boil, stirring constantly. Remove from heat and place bowl in another bowl filled with ice. Stir until cold. Add pecans and vanilla. Spoon mixture into the figs until filled so they are the size of fresh figs. Melt remaining chocolate over hot water. With dipping fork, dip each fig in the chocolate, coating half the fig. Rotate to remove excess chocolate. Place on wax paper, at room temperature to set. Makes about 18 to 20 stuffed figs.

For candy making use a pan with a heavy bottom and a wooden spoon.

Cookies and Small Cakes

The Colonial Room at the Smithsonian Institution, in Washington, D.C.

Grandmother Black's Tea Cakes

Cream together ½ cup butter, 1 cup sugar; blend in 1 egg; sift together and add to above mixture: ½ teaspoon salt, 2 teaspoons baking powder, 2 cups sifted flour, 1 teaspoon vanilla.

Let chill for at least one hour, then roll out small amounts of dough at a time and cut with a small cookie cutter. Bake on lightly greased cookie sheet in 400° oven for 8 to 10 minutes. If desired, blend together ¾ cup sifted confectioner's sugar and add 3-4 teaspoons of water. Color with food coloring and brush on the cookies while warm. May As Well Leave the Lid Off the Cookie Jar.

Some of my most cherished memories are the times of getting off the school bus to share the day's events with my Grandmother Black. As we ate warm tea cakes, she would tell me about my forefathers who came to this country so we could worship God in a free country.

*T*he joy of cookie making has been celebrated in America since the Dutch introduced the delicious snacks to their colonies. The word "cookie" came from the Dutch word "koekje," meaning "little cake." German and French settlers made similar sweets and the three methods gradually blended into the repertoire of Southern cuisine.

Although the English preferred the word "biscuit" to "cookie," they brought recipes for small cakes with them to Virginia. Martha Washington is known to have served Shrewsberry Cakes and Jumbles, a buttery cookie that was twisted into various shapes, during Christmas holidays at Mount Vernon.

Seasonings like ginger and many extracts were available in the colonies together with almonds and fruit. Molasses was the sweetener of necessity because sugar was expensive. Molds of different shapes and tin cookie cutters were used to make decorative designs.

Recipes arrived from many sources. Thomas Jefferson, the indefatigable Southern gourmet, discovered French macaroons and meringues in Paris while serving as minister to France and brought them home to Monticello. While president, Jefferson often requested a plateful of cookies with a decanter of wine for a late-night snack.

As always, Southerners were resourceful at using native products. Pecans were often featured in recipes and eventually peanuts came into vogue, notably in famous Peanut Butter Cookies. Southern peanuts and pecans are now America's favorite nuts.

Cookies are more popular than ever in today's South. Bake sales to raise money for charity are widely held and homemade cookies make excellent fund raisers. Cookies appear on almost any party table where the Southern sweet tooth is evident in pick-up desserts as well as savory hors d'oeuvres. Add the endless variety of recipes in regional cookbooks and it becomes obvious that Southern cookie making is still a joy.

Harrison County Heritage Sketch
Harrison County Conservation Society
Harrison County, Texas
(limited to 700 copies)

RIBBON COOKIES

A really pretty cookie that is nice for special occasions

1 cup margarine
1¼ cups sugar
1 egg, beaten
1 teaspoon vanilla
2½ cups flour
1½ teaspoons baking powder
½ teaspoon salt
¼ cup candied cherries, cut in
  small pieces
1 square unsweetened chocolate
¼ cup pecans
2 tablespoons poppy seed

Cream margarine and sugar; add egg and vanilla. Sift flour, baking powder, and salt. Add to creamed mixture. Mix well. Divide in three parts. Add cherries to one part, chocolate and pecans to another, poppy seed to the third part. Line a 12 x 4 inch pan with wax paper. Place dough with cherries on bottom, then the chocolate dough and nut mixture, and then the poppy seed mixture. Cover with wax paper. Chill in the refrigerator overnight. Cut loaf in half lengthwise. Slice thin cookies with a sharp knife. Bake on an ungreased cookie sheeet in a 375° oven for 10 to 12 minutes. Makes 6 dozen.

SANDIES

Pretty and festive on a party tray

1½ sticks butter
4 tablespoons confectioners'
  sugar
2 teaspoons cold water
1 teaspoon vanilla
2 cups flour
⅛ teaspoon salt
1 cup pecans, finely chopped
1 cup confectioners' sugar

Cream butter and sugar. Mix in water and vanilla. Add flour slowly, beating well after each addition. Mix in salt. Stir in pecans. Form balls approximately 1 inch in diameter with hands. Bake on greased cookie sheet at 275° for about 40 minutes. When done, roll in confectioners' sugar. Makes 3 dozen.

DELTA MELTING MOMENTS

A melt-in-your-mouth cookie from the Mississippi Delta

½ pound butter
5½ tablespoons confectioners'
  sugar
1¼ cup flour
½ cup cornstarch
¼ teaspoon almond extract
¼ teaspoon orange extract

Cream butter and sugar. Sift in flour and cornstarch. Mix together. Add flavorings and chill overnight. Shape into balls the size of walnuts and place on a greased cookie sheet. (Do not use butter on the cookie sheet; it will burn.) Flatten the balls with bottom of a small wet glass. Bake at 350° for 10 minutes. Cookies do not brown. Makes 2 dozen.

COOKIE GLAZE

1 cup powdered sugar
1 tablespoon melted butter
1 tablespoon lemon juice
1 tablespoon orange juice

Beat all ingredients together. Carefully remove cookies from pan and spread with cookie glaze while warm.

This recipe is from Heart Warming Recipes *by the Belzoni Garden Club in Belzoni, Mississippi, and was submitted by the cookbook committee.*

ELIZABETH MATTINGLY'S BUTTER COOKIES

Pretty party cookies with jelly centers

3 sticks butter, softened
1 cup sugar
3 egg yolks, beaten
3 cups flour
½ teaspoon vanilla or almond
   extract
Currant or other jelly

Cream butter and sugar; add beaten egg yolks. Gradually mix in flour and extract. Chill for 30 minutes or more. Pinch off dough and form into small balls. Place on greased cookie sheets; press a hole in the center of each ball with your finger. Fill holes with jelly. Bake in a preheated 350° oven for 15 to 20 minutes. Makes 5½ dozen.

SHREWSBERRY CAKES

A beautiful butter cookie with citron in the center

3 cups sugar
1½ pounds (6 sticks) butter
7 eggs
2 teaspoons vanilla
12 cups flour
4 ounces citron, cut into small
   pieces

Cream the sugar, butter, and eggs together. Stir in vanilla and slowly work in the flour. Chill in the refrigerator for 4 hours or overnight. Roll out to ¼-inch thickness on a floured board. Cut with a 2-inch round or scalloped cookie cutter. (Traditionally these are cut round and scalloped on the edges with thumb and finger.) Place a small piece of citron in the center of each cookie. Bake on a foil-lined cookie sheet or a greased cookie sheet, about 1 inch apart, in a preheated 350° oven for 10 to 12 minutes. Makes 12 dozen.

Note: Recipe may be halved successfully. To halve the egg, place 1 beaten egg in a cup and scoop out half.

HEBREW COOKIES

A century-old family secret

1 pound butter or margarine
1¼ cups sugar
3 eggs
3 cups pecans or walnuts
1 cup bourbon
8 to 8½ cups flour
2 cups confectioners' sugar
4 tablespoons cinnamon

Cream the butter and sugar until light. Add the eggs, nuts, and bourbon. Stir in enough flour for a medium-textured dough to roll like a pie crust. Chill the dough for 4 hours or overnight in the refrigerator. Place on a floured board and roll out as for pie dough ⅛ to ¼ inch thick. Cut into ¾ x 2 inch strips. Bake in a preheated 400° oven for 10 to 15 minutes or until firm to the touch. Mix confectioners' sugar and cinnamon together. Roll cookies, while still hot, in the sugar-cinnamon mixture. Makes well over 100 cookies. Store in tins.

Over eighty years ago Mrs. Perkins and Mrs. Henshaw of Jackson, Mississippi, had an aunt who hand stitched beautifully. A neighbor asked her to make a baby bonnet for a new family arrival. The aunt told her that she would not take any amount of money for the bonnet and would only make it if the neighbor would give her the recipe for Hebrew Cookies, a treasured family secret. Now it is a treasured recipe in Mrs. Perkins' and Mrs. Henshaw's family though there is some disagreement on how it should be made. One sister likes her Hebrew Cookies one-eighth of an inch thick while the other likes hers one-fourth of an inch thick. Either way, they both agree that they are the best cookies that they have encountered in their eighty-odd years. Neither sister remembers why the cookies were named Hebrew Cookies.

LEMON THINS

The crisp, lemony flavor goes perfectly with tea

½ cup butter, softened
½ cup sugar
2 eggs, well beaten
1 cup flour, sifted
1 teaspoon lemon extract

Cream butter, add sugar gradually, and beat until fluffy. Add beaten eggs and mix well. Gradually beat in flour and lemon extract. Drop with a teaspoon onto oiled cookie sheets, leaving 2 inches between each cookie. Bake in 350° oven until brown around edges. Cool slightly. Remove with a spatula to wire racks to cool well. Makes 4 dozen.

Never place cookie dough on a hot cookie sheet. It should be completely cool.

AUNT PITTYPAT'S JUMBLES

A favorite since Martha Washington's time

1¼ cups sugar
¾ cup margarine
3 eggs
4½ cups flour
3 teaspoons baking powder
½ teaspoon mace
⅔ teaspoon salt
3½ tablespoons orange juice
2 tablespoons lemon juice
1 cup pecans or walnuts, chopped

Cream the sugar and margarine. Add the well-beaten eggs one at a time, then add flour, baking powder, mace, and salt sifted together, alternately with the orange and lemon juice. Taste for seasoning and add more juice if necessary. Stir in the chopped nuts. Chill dough several hours or overnight. Turn onto a slightly floured board and roll ¼ inch. Cut into jumbles with a 2-inch doughnut cutter. Pull them slightly to make more oblong than round. Place on a greased baking sheet, leaving a little space between them, about ½ inch. Bake in a 350° preheated oven for 12 to 15 minutes or until firm to the touch. Makes about 4 dozen. For variety divide the dough into three portions. Mix ingredients as directed, then finish in one of the following ways:

Brush tops of cut cookies with egg wash (see index for recipe) and sprinkle with granulated sugar, then bake.

Brush tops of cut cookies with egg wash and place chopped or split almonds on each jumble, then bake.

Add ½ cup seedless raisins to mixture before rolling and cutting.

MARYLAND BLACK PEPPER COOKIES

Their spicy taste goes well with lemonade or iced tea

4 eggs, separated
1½ cups brown sugar
2 cups flour
¼ teaspoon salt
2 teaspoons cinnamon
1 teaspoon cloves
½ teaspoon black pepper
½ teaspoon soda
½ teaspoon baking powder
1 cup raisins
1 cup walnuts, chopped

Beat egg whites and yolks separately, combine and beat together. Slowly mix in brown sugar. Sift flour with salt, cinnamon, cloves, black pepper, soda, and baking powder. Blend into egg mixture. Stir in raisins and walnuts. Drop by teaspoonsful onto buttered cookie sheet. Bake at 350° for approximately 10 minutes. Makes 7 dozen small cookies.

ALPHABET COOKIES

Twist into letter shapes

1 cup butter or margarine
1 cup sugar
2 eggs
1 teaspoon vanilla
4 cups pastry flour
Grated rind of 1 lemon
1 scant tablespoon crushed
 cardamom

Cream the butter and sugar together; add well-beaten eggs and vanilla. Mix flour with lemon rind and crushed cardamom; add to batter. Knead the mixture in the bowl with hands until thoroughly mixed. Chill for a few hours. Cut off a small portion and with the palms of the hands, roll it into a long cylindrical strip about ½ inch thick. Form the dough into any letters desired and bake on a greased baking sheet at 450° for about 10 minutes. Dough will be firm to the touch. The amount will depend on size of letters desired but should get you through the alphabet several times.

NUT HOOPS

These bring back delicious memories

¾ cup sugar
1 cup butter or margarine
3 egg yolks
1 teaspoon vanilla
3½ to 4 cups flour
1 egg white, beaten to a froth
¼ cup walnuts, finely chopped

Cream sugar with butter. Beat in yolks and add vanilla. Slowly work in flour and knead until well mixed. This makes a stiff dough. Roll out ¼ inch thick and cut into rings with a doughnut cutter. Brush with beaten egg white and sprinkle with chopped nuts. Bake at 350° for 10 to 12 minutes or until slightly brown. Makes about 6 dozen.

PECAN CRISPS

Rich and crunchy — a pecan-lover's dream

1 cup margarine
2½ cups brown sugar
2 eggs, beaten
2½ cups flour
⅛ teaspoon salt
½ teaspoon soda
1 cup pecans, chopped
1 teaspoon vanilla

Cream margarine and sugar. Beat in eggs. Sift together flour, salt, and soda. Blend gradually into creamed ingredients. Stir in nuts and vanilla. Drop by teaspoonsful on greased cookie sheet and bake at 350° for approximately 15 minutes. Makes 10 dozen.

CARAMEL PECAN BARS

One of the best recipes in the book

1 cup butter or margarine
1½ cups brown sugar
2 cups flour
1 cup pecans, chopped
1 12-ounce package milk
   chocolate chips

Beat ½ cup butter and 1 cup brown sugar. Mix in flour. Mixture will be consistency of coarse meal. Press into ungreased 13 x 9 inch pan. Scatter pecans over mixture. Melt ½ cup butter in saucepan. Stir in ½ cup brown sugar and bring to a boil over medium heat. Boil 1 minute, stirring constantly. Pour over pecans and crust. Bake approximately 20 minutes, until golden brown and bubbly. After removing from oven, sprinkle milk chocolate chips over top while hot. When chocolate begins to melt, spread it over surface. Cool; cut into squares. Refrigerate 30 minutes. Pack in tins. Makes 3 to 4 dozen.

GEORGIA PEANUT COOKIES

A yummy drop cookie

½ cup margarine
1 cup sugar
2 eggs
2 cups sifted flour
2 teaspoons baking powder
½ teaspoon salt
¼ cup milk
1½ cups chopped peanuts

Cream together margarine and sugar. Add beaten eggs and blend thoroughly. Sift flour, measure, add baking powder and salt, and sift again. Add alternately with milk to creamed mixture. Add nuts and mix only enough to blend. Drop by teaspoonsful onto greased baking sheet. Bake in 400° oven about 10 minutes. Makes 8 dozen 1½-inch cookies.

Always preheat the oven and use only one rack. Pans should be at least 2 inches from oven walls. If using two smaller pans, see that they are spaced evenly from each other.

PEANUT BUTTER COOKIES

Serve with milk for an after-school treat

1 cup margarine, softened
1 cup smooth peanut butter
1 cup sugar
1 cup brown sugar
2 eggs, well beaten
2½ cups sifted flour
1½ teaspoons baking soda
1 teaspoon baking powder
½ teaspoon salt

Cream margarine and peanut butter until smooth. Add sugars gradually and cream thoroughly. Add well-beaten eggs to mixture. Sift flour once before measuring. Then, sift flour, soda, baking powder, and salt together and add to creamed mixture. Chill dough. Form into walnut-size balls. Place on greased baking sheets. Flatten with a fork dipped in flour, making a criss cross pattern. Bake at 350° for 10 to 12 minutes. Makes 6 to 8 dozen.

PEANUT BLOSSOMS

Pretty to serve; satisfying to eat

½ cup butter or margarine
½ cup crunchy peanut butter
½ cup granulated sugar
½ cup brown sugar
1 egg
1⅓ cups flour
1 teaspoon baking soda
½ teaspoon salt
2 tablespoons milk
1 teaspoon vanilla
Granulated sugar
48 chocolate kisses, unwrapped

Cream together margarine and peanut butter. Beat in sugars. Add egg. Sift flour, soda, and salt and add to mixture alternately with milk. Mix in vanilla. Form teaspoons of dough into balls. Roll balls in granulated sugar and place on ungreased cookie sheet. Bake at 350° for 12 minutes or until light brown. As soon as cookies are removed from oven, press a kiss in the center of each, firmly, so that cookie cracks around edge. Makes 4 dozen.

CRY BABIES

Molasses was cheaper than sugar in the Old South

½ cup shortening
½ cup sugar
½ cup molasses
1 egg, slightly beaten
1½ teaspoons ginger
¼ teaspoon salt
⅓ cup boiling water
1½ teaspoons baking soda
2 cups flour

Cream shortening and sugar well, beat in molasses, and add slightly beaten egg. Add ginger, salt, boiling water, and baking soda. Mix thoroughly. Stir in flour. Drop by teaspoonsful onto greased cookie sheets at least 2 inches apart. Bake at 350° for 10 to 12 minutes or until babies are done, but still soft. Makes 3 dozen.

BELL-RINGER MOLASSES COOKIES

Serve with mild cheddar cheese at your next cocktail party

2 cups brown sugar
1 cup shortening
1 egg
1 cup molasses
4 cups all-purpose flour
½ teaspoon salt
2 teaspoons baking soda
1 teaspoon cinnamon
½ teaspoon cloves
1 teaspoon vanilla
1 teaspoon lemon extract

Cream sugar, shortening, egg, and molasses (buy dark Jamaican molasses for best flavor). Sift together dry ingredients and gradually add to the creamed mixture. Add vanilla and lemon extract. Chill dough. Form 1-inch balls and place on greased cookie sheet. Bake at 350° for about 12 minutes. May be sprinkled with sugar as soon as removed from oven. Cool cookies slightly before handling. Makes 5 to 6 dozen.

These cookies are sold every fall at the Oktoc Country Store during a fund-raising celebration in Oktoc, Mississippi. They taste even better with cool apple cider.

SIX-FLAVOR REFRIGERATOR COOKIES

Makes one roll each of plain, chocolate, coconut, fruit, nut, and spice

6 cups flour, sifted
4 teaspoons baking powder
½ teaspoon salt
1½ cups margarine
3 cups brown sugar
2 eggs, well beaten
2 teaspoons vanilla
2 squares (2 ounces) chocolate
⅓ cup shredded coconut
⅓ cups currants, raisins, or
    chopped dried fruit (dates,
    apricots, prunes, or figs)
⅓ cup nuts, finely chopped
    (almonds, pecans, peanuts, or
    walnuts)
½ teaspoon cinnamon
½ teaspoon nutmeg

Sift flour, baking powder, and salt. Cream margarine and sugar until fluffy. Add eggs and vanilla. Slowly and gently work flour mixture into creamed mixture. Divide into six equal portions. Leave one portion plain and make variations of remaining dough. Shape into rolls and chill overnight. When firm slice very thin and bake in a 375° oven for 10 to 12 minutes. Makes 10 dozen cookies.

Chocolate: Add 2 ounces melted chocolate to one portion of dough and roll.

Coconut: Add ⅓ cup shredded coconut to one portion of dough.

Fruit: Add ⅓ cup of your chosen fruit (soften figs by steaming or boiling in water) to one portion of dough.

Nut: Add ⅓ cup finely chopped almonds, pecans, peanuts, or walnuts to one portion.

Spice: Add ½ teaspoon cinnamon and ½ teaspoon nutmeg to one portion of dough.

ROBERT E. LEE COOKIES

Spicy molasses cookies with a fragrance that permeates the entire house

1½ cups (3 sticks) butter or
   margarine, melted
½ cup molasses
2 cups sugar
2 eggs
4 cups flour
4 teaspoons soda
2 teaspoons cinnamon
1 teaspoon ginger
1 teaspoon cloves

Melt the butter and add molasses, sugar, and eggs. Beat well. Sift together and add to the mixture the flour, soda, cinnamon, ginger, and cloves. Refrigerate dough for several hours. Break off pieces of dough (heaping teaspoon-sized) and roll into small balls. Roll balls in sugar. Place on an ungreased cookie sheet about 1½ inches apart. Bake in a preheated 350° oven until firm and brown, about 8 to 10 minutes. Makes 10 dozen.

This recipe came from Stratford Hall, Virginia. It is said to be a favorite cookie of the Lee family, especially young Robert E. Lee. The cookies are baked at the Lee Plantation and served with warm apple cider to visitors.

CHERRY WINKS

As pretty and colorful as they are good

2¼ cups flour
1 teaspoon baking powder
½ teaspoon baking soda
½ teaspoon salt
¾ cup margarine
1 cup sugar
2 eggs
2 tablespoons milk
1 teaspoon vanilla
1 cup chopped pecans
1 cup chopped dates
1 12-ounce jar maraschino
   cherries

Sift together the flour, baking powder, soda, and salt. Blend the margarine, sugar, eggs, milk, and vanilla. Add dry ingredients to the creamed mixture. Stir in the chopped pecans, dates, and ⅓ cup chopped cherries. Grease a baking sheet and drop cookie batter from a teaspoon about one-half full. Place a piece of cherry (½ or ⅓) in the center of each cookie. Bake at 350° for 12 to 15 minutes. Makes about 4 dozen.

Grease cookie sheets with unsalted fats. For delicate cookies, use a greased parchment or foil liner from which they peel off easily when slightly cooled.

MOTHER'S COCONUT CRUNCHIES

A wholesome, comforting snack

½ cup shortening
½ cup sugar
½ cup brown sugar
1 egg
½ teaspoon vanilla
1 cup flour
¼ teaspoon baking soda
½ teaspoon baking powder
⅛ teaspoon salt
1 cup quick oatmeal
1 cup corn flakes
1 cup angel flake canned coconut

Cream shortening with sugars. Add egg and vanilla. Sift together flour, soda, baking powder, and salt. Slowly beat into shortening mixture. Stir in oatmeal, corn flakes, and coconut. Form into walnut-sized balls, place on buttered cookie sheet 2 inches apart, and flatten with heel of your hand. Bake in 350° oven 15 to 20 minutes or until golden. Makes 5 dozen.

BILLYE TAYLOR'S RAISIN COOKIES

A raisin-filled cookie of German origin

2 cups brown sugar, packed
1 cup (2 sticks) butter
3 eggs
1 teaspoon vanilla
4½ cups flour, unsifted
1 teaspoon baking soda
⅛ teaspoon salt

Cream sugar with softened butter. Add slightly beaten eggs and vanilla. Add flour mixed with soda and salt to the creamed mixture gradually. Chill dough overnight in the refrigerator. Remove a small portion at a time from the refrigerator and roll out thin on a lightly floured board. Cut half the cookies 1½ inches round for the bottom layer and 2 inches round for the top of the cookie. Put 1 tablespoon chilled filling on bottom round and cover with top round. Seal edges with a fork. Place on an ungreased cookie sheet and bake in a 325° oven for 10 minutes. Cool on racks and store in airtight cookie tins for several weeks; they will keep up to a month. Makes about 6 dozen cookies.

FILLING

2 cups brown sugar
3 cups seedless raisins
3 tablespoons cornstarch
2 cups water

Boil together the brown sugar, raisins, cornstarch, and water until raisins are plumped and mixture is thickened. Chill overnight. It is important that the filling be kept well chilled while making cookies, otherwise the filling will not be thick enough to stay on cookie while assembling.

LITTLE LEAGUE OATMEAL COOKIES

Also a winner with the little Miss Teaset crowd when iced and sprinkled with coconut

1½ cups sifted flour
1 cup sugar
½ teaspoon baking soda
1 teaspoon salt
½ teaspoon nutmeg
¾ teaspoon cinnamon
¾ cup margarine
1 egg, well beaten
1 cup mashed ripe banana (2 to 3 bananas)
1¾ cups rolled oats, uncooked
½ cup chopped pecans or walnuts
½ cup raisins
1 cup chocolate chips

Sift into mixing bowl flour, sugar, soda, salt, nutmeg, and cinnamon. Cut in margarine. Add egg, bananas, rolled oats, nuts, raisins, and chocolate chips. Beat until thoroughly blended with a spoon. Drop by teaspoonsful about 1½ inches apart, onto ungreased cookie sheet. Bake in a 400° oven about 15 minutes, or until edges are browned. Remove from pan immediately and cool on a rack. Makes about 3½ dozen cookies.

BANANA ICING

¼ cup mashed ripe banana
½ teaspoon lemon juice
⅛ teaspoon salt
2 tablespoons softened butter or margarine
2½ cups sifted confectioners' sugar
1 cup grated coconut

Mix the mashed banana with the lemon juice and dash of salt. Cream in the softened butter or margarine. Gradually beat in the confectioners' sugar. Beat until fluffy. Ice the cookies and sprinkle with tinted coconut. To tint coconut, shake white coconut in a covered jar or plastic bag with a few drops of vegetable coloring until tinted. Pink and green are especially nice.

LEE ANN HAYES DATE NUT FINGERS

Festive addition to a party platter

1 stick butter
2 cups brown sugar
2 eggs
1⅓ cups flour
1 teaspoon vanilla
1 teaspoon almond extract
1 cup walnuts, chopped
1 8-ounce package seeded, chopped dates
Confectioners' sugar

Cream butter and sugar. Add eggs. Mix in flour, vanilla, and almond extract. Stir in walnuts and dates. Pour into greased 3-quart glass dish. Bake at 325° for 30 minutes. Cut into rectangular fingers. Sprinkle with confectioners' sugar while still warm. Makes 40.

DATE PINWHEEL COOKIES

A festive cookie — good anytime

1 cup chopped dates
2 cups brown sugar, firmly
   packed
½ cup water
⅔ cup margarine
2 eggs
1 teaspoon vanilla
4 cups flour
1 teaspoon baking soda
¼ teaspoon cream of tartar
½ teaspoon salt

Make the filling by placing dates, ½ cup of the brown sugar, and water in a saucepan. Simmer about 8 minutes, or until mixture thickens, stirring constantly. Remove from heat and cool. Cream margarine and the remaining sugar until light. Beat in eggs and vanilla. Sift flour, measure, and sift again with the soda, cream of tartar, and salt. Stir flour mixture into margarine mixture gradually to make a stiff dough. Divide dough in half. Roll out each portion on a lightly floured board, making a rectangle about 8 x 10 inches and ¼ inch thick. Spread each with half the cooled date filling. Roll like a jelly roll. Wrap in wax paper and chill thoroughly for 12 hours or overnight. Cut slices ¼ inch thick with a sharp knife. Place on an ungreased baking sheet. Bake in a 400° oven for 8 to 10 minutes. Makes 7 to 8 dozen.

PECAN SOUFFLÉ TASSIES

Perfect for any party, they make their own crust

1 cup sugar
4 eggs
2 cups milk
½ cup melted margarine
½ cup flour
1 teaspoon vanilla
1 cup pecans, chopped
72 small pecan halves for garnish

Place sugar, eggs, milk, margarine, flour, vanilla, and 1 cup chopped pecans in a blender. If blender will not contain the entire mixture, reserve some of the milk to add later. Pour mixture into greased miniature muffin pans, about half full. Place a pecan half on top of each pie. Bake in a preheated 300° oven for 30 to 35 minutes or until a knife in the center comes out clean. Makes about 72 tassies.

To soften hard, dry cookies, put them with a piece of bread into a tightly closed container. Replace the bread every few days, for it molds easily.

HEDGEHOGS

A Creole specialty — delicate and delicious

2 cups walnuts or pecans
1 cup (8-ounce package) pitted
  dates
1 cup brown sugar
2 eggs
1½ cups shredded coconut

These are best done in a food processor though ingredients may be chopped by hand and blended with a mixer. Process nuts until fine and remove from the workbowl. Process dates until they are well chopped or they form a ball. Without removing from the processor, mix brown sugar and egg with the dates. Process just until blended. Add the nuts and ½ cup coconut. Process until stiff and forms a ball. Shape into rolls 1 inch long and ½ inch thick. Roll each cookie in the remaining 1 cup coconut. Place on a greased cookie sheet. Bake at 350° for 15 to 20 minutes or until the coconut is a delicate brown. Remove and cool. Store in an airtight tin for at least a week. Makes about 2 dozen.

CALAS TOUT CHAUD

Spicy deep-fried rice balls

⅔ cup long grain rice
1½ cups water, boiling
1½ cups flour
1½ teaspoons baking powder
1 teaspoon cinnamon
½ teaspoon nutmeg
2 eggs
1½ tablespoons sugar
½ teaspoon vanilla
Oil for frying
Confectioners' sugar
Maple or other syrup or honey

Cook rice in boiling water according to manufacturer's directions. Cool to room temperature. Mix together flour, baking powder, cinnamon, and nutmeg. Beat eggs in a separate bowl; beat in sugar, add vanilla. Stir rice into egg mixture. Gradually stir in flour mixture. Make 12 small rice balls by wetting your hands and forming them by squeezing and shaping the mixture. Fry them in deep fat at 350° until golden and crunchy. Sprinkle with confectioners' sugar. Serve with syrup. Makes 12 balls.

Calas were sold in the French Quarter on Sunday mornings by turbanned black women. "Belles calas tout chauds," they would cry, arousing sleepy residents who ate the crisp sweets for breakfast.

If you have frozen baked cookies, thaw them unwrapped. Heat them for a moment on a cookie sheet in a 300° oven to restore crispness.

CHARLOTTE CHARLES' TOP HATS

Make them small for pretty party pick-ups

½ cup shortening
½ cup granulated sugar
½ cup light brown sugar
1 egg
½ teaspoon vanilla
1 cup flour
½ teaspoon baking soda
¼ teaspoon salt
1 cup cornflakes, crushed
1 cup quick cooking oats
½ cup grated coconut

Beat shortening and granulated and brown sugars until light and creamy. Add egg and vanilla. Sift together flour, baking soda, and salt and blend into mixture. Crush cornflakes in food processor or blender and stir into mixture. Add oats and coconut. Remove one-third of dough; shape remaining two-thirds of dough into balls, using a level teaspoon. Place on greased cookie sheets. Flatten with bottom of glass which has been covered with a dish towel, moistened, and dipped in flour. Bake at 350° for 10 to 12 minutes. Shape reserved dough into balls, using half teaspoons. Bake little balls on greased cookie sheets at 350° for 8 minutes. Cool. For miniature, party-size Top Hats, use ½ teaspoon batter for bottom layers, ¼ teaspoon for balls.

CHOCOLATE FILLING

1 cup semisweet chocolate
   morsels
½ cup confectioners' sugar
1 tablespoon water
1 3-ounce package cream cheese,
   softened

Melt chocolate with sugar and water in double boiler over hot water. Cool slightly. Beat cream cheese until smooth and blend in chocolate mixture. Spread filling over large cookies and top with small ones. Makes 3½ dozen standard-size cookies.

CHOCOLATE MERINGUE COOKIES

A chocolatey, chewy cookie with a crinkly top

3 egg whites
1 cup confectioners' sugar, sifted
1 6-ounce package semisweet
   chocolate pieces, melted
½ teaspoon vanilla
⅓ cup saltine crackers, finely
   crumbled

Beat egg whites until stiff but not dry. Add sugar slowly, beating well. Fold in the cooled melted chocolate and vanilla. Stir the finely crumbled saltines into the mixture. Drop by teaspoonsful onto a greased cookie sheet or a foil-lined sheet 2 inches apart. Bake at 350° for about 15 minutes or until firm to the touch. Makes about 3 dozen.

PAT ROSS'S LADYFINGERS

Homemade ladyfingers are a real treat

3 egg yolks
9 tablespoons sugar, divided
⅛ scant teaspoon salt
½ teaspoon vanilla
¾ cup sifted cake flour
3 egg whites
Confectioners' sugar

Have eggs at room temperature. Preheat the oven to 325°. Butter a cookie sheet or have ladyfinger pans prepared. Beat the egg yolks, 6 tablespoons of sugar, and salt together until thick and lemon-colored and will hold the ribbon stage. Add the vanilla. Sift the cake flour and measure. Carefully and gradually fold it into the egg yolk-sugar mixture. Beat the egg whites until they reach soft peaks and then add 3 tablespoons sugar (1 tablespoon at a time, beating after each addition). Beat until stiff. Stir about one-third of the egg whites into yolk mixture and fold in the rest. Put the batter into a pastry bag with a ½-inch tip and press 4-inch-long cookies onto a buttered baking sheet. Sprinkle with confectioners' sugar and bake until lightly brown (about 9 to 10 minutes). Let them cool on the baking sheets for about a minute, then transfer to racks and let cool completely. Store in an airtight container. Makes 2½ dozen.

CHOCOLATE-COVERED CHERRY COOKIES

That "something different" which makes a party

3 cups flour
1 cup unsweetened cocoa
½ teaspoon salt
½ teaspoon baking powder
½ teaspoon baking soda
1 cup margarine, softened
1¾ cups sugar
2 eggs
2½ teaspoons vanilla
2 (10-ounce) jars maraschino
  cherries
1 (12-ounce) package semisweet
  chocolate pieces
1 cup sweetened condensed milk

Stir together flour, cocoa, salt, baking powder, and soda. Cream margarine and sugar. Add eggs and vanilla and beat well. Gradually add flour mixture to butter mixture. Beat well. Shape dough into small balls and place on ungreased cookie sheets. Press center of each ball with middle finger. Drain cherries, reserving juice. Place a cherry in the center of each cookie. Combine chocolate pieces and condensed milk in the top of a double boiler. Heat until chocolate is melted. Stir in 8 teaspoons reserved cherry juice. Spoon about 1 teaspoon frosting over each cherry, spreading to cover well. You may thin frosting by adding more cherry juice. If you run out of cherries, insert pecan halves. Bake at 350° for 10 minutes. Cool on wire racks. Makes about 88.

CHOCOLATE ALMOND BALLS

Bite-sized balls of buttery chocolate

2 squares semisweet chocolate
1 tablespoon milk
¾ cup butter
½ cup sugar
2 teaspoons vanilla
2 cups flour
1 teaspoon baking soda
½ teaspoon salt
½ cup slivered almonds
Confectioners' sugar

Melt chocolate and milk in top of a double boiler. Cool. Cream butter and sugar and add vanilla. Mix in chocolate mixture. Blend in flour, soda, salt, and stir in almonds. Chill for approximately 3 hours. Shape dough into small balls. Bake on ungreased cookie sheets in 350° oven for approximately 15 minutes. Roll in confectioners' sugar while still slightly warm. Makes 4 dozen.

MAIDS OF HONOR

An English teatime favorite adopted by the South

¾ cup butter or margarine,
  softened
½ cup sugar
2 cups flour
¼ teaspoon salt

Preheat oven to 350°. Grease bottoms and sides of 3½ dozen miniature muffin tins. Cream butter or margarine with sugar and gradually mix in flour and salt. Pinch off small pieces of dough and press into tins, forming a cup. Set aside.

FILLING

2 eggs
½ cup sugar
2 tablespoons flour
2 tablespoons butter, melted
½ cup almond paste
1½ tablespoons sherry
⅛ teaspoon nutmeg
Raspberry or strawberry
  preserves

Beat eggs well and add sugar and flour slowly. Mix in butter, almond paste, sherry, and nutmeg. Spoon ½ teaspoon of preserves into each muffin cup. (Be careful not to put in too much.) Fill muffin cups with custard. Bake at 350° for approximately 30 minutes. Makes 3½ dozen.

These delicious tarts were brought to the mid-Atlantic South by English settlers, and became quite popular. Some claim the very old sweet was named for the maids of honor at the court of Elizabeth I. Other sources report they were first baked by Anne Boleyn for the court of Henry VIII when she was maid of honor to Catherine of Aragon. Whether they helped Anne lure Henry from Catherine is open to debate.

COCONUT MACAROONS

From the Cloister Hotel at Sea Island, Georgia

5 ounces almond paste
20 ounces (2½ cups) granulated
**   sugar**
1 cup (about 8) egg whites
1 teaspoon vanilla extract
10 ounces coconut, shredded
1½ ounces (3 tablespoons) all-
**   purpose flour**

Break up almond paste into small pieces. Add sugar a little at a time, using a mixer or hands, until completely mixed and looks like coarse meal. Gradually add the egg whites, scraping down the bowl at least once. Add vanilla. Place bowl in a hot water bath (to heat), stirring the mixture constantly. Heat until the mixture is too hot to touch. Set aside. Blend coconut and flour. Then mix all ingredients together using a wooden spatula. Drop by teaspoonsful or fill a pastry bag with the mixture and drop through a number 8 star tube onto a paper pan liner or brown paper that has been cut to fit your cookie sheet. Bake in a pre-heated 350° oven until golden brown, about 15 to 20 minutes. Let the macaroons cool completely before removing them. Let them dry a little on racks. Store in airtight tins. Makes about 4 dozen.

Note: The coconut might be dry at times and therefore will absorb more moisture, causing the mixture to be too stiff and hard to pipe out. This can be corrected by adding a little more egg white to the mixture. Pat Ross, a noted cooking instructor, advises that if dough is not stiff enough you may add ground almonds to the dough to stiffen it. This also gives it an interesting crunch.

MAMA SUGAR'S OATMEAL SHORT'NIN BREAD

Nourishing and not too sweet

1½ cups unsifted flour
⅔ cup quick-cooking rolled oats
⅔ cup brown sugar
1 cup (2 sticks) butter or
**   margarine**

Combine flour with oats in a bowl. Add sugar and stir in the butter or margarine. Mix with your fingers until well blended and crumbly. Press firmly and evenly into a lightly buttered pie pan. Bake in a 300° oven for about 45 minutes. Cut into thin wedges while still warm and cool them in the pan. Serves 12.

BINNY'S BEIGNETS

New Orleans French Market doughnuts

1 package yeast
¼ cup warm water
⅓ cup sugar
1 cup warm milk
½ teaspon salt
2 tablespoons corn oil
4–5 cups flour
2 eggs, beaten
Oil for frying
Confectioners' sugar

Dissolve yeast in warm water. Add sugar; mix in warm milk, salt, corn oil, and part of flour. Mix well. Alternately add eggs and enough flour to make a soft, non-sticky dough. Knead well and place in a covered, greased bowl for 30 minutes. Divide dough in half. Keep unused part of dough covered. Roll out to ¼ inch thickness and cut into rectangles 2 x 3 inches. At this point you may refrigerate overnight or freeze for a few weeks. Cook only 3 or 4 at a time in deep fat heated to 360°, turning often. Drain well and serve with confectioners' sugar. Makes 3 to 4 dozen.

STRAWBERRY KISS MERINGUES

From historic Stagecoach Inn in Saledo, Texas

7 egg whites
⅛ teaspoon salt
½ teaspoon cream of tartar
1½ cups sugar, sifted
1 teaspoon vanilla
¾ cup sugar

Place the egg whites, at room temperature, in a bowl; add salt and cream of tartar. Use wire whisk and beat until they are very stiff. Add sifted sugar ½ teaspoon at a time. Continue to beat, then add vanilla. Fold in the ¾ cup sugar. The Inn uses a pastry bag to form a circle of the meringue mixture (use large nozzle). A spatula or spoon may also be used to form ovals. The meringues may be shaped on wax paper covering a baking sheet – allow 3 inches between each one. Bake slowly at 225° for 45 to 60 minutes. The meringues may dry in the oven with slightly open door for about 10 minutes after heat is turned off. Makes about 3 dozen meringues. The Inn makes a dessert by filling the meringues with a scoop of vanilla ice cream and topping them with sweetened, crushed strawberries. Make the meringues slightly larger than cookie-size when doing this.

The Stagecoach Inn was originally a stage stop built in 1852 around a five-hundred-year-old oak tree. It is now a hotel and restaurant.

PENUCHE LACE TULIPE COOKIES
DAIRY HOLLOW HOUSE

From a bed and breakfast inn in the Ozarks

½ **cup butter**
⅔ **cup light brown sugar**
½ **cup light corn syrup**
1 **cup unbleached white flour**
1 **tablespoon plus 1 teaspoon**
  unsweetened cocoa
½ **teaspoon vanilla**
⅓ **cup regular oatmeal**

Preheat oven to 375°. Grease two cookie sheets. Combine first three ingredients in a heavy saucepan and bring to a boil. Remove from heat. In a separate bowl, combine flour and cocoa. Add corn syrup mixture and beat in vanilla and oatmeal. Batter will be like a thick, sticky syrup. Drop two heaping tablespoons batter, widely separated, onto prepared cookie sheet. Place in oven. Bake for 6 to 7 minutes. Put the second cookie sheet with its 2 spoonsful of batter in the oven while the first batch cools for about 30 seconds. Get out two stemmed wine glasses and a long, thin-bladed pancake-turner-type spatula. Working carefully, pry a still-soft cookie from sheet with the spatula and *immediately* drape over flat stem-base of wine glass. Cookie will fold down over sides in an irregular flower shape that is flat on the bottom. Let cookie cool while on wine glass. Do the same with second cookie. Repeat with remaining batter. Serve filled with one of the following: chocolate mousse flavored with Drambuie; vanilla ice cream with hot fudge sauce or fresh berries marinated in Chambord liqueur; persimmon or apricot purée folded into sweetened whipped cream; chopped bananas and toasted pecans folded into whipped cream sweetened with brown sugar. We like to pour a pool of either custard sauce or raspberry sauce on a dessert plate, set the filled tulipe atop this, and garnish the whole thing with a mint leaf or a twist of orange. Makes 1½ to 2 dozen.

Dairy Hollow House is a restored 1880s farmhouse and cottage with accommodations for fifteen people and fantastic food, located in the Victorian resort town of Eureka Springs, Arkansas.

*W**hen using brown sugar always pack the sugar into the measuring cup.*

CREOLE LACE COOKIES

Pecan lace cookies from Lee Barnes Cooking School in New Orleans

1⅓ cups pecans, chopped
1 cup sugar
4 tablespoons flour
⅓ teaspoon baking powder
⅛ teaspoon salt
½ cup (1 stick) butter, melted
2 teaspoons vanilla
1 egg, beaten

Mix well the pecans, sugar, flour, baking powder, and salt. Add the melted butter, vanilla, and egg. Drop onto foil-lined cookie sheet in scant teaspoonsful. Place about 3 inches apart. Bake in a 325° oven for 8 to 12 minutes, depending upon your oven. Let cool. Peel off the foil. Makes about 4 dozen.

REBA'S LEMON LOVE NOTES

A must on your cookie list

¾ cup flour
⅓ cup butter
2 eggs
1 cup brown sugar
¾ cup shredded coconut
½ cup pecans or walnuts, chopped
⅛ teaspoon baking powder
½ teaspoon vanilla
1 teaspoon grated lemon rind
1½ tablespoons lemon juice
⅔ cup confectioners' sugar

Mix together flour and butter to a fine crumb. Sprinkle evenly in an 11 x 7 inch pan. Bake in a 350° oven for 10 minutes. Beat eggs, mix in brown sugar, coconut, chopped nuts, baking powder, and vanilla. Spread on first mixture as you take it from the oven; return to oven and bake 20 more minutes. Mix lemon rind and juice. Add confectioners' sugar to make a creamy mixture. Spread over top as soon as pan is taken from oven. Cool and cut into squares. Makes 24 squares.

BAKED FUDGE

Serve this old Georgia recipe with whipped cream or ice cream

½ cup butter
3 squares (3 ounces) chocolate
1 cup sugar
2 eggs
½ cup flour
1 teaspoon vanilla
⅔ cup pecans or walnuts, finely chopped

Melt butter and chocolate in the top of a double boiler over hot water; remove from fire; add sugar and unbeaten eggs. Beat until well blended. Add the other ingredients; pour into a greased and floured square cake pan to the depth of ½ inch. Bake in a 325° oven until firm as a custard, about 45 to 50 minutes. It firms when refrigerated several hours. Chill and cut into squares. Makes 12 squares.

BROWNIE CUPS

Perfect pick-up for a cocktail buffet

1 cup butter or margarine,
   softened
6 ounces cream cheese, softened
1 cup flour

Blend butter and cream cheese until smooth. Add flour gradually. Form into a ball; chill 1 hour. Press into 3½ dozen greased miniature muffin tins. Set aside. Preheat oven to 350°.

FILLING

2 eggs
¼ teaspoon salt
½ cup sugar
¾ cup milk chocolate chips
½ cup pecans, chopped
½ teaspoon vanilla

Beat eggs well; mix in salt and sugar. Chop chocolate chips in food processor until fine. Stir chocolate, pecans, and vanilla into batter. Spoon into pastry shells. Bake 20 minutes. May be topped with tiny dollops of sweetened whipped cream. Makes 3½ dozen.

MILDRED BROWN'S CRÈME DE MENTHE BROWNIES

Pretty party pick-up from a talented caterer

2 eggs
¼ pound butter, melted
1 cup sugar
2 1-ounce squares unsweetened
   chocolate, melted
2 tablespoons crème de menthe
½ cup flour, sifted
½ cup pecans, ground

Combine eggs, butter, and sugar; beat well. Blend in chocolate and crème de menthe. Stir in flour and ground pecans. Pour into well-greased 9-inch square pan. Bake for 30 minutes at 350°. Cool in pan.

TOPPING

2 tablespoons butter, softened
1 cup confectioners' sugar
1 tablespoon milk
1 teaspoon peppermint extract
1 or 2 drops green food coloring

Beat butter in mixer until soft and gradually add sugar, milk, and peppermint extract. Tint with green food coloring. Spread thinly onto cake.

GLAZE

1 tablespoon margarine, melted
1 1-ounce square unsweetened
   chocolate, melted

Stir melted margarine and chocolate together. Drizzle over icing. Cut into small squares. Makes 2½ dozen.

CORRINE'S SOUTHERN BELLE BROWNIES

Iced brownies that are perfect for parties or bake sales

1 cup butter or margarine
½ cup cocoa
2 cups sugar
4 eggs
2 cups flour
½ teaspoon baking powder
¼ teaspoon salt
3 teaspoons vanilla

Melt ½ cup butter or margarine with cocoa in the top of a double boiler. Set aside to cool. Cream the other ½ cup butter or margarine with sugar. Add the cocoa mixture. Add eggs and beat well. Sift flour, baking powder, and salt together. Add to the above mixture a little at a time. Stir in vanilla. Pour batter into a greased 11 x 12 inch or 10 x 15 inch pan. Bake in a 325° oven for 35 minutes. When cool frost with One-Minute Fudge Frosting. Makes about 24 brownies.

ONE-MINUTE FUDGE FROSTING

¼ cup butter or margarine
¼ cup cocoa
¼ cup milk
1 cup sugar
2 teaspoons vanilla
½ cup pecans

Melt butter or margarine and cocoa. Add milk and sugar. Bring to a rolling boil. Boil for 1 minute. Remove from heat, add vanilla. Beat while hot until it begins to thicken. Add nuts and spread on brownies. If any icing is left drop on wax paper and place a pecan on the top. It makes great candy.

PAM MAYFIELD'S BLONDE BROWNIES

Everyone will want the recipe

1 cup flour
½ teaspoon baking powder
⅛ teaspoon baking soda
½ teaspoon salt
1 cup chopped pecans
½ cup margarine
1 cup brown sugar
1 egg, slightly beaten
1 teaspoon vanilla
½ of a 6-ounce package chocolate
  chips (3 ounces)

Sift together the flour, baking powder, baking soda, and salt. Add the chopped pecans. Set aside. Melt the margarine; add brown sugar and beaten egg. Stir in the vanilla. Add the flour mixture, stirring well. Turn into a greased and floured 8 x 8 x 2 inch cake pan. Sprinkle with the chocolate chips and bake at 350° for 20 to 25 minutes. Cool in the pan. Makes 16 squares. Pam usually doubles the recipe and puts it in a 9 x 13 inch pan.

VICKSBURG BUTTER CREME BROWNIES

Slice into fingers instead of squares for a party treat

1 square semisweet chocolate
¼ cup butter
1 egg
½ cup sugar
¼ cup flour
¼ cup pecans, finely chopped

Melt chocolate and butter together over hot water and cool slightly. Beat egg until frothy. Stir into chocolate mixture. Add sugar. Blend well. Add flour and nuts and stir until well blended. Pour into 8 x 8 inch pan. Bake 13 to 15 minutes at 350°. Cool and cover with butter creme filling. Makes 2 dozen.

BUTTER CREME FILLING

1 cup confectioners' sugar
2 tablespoons butter, softened
¼ teaspoon vanilla extract
1 tablespoon heavy cream or
    evaporated milk

Cream together and spread over brownie layer. Put pan in refrigerator for 10 minutes. Remove and spread with glaze.

GLAZE

2 tablespoons butter
2 squares semisweet chocolate

Melt butter and chocolate together. Spread gently over filled brownie layer being careful not to disturb filling. Chill in refrigerator until glaze sets. Cut into small finger strips. Can be frozen. Food coloring may be added to creme filling for different holidays and occasions.

This delicious brownie is used with the permission of the Vintage Vicksburg Cookbook committee. It is the recipe of Mrs. Earl (Edith) Lundy.

TOFFEE-TOPPED SQUARES

A short'nin bread that tastes like toffee candy

¼ cup butter
6 tablespoons sugar, divided
1 cup self-rising flour
¼ cup butter
1 14-ounce can sweetened
    condensed milk
¼ cup pecans or walnuts,
    chopped
½ teaspoon vanilla
4 ounces sweet chocolate, melted
1 tablespoon water

Cream ¼ cup butter with 4 tablespoons sugar. Blend in flour. Spread evenly in a greased 8-inch pan. Bake at 350° for 20 minutes. Mix together ¼ cup butter, 2 tablespoons sugar, sweetened condensed milk, and pecans or walnuts. Add vanilla. Pour over shortbread and cool. Melt chocolate with the tablespoon water and spread over the toffee. Cool and cut into small squares. Makes 12 to 16.

CARAMEL BROWNIES

Good!

2 cups sugar
1 cup (2 sticks) butter
4 egg yolks, beaten
3 cups cake flour
2 teaspoons baking powder

Cream sugar and butter until light and fluffy. Add beaten egg yolks. Sift flour and baking powder together. Slowly stir in the batter. Spread the batter mixture over the bottom of a greased and lightly floured 10½ x 15½ x 2½ inch pan. Mix the icing and spread over the batter. Bake at 350° for 50 to 60 minutes.

ICING

4 egg whites
2 cups dark brown sugar
1 cup pecans, finely chopped
1½ teaspoons vanilla

Beat egg whites until stiff. Slowly stir in the dark brown sugar. Mix in the pecans and vanilla. Makes about 48 squares.

BOBBYE J. PORTER'S GINGERBREAD MEN

A food-processor recipe from the owner of the Post House Restaurant in Natchez

2 cups unbleached flour
1 cup cake flour
2 teaspoons ground ginger
1½ teaspoons cinnamon
1 teaspoon baking powder
¾ teaspoon salt
½ teaspoon baking soda
½ teaspoon grated nutmeg
½ teaspoon cloves
½ teaspoon cardamom
½ teaspoon dry mustard
1 egg
½ cup sugar
½ cup brown sugar, firmly
   packed
½ cup unsalted butter, room
   temperature
¼ cup (2 tablespoons) dark
   molasses
½ cup confectioners' sugar
Currants, pine nuts, cinnamon
   candies (optional decorations)

With steel knife in food processor, combine first 11 ingredients and blend well 5 seconds. Transfer flour mixture to medium bowl and set aside. Mix egg, granulated sugar, brown sugar, and butter in a workbowl 1 minute. Add molasses and blend 15 seconds. Return flour mixture to workbowl and mix using off and on turns until flour is incorporated. Do not overprocess. Transfer dough to plastic bag and flatten into disc. Seal tightly and chill at least 4 hours or overnight. Preheat oven to 250°. Dust pastry sheet with confectioners' sugar. Divide dough into 4 equal portions. Roll out to thickness of ¼ inch. Cut with 1½ inch cookies cutter. Bake 12 minutes. Store in airtight container. Can use gingerbread man cutter and decorate if desired. Makes 22 gingerbread men.

DUTCH GINGER THINS

A colonial delight

1¼ cups sifted flour
½ cup sugar
½ cup butter or margarine
1 egg, separated
¼ teaspoon vanilla
¼ cup sliced preserved ginger, ⅛ inch thick, well drained
1 teaspoon preserved ginger syrup

Sift flour and measure. Mix in the sugar. Cut in butter or margarine. Beat the egg yolk slightly and stir into the mixture. Add vanilla. Work dough with hands until smooth. Roll out dough on a floured board to about ⅛ inch thick. Cut with a 2½-inch scalloped or round cookie cutter. Place on an ungreased cookie sheet. Press a ginger slice into each cookie center. Beat egg white with ginger syrup. Brush cookies with mixture. Bake in a 375° oven for 10 to 12 minutes until lightly browned. Makes about 2 dozen.

CANDY-CANE COOKIES

Decorate the tree or tuck into bows on Christmas gifts

3½ cups flour
1¼ cups (2½ sticks) butter or margarine, softened
1 cup confectioners' sugar
1 teaspoon vanilla extract
¼ teaspoon salt
1 egg
½ teaspoon red food coloring
½ teaspoon peppermint extract
¼ cup granulated sugar
2 to 3 drops red food coloring (optional)

Combine the flour, butter, confectioners' sugar, vanilla extract, salt, and egg with an electric mixer at low speed until well blended. Remove half of the dough from the bowl and set aside. Knead in red food coloring and peppermint extract until well blended. On a lightly floured board, roll 1 rounded teaspoonful plain dough into a 4-inch rope. Repeat, using 1 teaspoon red dough. Place ropes side by side and gently twist together pinching ends to seal. Curve one end of rope to form handle of candy cane. Place cookie on ungreased cookie sheet with spatula. Repeat with remaining dough. Sprinkle cookies with granulated sugar that has been tinted red with the food coloring, if desired. Place in a preheated 375° oven for 10 to 12 minutes or until lightly browned. Cool cookies on a rack and store in a tightly covered tin for up to one week. Makes about 4 dozen.

LIZZIES

Fruit and nuts look like jewels in a miniature cake confection

1 cup butter, room temperature
1 cup brown sugar
4 eggs
3 cups flour
1 teaspoon nutmeg
1 teaspoon cinnamon
¼ teaspoon ground cloves
4 cups pecans (3 cups chopped, 1
  cup halves)
1 cup candied cherries, chopped
  into fourths
½ cup citron
1 8-ounce box pitted dates,
  chopped
1 cup candied pineapple, cut into
  small wedges
3 tablespoons milk
½ cup blackberry wine or orange
  juice (⅓ cup bourbon may be
  substituted)

Cream butter and sugar well. Add eggs one at a time, beating well after each addition. Add ½ cup flour and mix well. Add spices. In a separate bowl place nuts (both pieces and halves) and cut-up fruit and add ½ cup flour, stirring to coat all of the pieces well. Fold fruit mixture into creamed mixture. Add milk, wine, orange juice or bourbon, and balance of flour. Mix batter well. Drop by teaspoonsful onto foil-lined cookie sheet or into tiny paper cups for miniature cakes. Bake for 20 minutes at 350° or until light brown (they will still be soft). Makes about 10 dozen.

It is unknown where Lizzies got their name. They have been a popular fruitcake cookie for as long as anybody can remember.

Sprinkle small squares of fruitcake with sherry or bourbon. Coat with confectioners' sugar. Nice for parties or to serve with tea.

OVERNIGHT SLICED FRUIT COOKIES

A delicious cookie recipe from the past

¾ cup butter
2 cups light brown sugar
3 eggs
1 teaspoon baking soda
1 tablespoon water
¼ cup finely chopped citron
¼ cup finely chopped raisins
¾ cup pecans, finely chopped
¼ teaspoon almond extract
3½ cups flour
Sugar

Put butter in a mixing bowl and set the bowl over hot water until the butter softens; remove the bowl, add brown sugar and eggs, and beat until the mixture is blended. Dissolve soda in the tablespoon water. Add to the butter-sugar mixture. Add fruits, nuts, and almond extract and stir in the flour. Turn into a greased bread pan. Set the pan in the refrigerator overnight or longer. When ready to bake the cookies, turn the dough onto a bread board and cut into very thin slices. Place on a greased baking sheet, sprinkle with sugar, and bake in a hot oven at 425° for 12 to 15 minutes. Leave plenty of room between the cookies as they spread. Makes about 3½ dozen. If smaller cookies are desired, the cookie dough may be placed in small bread pans or rolled in wax paper and refrigerated. This recipe makes the large, old-fashioned kind.

BENNE SEED COOKIES

Sesame seeds are called benne seeds in the South and are considered to be lucky

1½ cups butter, room temperature
3 cups brown sugar
4 eggs
2½ cups flour
½ teaspoon baking powder
1 cup benne seeds (sesame seeds), toasted
2 teaspoons vanilla

Cream butter with brown sugar and eggs. Sift flour with baking powder and add to the batter. Mix well. Add the toasted benne seeds and vanilla. Drop by ¼ to ½ teaspoonsful about 2 inches apart onto a foil-lined cookie sheet. Bake at 325° about 15 minutes or until brown. This amount makes about 15 dozen wafer-thin cookies the size of a silver dollar. The recipe may be halved if you do not want as many cookies. They keep well in tins for weeks and are addictive!

Note: To toast benne seeds place in an iron or heavy skillet and cook over low heat, stirring constantly, until light golden. You may also place in a 300° oven for 15 minutes, stirring occasionally.

Benne seeds date from the days of slavery. They were brought into the country from Africa aboard the slave ships. The word benne is derived from an African language.

FRESH BLUEBERRY TASSIES

Blueberries with currant jelly and sour cream

½ cup (1 stick) unsalted butter,
   softened
⅓ cup sugar
⅓ cup ground almonds
2 egg yolks
½ teaspoon vanilla
¼ teaspoon salt
1⅓ cups flour

Beat butter until fluffy. Beat in sugar, almonds, egg yolks, vanilla, and salt until blended. Stir in flour just until blended. Divide dough into 24 balls. Place in 1½-inch greased tart pans. Lightly press to cover bottom and sides. Prick dough with fork; chill ½ hour. Bake in preheated 350° oven 15 to 18 minutes. Cool; carefully remove tart shells. Will keep several days in tins. A delicious crust that can be used for any filling requiring a pre-baked, sweet crust.

FILLING

1 quart fresh blueberries
10-ounce jar currant jelly
1 pint sour cream

Wash and pat dry the blueberries. Divide berries among the 24 tart shells. Melt currant jelly over low heat and cool. Pour over the berries and spread a layer of sour cream on the top of each tassie. Makes 24.

MEXICAN FRUIT WAFERS

Cinnamon-scented with a chocolate brandy glaze

2 tablespoons flour
¼ teaspoon salt
¼ teaspoon cinnamon
⅛ teaspoon baking powder
⅛ teaspoon ground cloves
⅛ teaspoon nutmeg
1 cup sugar
2 eggs
1 cup almonds, blanched and
   finely chopped
¼ cup chopped candied orange
   peel
1 teaspoon grated lemon rind

Sift flour, salt, cinnamon, baking powder, cloves, and nutmeg together and set aside. Mix sugar and eggs until just blended. Add flour mixture, almonds, orange peel, and lemon rind. Drop by teaspoonsful 2 inches apart on brown paper lined cookie sheet. Bake at 400° for 7 minutes. Cool 7 minutes and peel cookies off paper. If cookies stick to paper, lift paper from cookie sheet and lay a damp cloth on cookie sheet. Place paper and cookies on cloth. Return to the oven 3 to 4 minutes, until paper softens with steam. Remove from oven and lift cookies off with a spatula immediately.

CHOCOLATE BRANDY GLAZE

6 ounces semisweet chocolate
   morsels
3 tablespoons butter or margarine
¼ cup brandy

Melt chocolate and butter or margarine over hot, not boiling, water. Remove from heat. Blend in brandy. Spread on cookies. Makes 5½ dozen.

SHERRY CAKES

Bake these dainty treats in miniature muffin pans

1 egg, separated
¾ cup sugar
1⅛ cups self-rising flour
¼ cup corn oil
½ cup milk
¾ teaspoon vanilla

Preheat the oven to 350°. Combine egg yolks and sugar by gradually adding sugar to egg yolks while beating with electric mixer until light yellow in color. Add remaining cake ingredients except egg whites. Mix well. Beat egg whites until stiff but not dry. Fold beaten egg whites into the batter. Grease tiny muffin pans. Pour batter into the tins two-thirds full. Bake for approximately 15 minutes or until golden. Remove cakes while still warm and arrange in a flat shallow pan.

SAUCE

1 cup sugar
½ cup water
¾ cup golden sherry
⅛ teaspoon anise extract
Whipped cream for garnish

Combine sugar and water; boil until sugar dissolves. Remove from heat; stir in the golden sherry and anise extract. Pour over warm cakes and allow to cool. Chill overnight. When ready to serve top with a dollop of whipped cream. Makes about 3½ dozen small cakes.

LANE CUPCAKES

Miniature Lane Cakes

1 cup (2 sticks) butter
2 cups sugar
4 eggs, separated
3 cups cake flour, sifted
1 tablespoon baking powder
½ teaspoon salt
1 cup milk
1½ teaspoons vanilla

Cream butter and sugar together until light. Add well beaten egg yolks and beat until fluffy. Sift together the flour, baking powder, and salt. Add flour mixture alternately with milk to the butter mixture, beating well after each addition. Add vanilla. Beat egg whites until stiff but not dry. Fold beaten egg whites into the batter. Grease and lightly flour muffin tins. Fill two-thirds full. Lightly pat filled cake pans on counter top to distribute batter. Bake at 350° for about 25 minutes. Makes 36 to 42 cupcakes or 2 9-inch butter cakes. When cupcakes are cool, trim them and hollow out center of the bottom of the cakes with a paring knife. Fill hollowed center with 1 teaspoon Lane Cake Filling (see index for Lane Cake). Ice sides with Seven-Minute Frosting (see index for recipe).

FORGOTTEN KISSES

Chocolate and nuts seem to be suspended in these crisp meringues

3 egg whites
¾ cup sugar
⅛ teaspoon salt
1 teaspoon white vinegar
1 (6-ounce) package semisweet
  chocolate chips
½ cup pecans or walnuts, finely
  chopped

Beat egg whites until they begin to get stiff. Add sugar a little at a time; beat until stiff peaks form. Beat in salt and vinegar. Fold in chocolate chips and nuts. Drop by teaspoonsful onto a foil-lined baking sheet. Bake for 20 minutes at 250°. Turn off heat and leave in oven 3 hours or overnight without opening door. Makes about 80.

PATSY MCINTYRE'S ORANGE BLOSSOMS

Raisin-gem muffins with an orange glaze

1½ cups seedless raisins
½ cup pecans or walnuts,
  chopped
1 tablespoon grated orange rind
½ cup margarine
1 cup sugar
2 eggs, slightly beaten
1 teaspoon vanilla
2 cups sifted flour
½ teaspoon salt
1 teaspoon baking soda
1 cup buttermilk or sour milk

Chop or grind raisins and nuts together. Add orange rind. Cream margarine; add sugar. Beat until fluffy and light. Add eggs, beating well after each addition. Stir in vanilla. Mix flour and salt. Add soda to buttermilk. Slowly stir in the flour and buttermilk alternately. Mix well after each addition. Fold in raisin mixture. Fill 3-inch greased and floured muffin tins two-thirds full and bake in a preheated 350° oven for 40 to 50 minutes. Cool 5 minutes. Remove from tins. Dip the tops in a glaze. Makes 24 muffins.

GLAZE

¼ cup sugar
3 tablespoons orange juice

Mix the sugar with the orange juice and let stand 30 minutes.

The muffin, once called a "little muff" to keep the hands warm, has become a Southern favorite. Muffins and the peddlers who sold them are believed to be an English tradition. According to the English history texts, muffin men could be found on London streets from the late nineteenth century up until the beginning of World War II. The English called their muffins "tea cakes." The tea cakes actually resembled our modern English muffins.

ROXBURY CAKES

Fruited spice cakes handed down from English ancestors

½ cup butter
½ cup granulated sugar
½ cup brown sugar
2 egg yolks
½ cup milk
1½ cups flour
1½ teaspoons baking powder
½ teaspoon allspice
½ teaspoon cinnamon
¼ teaspoon cloves
¼ teaspoon nutmeg
¼ cup pecans, coarsely chopped
¼ cup chopped citron
¼ cup chopped candied cherries
½ cup chopped raisins
1 teaspoon vanilla
2 egg whites, beaten
Confectioners' sugar for dusting

Cream the butter and sugars together; add the egg yolks; beat until blended. Add the milk alternately with the flour, baking powder, and spices, which have been sifted together. Add the nuts, fruit, vanilla, and fold in the beaten egg whites (beaten until soft peaks form). Pour the batter into greased muffin tins about two-thirds full. Bake in a 350° oven for 25 to 30 minutes. Dust the cakes with powdered sugar while they are still warm. Makes 1 dozen large, 2 dozen small, or 3 dozen tiny cakes.

Custards, Puddings, and Molds

The kitchen at the Hermitage, President Andrew Jackson's home in Nashville, Tennessee.

Bird's Nest Pudding

Orange jelly (gelatin)
Orange peel
Sugar
Cornstarch pudding
Thick cream

Make an orange jelly nest by turning a pie dish upside down in the bottom of a two-quart round tin basin, pouring the jelly in the basin over the pie dish, and storing away in the ice house to harden.

Pare the rind from four oranges in very thin strips to resemble straw; preserve them with sugar.

Have ready some egg shells that have been emptied from a small hole at the top, fill them with a cornstarch pudding, stand in a pan of Indian meal to prevent them from falling over, and put in a cold place to harden. When the jelly is firm turn it out on a glass dish, put the straws in it around the outside space left by the pie dish, and fill the nest with whipped cream, representing feathers. Break the shells away from the eggs and put them in center of nest.

*S*outherners who settled along the Atlantic coast were as passionate about puddings as their English ancestors. During the early 1700s, plum and other fruit puddings were the desserts of choice. Later in the century, many colonists prospered; soon hardscrabble farms expanded into lush plantations, resulting in an abundance of farm-fresh eggs, heavy cream, and homegrown fruit and nuts. Plantation wives used these riches to make creamy English desserts: trifle, tipsy parson, baked and boiled custard.

Southerners may have inherited their love for puddings from the English, but the French also left their mark. When Thomas Jefferson returned from serving as minister to France, he brought home a wealth of recipes for French puddings and molds: charlotte russe, floating island, and wine jelly. These unfamiliar dishes were welcomed enthusiastically by early Virginia hostesses who were fond of serving a lavish assortment of pretty desserts. Mousses and charlottes could be made as fancy as one pleased with the popular fluted metal molds. Shimmering, jewel-toned jellies, supported by the addition of gelatinous boiled calves' feet, also made spectacular displays.

Sumptuous creams and molds were relished by the genteel society of Charleston. Suprisingly, they held up well in the city's notoriously humid weather. Charlestonians had disdain for one pudding, however; they disliked the idea of eating sweetened rice and would have nothing to do with rice pudding. Elsewhere in the South, the average citizen preferred rice, fruit, or bread pudding to creamy custard.

Today we regard charlottes, trifles, and plum pudding as celebration desserts — reserved for holidays and special occasions. Simpler fare like banana pudding, floating island, and kiss custard are comfort foods whose soothing taste fills us with nostalgia. Together with other refrigerator desserts they will remain popular for a long time.

APPLE CHARLOTTE WITH BRANDY SAUCE

Joe Middleton's interpretation of this classic dessert

8 to 10 slices firm-textured white bread, trimmed of crusts, buttered on one side
8 green tart apples
4 tablespoons butter
¼ cup sugar
Grated rind of 1 lemon
1 teaspoon cinnamon
1 teaspoon ground ginger
½ teaspoon ground cloves
3 ounces applejack or Calvados

Preheat oven to 400°. Line the bottom and sides of a 1½-quart charlotte mold or casserole with the bread slices, buttered side to the mold. Peel, core, and slice the apples. Melt the butter in a large skillet. Add the sliced apples, sugar, grated lemon rind, cinnamon, ginger, cloves, and applejack. Fry slowly until the apples are slightly softened. Pour the apples into the mold, allowing the excess to form a mound around the rim. Bake for 20 minutes, then cover with aluminum foil and continue cooking for another 20 minutes or until the apples are completely cooked and the edges of the bread have browned slightly. Cool for at least 1 hour before unmolding and serve with brandy sauce. Serves 6.

BRANDY SAUCE

½ cup apricot glaze (if not available see note)
1 ounce brandy
1 cup apple juice
Juice of 1 lemon
⅛ teaspoon ground ginger
1 teaspoon cornstarch

Combine apricot glaze, brandy, ¾ cup apple juice, lemon juice, and ginger in a saucepan and bring to a boil. Add cornstarch to the remaining ¼ cup apple juice to dissolve. Return to a boil. Remove from heat and serve warm.

Note: To make an apricot glaze, heat ½ cup apricot jam or preserves with 1 teaspoon water until it melts, then put through a strainer to remove any lumps.

Joe Middleton is one of the South's favorite chefs, caterers, and cooking school teachers. He has been a chef at the Hyatt Regency in Houston; the Routh Street Café, Dallas; the Waldorf Astoria in New York; and Commander's Palace in New Orleans. He has taught cooking in Lee Barnes Cooking School in New Orleans, Anna Muffaleto's Cordon Bleu Cooking School in New York, and has taught culinary arts at Tulane University in New Orleans.

A̶lmost any bowl that splays out at the sides can be used for a pudding mold. For straight-sided desserts use a springform mold.

MEXICAN FLAN

From Sheila Palmer — a Jackson, Mississippi food specialist

¼ cup sugar
6 whole eggs plus 2 yolks
½ teaspoon cinnamon
1 teaspoon vanilla
2 12-ounce cans light evaporated
    milk
1 14-ounce can sweetened
    condensed milk
Sliced almonds for garnish
½ pint heavy cream, whipped

Cook sugar in a heavy skillet over low heat until it browns and turns to liquid. Remove from heat and allow to cool completely in a large loaf (bread) pan. Beat eggs well; add cinnamon, vanilla, and milks. Pour into the cooled caramelized sugar in the loaf pan. Set the pan in a pan of hot water, 1 inch deep. Bake at 325° approximately 50 minutes or until a cake tester comes out clean. Completely cool on a rack at room temperature. Cover and store in the refrigerator. Prior to serving loosen sides with a table knife and invert onto a serving plate. Pour caramelized sauce from the pan over and garnish with sliced almonds and whipped cream. Slice like bread to serve. Serves 12.

RICE PUDDING

A tasty top-of-the-stove method that you make ahead

½ cup long grain white rice
1 cup water
4¼ cups milk
¼ cup white raisins
3 egg yolks
½ cup sugar
2 teaspoons vanilla
⅛ teaspoon salt
1 teaspoon cinnamon
½ teaspoon nutmeg

Combine rice and water in a 2-quart saucepan. Bring to boil and boil 8 to 10 minutes or until water is absorbed. Stir in milk and return to boiling. Lower heat and simmer, stirring often, for 25 minutes. Add raisins and cook 5 to 10 minutes longer or until rice is tender. Beat yolks in a small bowl until frothy. Whisk in sugar, vanilla, and salt. Stir in ⅓ cup hot rice mixture into yolks and return mixture to saucepan. Cook over very low heat for 2 minutes or until slightly thickened. Mixture should be loose and creamy. Pour into 1½-quart casserole dish; cover surface of pudding with plastic wrap (place plastic wrap on rice surface). Refrigerate overnight. When ready to serve, remove plastic wrap and sprinkle with cinnamon and nutmeg. Bake in a preheated 425° oven for about 5 minutes or until crusty on top. Serves 8.

OZARK PUDDING

A favorite of President and Mrs. Truman

2 eggs
1½ cups sugar
4 tablespoons flour
½ teaspoon baking powder
½ teaspoon salt
1½ teaspoons vanilla
1 cup nuts, chopped (pecans or
  walnuts)
1 cup chopped apples
Vanilla ice cream or whippped
  cream (optional)

Beat eggs until light. Add sugar slowly; beat until smooth. Mix in flour, baking powder, salt, and vanilla. Stir in nuts and apples. Bake in a greased, floured 8-inch square pan at 350° for 25 to 30 minutes. Serve warm — plain or topped with vanilla ice cream or whipped cream. Serves 6.

BREAD PUDDING WITH RUM SAUCE

The ultimate comfort food

6 slices day-old bread
1 teaspoon cinnamon
½ cup seedless raisins
2 tablespoons butter, melted
4 eggs
½ cup plus 2 tablespoons sugar
2 cups milk
1 teaspoon vanilla

RUM SAUCE

2 cups milk
½ stick butter
½ cup sugar
2 tablespoons flour
1 tablespoon cooking oil
1 teaspoon nutmeg
1 teaspoon vanilla
3 tablespoons rum, or to taste

Break bread into small pieces in a baking dish. Sprinkle cinnamon over bread and add raisins and melted butter. Toast bread mixture lightly in oven set at 350°. Mix eggs, sugar, milk, and vanilla and pour over bread mixture. Bake for about 30 minutes at 350° or until solid. Serves about 8.

Place milk, butter, and sugar in saucepan. Let come to a boil. Thicken with roux made of flour and oil. Remove from heat. Add nutmeg, vanilla, and rum. Serve over pudding.

This recipe is from Mary Mahoney's Old French House Restaurant, located in a beautiful two-hundred-year-old house on the Mississippi Gulf Coast.

SWEET POTATO PUDDING

Not too sweet, with a delicate flavor

2 cups sweet potatoes, mashed
2 tablespoons sugar
1 teaspoon allspice
½ teaspoon salt
1 egg
⅓ cup milk
¼ cup melted butter
¼ cup grated coconut
¼ cup raisins

Mash sweet potatoes with a mixer until smooth. Add sugar, allspice, and salt. Beat egg and mix with milk; add to potato mixture. Stir in melted butter, coconut, and raisins. Place mixture in a pie plate and bake in a preheated 375° oven for 20 minutes. Serves 4.

This recipe is from the Mount Calvary Missionary Baptist Church, Tougaloo, Mississippi. It was contributed by Mrs. Katie Rhone.

MEXICAN BREAD PUDDING

Capirotada (Kah-pee-roh-tah-thah) is a Southwestern favorite

1½ cups brown sugar, firmly
  packed
1 teaspoon cinnamon
1½ cups water
5 cups French bread cubes, cut ½
  inch square
1 cup golden raisins
2 cups tart apples, cut into ¼-inch
  cubes
¾ cups walnuts, chopped
1¼ cups sharp cheddar cheese,
  cut into ¼-inch cubes
3 teaspoons butter
Sweetened whipped cream or ice
  cream

Combine brown sugar, cinnamon, and water in a small pan; boil gently until sugar dissolves. Pour hot syrup over bread cubes and toss gently. Add raisins, apples, walnuts, and cheese; toss again until blended. Spoon into 3-quart shallow casserole, greased with the 3 tablespoons butter. You may let the pudding stand until about 20 minutes before you plan to serve it. Bake in a preheated 375° oven for 15 minutes, or until heated through. Serve warm, with whipped cream or ice cream. Serves 12 to 16.

This pudding has many variations, but it always has fruit and cheese in it.

If adding liqueurs to a custard as a flavoring, allow an extra egg yolk for every 2 tablespoons of liqueur.

BINNY WEBB'S BREAD PUDDING

An elegant version of a cozy dish

½ cup dried apricots, chopped
   with scissors
½ cup seedless dark raisins
2 cups water, boiling
¼ cup Kirsch
1 quart milk
5 eggs
4 egg yolks
1 cup sugar
1 teaspoon vanilla
1 cup heavy cream
10 slices French bread, cut ¼ inch
   thick
3 tablespoons unsalted butter,
   softened
2 tablespoons confectioners'
   sugar

Preheat oven 325°. Place apricots and raisins in a bowl and pour boiling water over them. Let stand five minutes and drain. Mix fruit with Kirsch. Place a large pan partially filled with water in oven. Bring milk to a boil. Mix eggs, egg yolks, sugar, and vanilla together with a wire whisk. Add cream to the milk and mix well. Gradually add this to the egg mixture. Strain through a fine sieve. Butter a 2-quart rectangular or oval baking dish. Place fruit in bottom. Butter bread and place, buttered side up, on top of the fruit. Pour milk mixture through strainer over bread. Place baking dish in the bottom third of the oven in pan of water. The water should cover half the dish. Bake 45 to 60 minutes or until a knife inserted in the middle of the pudding comes out clean. Sprinkle confectioners' sugar on top and glaze under the broiler, watching carefully that it doesn't burn. Serve at room temperature with Cognac Sauce. Serves 6 to 8.

COGNAC SAUCE

3 egg yolks
1 cup sugar
1 teaspoon vanilla
1½ cups milk
1 tablespoon cornstarch
3 tablespoons water
1 ounce cognac

Beat yolks and add sugar and vanilla. Heat milk to the boiling point and gradually add to the eggs. Cook over low heat until mixture is very hot. Combine water and cornstarch and add to the mixture. Stir until sauce coats a spoon. Remove from heat and stir in brandy. This sauce can also be used over fruit or pound cake.

In the early days bread pudding was known as a poor man's dessert. The creativity of frugal Southern cooks was challenged by having to decide how to make a dessert out of leftover bread, milk, eggs, and butter. Resourceful housewives used dried or fresh fruit and whatever spirits they had on hand for flavoring. Creole cooks raised bread pudding to a loftier position with recipes like this.

Add lemon juice and crushed mint leaves to taste to apricot preserves for a delicious cake, bread pudding, or ice cream topping.

NANIE'S PLUM PUDDING

Make it your Christmas specialty

1½ cups sugar
4 eggs
3 cups raisins
2 cups flour, sifted
1½ cups margarine or butter, cold
1½ cups bread crumbs
⅓ cup milk
½ cup citron (optional)
1 rounded teaspoon baking
   powder
1 teaspoon nutmeg
1 teaspoon ground cloves
1 teaspoon cinnamon
½ tablespoon orange marmalade

Cream sugar and eggs, one egg at a time. Add raisins that have been coated with flour. Slice cold butter and add to mixture, then add other ingredients. Put aside about 1 cup of the plum pudding mixture for the sauce. Cook in plum pudding steamer for 3 hours. Check water level every hour.

SAUCE
1 cup plum pudding mixture
5 cups water
1 cup sugar
Rind of 1 or 2 oranges, cut in
   small pieces

Cook until thickened. Spoon over pudding. Serves 12 to 14.

From Vintage Vicksburg, *compiled by the Junior Auxiliary of historic Vicksburg, Mississippi.*

If lady fingers are used to line a mold, split and place the curved sides against the form. To make an even top, slice each section to a point by cutting it diagonally and placing it with the pointed end toward the middle. You may also cut a small round for the center.

QUEEN PUDDING

A bread pudding with jam and meringue topping

4 slices day-old bread, crusts
   trimmed
2 tablespoons (¼ stick) butter,
   room temperature
Cinnamon
Freshly grated nutmeg
½ cup raisins
2 cups milk
4 egg yolks
¼ cup sugar
1 teaspoon vanilla
⅔ cup strawberry jam
4 egg whites
¼ cup sugar

Preheat oven to 350°. Lightly butter shallow 1½-quart baking dish and set aside. Spread bread slices with butter, then sprinkle lightly with cinnamon and nutmeg. Cut each slice into fourths. Arrange in a preheated dish. Sprinkle with raisins. Combine milk, egg yolks, ¼ cup sugar, and vanilla in medium bowl and beat slowly until blended but not frothy. Pour mixture over bread. Set baking dish in shallow baking pan. Add enough hot water to pan to come 1 inch up sides of baking dish. Bake until pudding is set, about 40 to 45 minutes. Let cool for 5 minutes. Increase oven temperature to 400°. Meanwhile, heat jam in a small saucepan over medium-low heat until softened. Spread evenly over pudding. Beat egg whites in a medium bowl until foamy. Add remaining sugar, 2 tablespoons at a time, beating after each addition until stiff peaks form. Spread meringue evenly over jam, sealing to edge of dish. Bake until meringue is lightly browned, 6 to 8 minutes. Serve warm. Serves 6.

*T*o unmold gelatin puddings, have a chilled plate ready that is large enough to allow for the garnish. Moisten the dish slightly to prevent the gelatin from sticking. Use a thin knife at several points around the edge to release the vacuum, then reverse the mold onto the plate. If necessary, place a warm damp cloth over the mold for a few seconds. If the pudding is still not released shake the mold lightly, bracing it against the serving dish.

ANGEL PUDDING

A treasure from Mary Leigh's grandmother

2 eggs, separated
½ cup sugar
⅛ teaspoon salt
½ cup milk
1 tablespoon gelatin dissolved in
    ¼ cup water
¾ cup evaporated milk, well
    chilled
1 teaspoon vanilla
3 dozen chocolate wafers,
    crumbled

Cook egg yolks, sugar, salt, and milk in top of double boiler until thick. While hot, add dissolved gelatin. Cool. Whip chilled evaporated milk until stiff and add to egg mixture. Beat egg whites; add vanilla; fold gently into egg mixture. Sprinkle half of chocolate wafer crumbs onto bottom of greased, 8-inch baking dish. Pour liquid over crumbs. Sprinkle remaining crumbs over top. Chill. Serves 6 to 8.

CABINET PUDDING

Macaroons and cream compose a celebration dessert

2 tablespoons gelatin
1 cup cold water
6 eggs, separated
8 tablespoons sugar
½ cup sherry
½ teaspoon almond extract
1½ dozen macaroons, crumbled
1 cup pecans, chopped
1 10-ounce jar maraschino
    cherries, sliced
1 cup heavy cream, whipped
4 tablespoons sugar
½ teaspoon vanilla

Soak gelatin in cold water; then, heat until dissolved. Beat egg yolks, add sugar, slowly, and continue beating until creamy. Add sherry. Cook mixture in top of a double boiler over medium heat until thick. Cool. Meanwhile, beat egg whites until stiff. Combine whites, egg yolk mixture, and gelatin slowly on low speed of mixer. Add almond extract. Pour one-third of custard into a 1½-quart mold. Add layer of macaroon crumbs, chopped pecans, and sliced cherries. Alternate layers until there are 3 layers of each mixture; leave out ¼ cup macaroon crumbs. Whip cream; sweeten with sugar; flavor with vanilla; spread over pudding. Top with remaining crumbs. Refrigerate until serving time. Serves 12.

Add 1 tablespoon of any liqueur to ½ pint heavy cream whipped with ¼ cup confectioners' sugar to develop your own "spécialité de la maison".

TIPSY PARSON

A cherished recipe from a Natchez mansion

1 quart milk
4 egg yolks
5 tablespoons sugar
2 tablespoons flour
Pinch of salt
1 1-2-3-4 cake, baked in a sheet
    pan (see index for Coconut
    Cake)
½ cup (or more) bourbon
1 cup pecans, grated
1 cup seedless green grapes,
    halved
1 cup fresh or frozen grated
    coconut
½ cup maraschino cherries,
    halved
1 large can crushed pineapple,
    drained (optional)
1 cup heavy cream

Scald milk in double boiler. Combine egg yolks, sugar, flour, and salt. Gradually stir hot milk into egg mixture; return to double boiler. Cook over hot water, stirring constantly until mixture thickens. Strain and cool custard. Break cake into approximately 1-inch chunks. Place one-third of chunks into glass bowl. Drizzle one-third of bourbon over cake and add one-third of custard, soaking cake well, so it will not be dry. Add approximately one-third of pecans, grapes, coconut, cherries, and pineapple. Alternate layers twice more, saving a few pecans, grapes, and cherries. Whip cream, spread on top, and decorate with reserved fruit and nuts. Cover with plastic wrap and refrigerate at least 4 hours. Serves 8 to 10. A beautiful dessert that tastes better the next day.

Mrs. Richard Campbell of Edgewood, an antebellum Natchez home, has prepared this spectacular dessert every Christmas for many years. She inherited the recipe from her Grandmother Dale.

AUNT ELLEN'S DESSERT PARFAITS

Make ahead, refrigerate in parfait dishes

4 eggs, separated
1 cup sugar
⅛ teaspoon salt
½ to ¾ cup sherry
1 envelope gelatin
¼ cup cold water
1 pint heavy cream, whipped
14 macaroons, crushed

Beat egg yolks; mix in sugar, salt, and sherry. Soak gelatin in cold water for 5 minutes. Add to yolk mixture. Beat egg whites until stiff and fold into mixture. Fold in whipped cream; then, stir in crushed macaroons. Scoop into parfait glasses or a large serving dish and chill several hours. Serves 10 to 12.

FRANCES'S ANGEL BAVARIAN CREAM

A beauty from Mary Leigh's Virginia cousin

2 cups milk
4 eggs, separated
1 cup sugar
2 tablespoons flour
1/8 teaspoon salt
1 tablespoon gelatin
1/4 cup cold water
1 1/2 teaspoons vanilla
1 cup heavy cream, whipped
1 Angel Food Cake (see index for recipe)
1/2 pint heavy cream, whipped
4 tablespoons sugar
1 1/2 teaspoons vanilla

Scald milk in top of a double boiler. Meanwhile, beat egg yolks. Gradually add sugar, flour, and salt, beating until thick. Add a little milk to egg mixture, beating constantly. Transfer egg mixture to milk on the stove and cook until it thickens. While hot, stir in gelatin that has been soaked in cold water. Cool. Add 1 1/2 teaspoons vanilla. Beat egg whites until stiff. Fold into yolk mixture. Whip 1 cup heavy cream and combine with custard. Slice thin layers from top and bottom of angel food cake. Break the middle section into small chunks. Place top slice in bottom of an angel food cake pan. Pour in a layer of custard, then add a layer of cake chunks. Continue alternating custard and cake, ending with the slice of cake cut from the bottom. Refrigerate overnight. Unmold. Whip cream and flavor with 4 tablespoons sugar and 1 1/2 teaspoons vanilla. Ice cake. Refrigerate several hours until time to serve. Cut into slices. Top with strawberry sauce. Serves 10.

STRAWBERRY SAUCE

2 cups strawberries, sliced
2/3 cup sugar
2 tablespoons cornstarch
2 tablespoons cassis

Mash berries with a spoon. Add sugar and cornstarch; cook until thick. Stir in cassis. Cool. Chill until serving time. Makes 1 pint.

Use a double boiler for top-of-the-stove custards and sauces. Cook over — not in hot water.

EGGNOG REFRIGERATOR CAKE

Layers of eggnog and cake with whipped cream frosting

1 cup (2 sticks) butter
4 cups confectioners' sugar
6 eggs, separated
½ cup bourbon
1 cup pecans, chopped
**1½ pounds cake (angel food or
pound cake)**
**½ pint whipping cream,
whipped**

Cream butter and sugar. Beat egg yolks thoroughly. Add bourbon and mix well until egg yolks are "cooked" (the bourbon cooks them). Add this to butter mixture. Blend and add pecans. Beat egg whites until stiff. Fold into mixture. Line a tube pan or ring mold with wax paper. Place a layer of cake that has been broken into pieces the size of a quarter or nickle on the bottom of the pan or mold. Cover with a layer of the eggnog mixture. Repeat alternating until cake and eggnog are used. End with a layer of cake. Place in the refrigerator for 12 hours. When ready to serve lift out of pan and cover with whipped cream. Serves 16.

BOILED CUSTARD

The misnamed custard you should never let boil

1 quart milk
1 cup sugar
⅛ teaspoon salt
2 tablespoons cornstarch
4 large eggs
1-2 teaspoons vanilla

Scald milk in the top of a double boiler. Combine dry ingredients. Beat eggs and mix in dry ingredients. Beat a small amount of hot milk into the egg mixture, then add to remainder of milk in top of boiler. Cook, stirring constantly until it coats the spoon, being sure not to let the mixture boil. Cool. Add vanilla to taste. Chill. May be served plain by the bowlful or over cake or fruit. Serves 8.

T̰o test a custard for doneness, insert a knife near the edge of the cup. If it comes out clean, remove it as there is sufficient stored heat in the cups to finish cooking it. If knife is clean when inserted in the middle, place the cups in ice water to stop the cooking process immediately.

MAGGIE MCKEE'S CUP CUSTARD

Smooth and nourishing — a comforting custard

2 cups milk
2 cups light cream
6 egg yolks
3 whole eggs
½ cup sugar
2 teaspoons vanilla
½ teaspoon nutmeg

Pour milk and cream into a saucepan. Bring just to a boil; then cool. In a large bowl beat the egg yolks and whole eggs together and add the sugar. Mix in the milk a little at a time. Add vanilla and nutmeg. Pour into greased ¾-cup custard cups. Sprinkle more nutmeg lightly over custard. Place cups in pan filled two-thirds of the height of the cups with hot water. Bake at 325° for approximately 40 minutes. Remove cups from water and cool completely before refrigerating. Serves 7.

WILLIAMSBURG WINE JELLY MOLD WITH CUSTARD SAUCE

A dish ladies ate when they had "vapors" but were reluctant to drink wine

2 envelopes gelatin
½ cup cold water
2 cups boiling water
Dash of salt
¾ cup burgundy
⅔ cup sugar
2 tablespoons lemon juice

Dissolve gelatin in cold water. Stir boiling water into mixture and combine well. Stir in salt, burgundy, sugar, and lemon juice. Pour into 1-quart mold. Chill.

CUSTARD SAUCE

1½ tablespoons cornstarch
2 cups light cream, divided
4 egg yolks
½ cup sugar
1 teaspoon vanilla

Dissolve cornstarch in ¼ cup cream. Beat egg yolks until light. Stir in cornstarch mixture. Heat remaining cream and add sugar. Pour 1 cup hot cream and sugar over egg mixture, stirring constantly. Return remaining hot cream to low heat and stir in egg and cream mixture. Cook 5 minutes in a double boiler, stirring constantly until sauce is slightly thickened. Add vanilla. Chill. Serves 8.

MY MOTHER'S KISS CUSTARD

Mary Leigh's mother's version of floating island

3 eggs, separated
1 cup sugar
2 tablespoons flour
¼ teaspoon salt
4 cups milk
½ teaspoon vanilla
½ teaspoon almond extract
1 tablespoon sugar

Beat egg yolks; gradually mix in dry ingredients. Add milk slowly. Cook over low heat until mixture thickens, stirring constantly; will become firmer after chilling. Add vanilla and almond extract. Pour into a 6-cup glass baking dish. Beat egg whites, mixing in 1 tablespoon sugar. Spoon over custard in soft mounds. Place in broiler to brown tips of meringue. Chill. Serves 6.

MRS. BARKSDALE'S SHERRY CAKE

A beautiful refrigerator cake reserved for special occasions

4 eggs, separated
¾ cup sugar
1 cup sherry
1 tablespoon unflavored gelatin
⅓ cup cold water
1½ pints heavy cream
1 angel food cake
5 ounces moist, sweetened
  coconut
12 maraschino cherries

Separate yolks and whites of eggs. Set whites aside. In the top of a double boiler, beat the yolks with ½ cup sugar. Add ½ cup sherry and cook until custard thickens, stirring constantly. Dissolve gelatin in ⅓ cup cold water and whisk into the custard mixture. Cook until it coats the back of a spoon. Remove from heat and cool completely. Whip ½ pint of heavy cream. Set aside and thoroughly clean beaters. Beat the egg whites until soft peaks form; add ¼ cup sugar slowly and continue beating until stiff. Fold the egg whites into the whipped cream. Fold egg white and cream mixture into the cooled custard. Tear angel food cake into pieces the size of a quarter or a little larger. Grease a ring mold and layer cake, then custard; repeating until all is used, ending with a layer of cake. Drizzle ½ cup sherry over cake, distributing evenly. Cover and refrigerate at least 8 hours. When ready to serve, remove sherry cake from mold and ice with 1 pint of whipped cream. Sprinkle coconut over and decorate with cherries. Serves 12.

LEMON REFRIGERATOR CAKE

The ultimate dessert for lemon lovers

6 eggs, separated
1½ cups sugar, divided
¾ cup lemon juice
1½ teaspoons grated lemon rind
1 tablespoon plain gelatin
¼ cup cold water
1 10-inch angel food cake (or sponge cake)
1 cup heavy cream, whipped

Combine slightly beaten egg yolks, ¾ cup sugar, lemon juice, and rind. Cook over hot, not boiling, water until mixture coats a spoon. Remove from heat and stir in gelatin that has been soaked in the ¼ cup cold water. Beat egg whites until stiff and gradually add remaining sugar, beating constantly. Fold into custard. Tear cake into small pieces and arrange a layer in the bottom of a greased tube pan. Pour custard over cake and alternate layers of cake and filling until all is used. Cake should be on top. Chill until firm. Unmold and ice with whipped cream. Decorate with cherries or nuts, if desired. Candied violets also make a pretty garnish. Serves 12.

CRÈME BRÛLÉE

Impressive but easy — can be made ahead

16 ounces heavy cream
¾ cup sugar
8 egg yolks
2 teaspoons vanilla
8 tablespoons brown sugar

Heat the cream in a double boiler over simmering water until hot but not boiling. Stir in sugar and dissolve. Preheat oven to 325°. Beat egg yolks thoroughly. Gently add the hot cream and vanilla. Pour into eight 6- to 8-ounce ramekins and place them in a large pan filled with warm water. Water should come halfway up the side of dishes. Bake for approximately 1 hour and 15 minutes or until a dinner knife inserted around the edges comes out clean. Cool. Cover with plastic wrap and chill until cold. May be made to this point a day in advance. Sprinkle each custard with 1 tablespoon sifted brown sugar. Preheat the broiler. Broil the custards close to the heat for about a minute, watching constantly until sugar is caramelized. When cool, you may serve immediately or return to the refrigerator for several hours until serving time. Serves 8.

LEMON FLOATING ISLAND

A new twist for a Southern classic

3 tablespoons cornstarch
4 cups milk
4 egg yolks, beaten
¾ cup sugar
⅛ teaspoon salt
1 teaspoon lemon extract
3 teaspoons grated lemon rind

Dissolve cornstarch in 1 cup of milk. Beat egg yolks and mix in sugar and salt. Slowly add cornstarch mixture. Scald remaining three cups of milk in the top of a double boiler over boiling water. Slowly add egg mixture to milk and stir constantly until thickened. Cool. Add lemon extract and rind. Pour into an ovenproof dish.

FLOAT

4 egg whites
4 tablespoons sugar
¾ teaspoon vanilla

Beat egg whites until stiff; gradually add sugar, then vanilla. Scoop over custard and smooth carefully. Place in broiler until tips of meringue are brown. Chill. Serves about 8.

MOCHA MOUSSE WITH ORANGE SAUCE

From the Palate Restaurant in Jackson, Mississippi

1 pound marshmallows
1 cup strong coffee
1 heaping tablespoon instant
  coffee
3 tablespoons cocoa
1 pint heavy cream, whipped
Candied violet for garnish

Melt marshmallows, coffees, and cocoa in top of a double boiler over hot water, stirring constantly with a whisk. Cool. Fold in the whipped cream. Spoon into 12 buttered individual molds or a turk's-head mold and chill in the refrigerator.

ORANGE SAUCE

½ cup orange marmalade
2 tablespoons cornstarch
2 cups orange juice
1 teaspoon orange zest

Heat marmalade in the top of a double boiler. Stir cornstarch into the orange juice and gradually add to the marmalade. Add orange zest. Cook until thickened. Remove from heat and chill. To serve, unmold individual molds or turk's-head mold in a puddle of orange sauce or drizzle sauce over the top and down the sides. Pipe whipped cream on the top and garnish with a candied violet. Serves 12.

CHARLOTTE RUSSE

Sumptuous and elegant; your guests will remember it

1¼ cups milk
2 egg yolks, beaten
½ cup sugar
⅛ teaspoon salt
1¼ tablespoons gelatin
¼ cup cold water
2 egg whites, stiffly beaten
1 cup heavy cream
5 tablespoons confectioners'
  sugar
3½ tablespoons sherry
1 teaspoon vanilla
1 dozen ladyfingers, split

Scald milk in a double boiler over medium heat. Beat egg yolks; add sugar and salt. Remove milk from stove; stir in egg yolk mixture; return to stove and cook until it slightly thickens. Soak gelatin in cold water for 5 minutes. Add to milk mixture and cool. Beat and fold in egg whites. Whip cream and add confectioners' sugar. Fold into custard. Add flavorings. Line a 6-cup mold or serving bowl with split ladyfingers. Pour in custard. Chill until firm. Serve in dessert or sherbet dishes. Serve plain or top with whipped cream. Serves 6.

MAGGIE'S GRADUATION MOUSSE

From Laurin Stamm, food editor of **Vicksburg, Mississippi Evening Post**

18 ladyfingers, split
1 cup plus 2 tablespoons butter
3 cups confectioners' sugar
9 eggs, separated
⅓ cup milk
3 teaspoons vanilla extract
2 teaspoons almond extract
6 ounces unsweetened chocolate,
  melted
1 cup pecans, chopped
½ pint heavy cream, whipped
Semisweet chocolate bits, finely
  chopped for glaze

Line an 8 x 8 x 3 inch glass dish with wax paper. Arrange ladyfingers around the sides and bottom of dish. Cream butter; gradually add sugar, creaming until light and fluffy. Add egg yolks one at a time; beat until smooth after each addition. Blend in milk, vanilla, almond extract, and unsweetened chocolate well. Beat egg whites until stiff but not dry (not quite so much as for a meringue); fold into chocolate mixture. Add pecans. Pour into prepared dish. Refrigerate for 6 to 8 hours. To serve, invert onto serving platter. Remove wax paper. Cover top with whipped cream and chocolate. (Put chocolate bits in your food processor to chop finely.) Cut mousse into squares or slices. Serves 9.

When adding egg yolks to custard, add a little custard to the eggs first, then eggs to the rest of the custard.

TOMBSTONE PUDDING

This old dessert recipe is thought to be from Kentucky

2 dozen macaroons, crumbled
6 eggs, separated
2 teaspoons flour
1 cup sugar
6 ounces sherry
½ teaspoon lemon juice
6 tablespoons sugar
¼ pound almonds, blanched

Place macaroons on an ovenproof platter. The dessert should be served from the dish in which it is cooked. Beat egg yolks well, add flour and beat again. Add cup of sugar gradually, then the sherry. Mix and place in the top of a double boiler. Cook slowly, stirring constantly until mixture is the consistency of thick custard. Remove from heat and pour over macaroons. Beat egg whites until stiff, add lemon juice and remaining 6 tablespoons sugar. Spread over macaroons, smoothing with a knife. Stick almonds into meringue standing them on ends, leaving as much of each nut outside as possible. Place under low flame in broiler for a few minutes. Watch carefully until meringue is golden brown. Serves at least 12.

JOE MIDDLETON'S PRALINE SOUFFLÉ

A Creole soufflé served with Caramel Sauce

1 cup cream
5 tablespoons flour
½ cup dark brown sugar
4 egg yolks
½ cup roasted pecans, ground in
   processor
6 egg whites
⅛ teaspoon salt
½ teaspoon cream of tartar
2 tablespoons sugar

Combine cream, flour, and brown sugar in a small saucepan. Bring to a boil while whisking. Cool slightly. Add yolks and pecans. Set aside. In bowl of mixer beat egg whites with salt and cream of tartar. Beat to soft peaks. Slowly add sugar. Beat to stiff peaks. Fold whites into pecan mixture. Place soufflé into 6 chilled and buttered ramekins. Place in 400° oven. Bake for approximately 15 minutes. Serve immediately with Caramel Sauce.

CARAMEL SAUCE

1 cup dark brown sugar
¼ cup white sugar
½ cup white corn syrup
1 cup cream

Combine the brown sugar, white sugar, corn syrup, and cream. Bring to a boil. Remove from heat and cool. Serves 6.

NUT SOUFFLÉ

This prune-scented soufflé does not fall and may be made several hours in advance

8 egg whites
2 cups sugar
1 cup chopped pecans, finely
    chopped
4 cooked prunes, chopped
⅛ teaspoon salt
1 teaspoon vanilla

Beat egg whites until very stiff. Slowly fold in sugar a little at a time, beating well. Add finely chopped pecans, chopped prunes, and salt. Beat in vanilla. Lightly grease a 9-inch cake pan, fill with mixture, and place pan of hot water under the soufflé to prevent burning. Bake in a 300° degree oven for 45 to 60 minutes positioned in the center of the middle rack. Soufflé does not brown, but will be slightly firm to the touch on top. Cool and refrigerate until ready to serve. When soufflé is cold, serve with scoops of whipped cream. Serves 12 to 16.

ENGLISH TRIFLE

Brought to Virginia by early English settlers

4 egg yolks
¼ cup sugar
⅛ teaspoon salt
2 cups milk
1 teaspoon vanilla

Beat egg yolks gently. Gradually blend in sugar and salt. Scald milk and add slowly, with mixer on low speed. Place custard in top of double boiler and cook over simmering water, stirring constantly until slightly thickened. It should never boil and will be thin. Strain into bowl and cool. Add vanilla. Set aside.

1 16-ounce pound cake
½ cup sherry
8 ounces raspberry preserves or
    jam
¾ cup maraschino cherries,
    sliced
¾ cup toasted sliced almonds
1 cup whipping cream
3 tablespoons sugar
½ teaspoon vanilla

Cut pound cake into 15 or 16 thin slices. Trim crust. Arrange slices neatly around sides and on bottom of glass or crystal bowl. Spoon half of sherry on cake slices including those on sides. Pour half of custard over cake. Dribble one-half of raspberry preserves evenly over custard. Sprinkle ¼ cup cherries and ¼ cup almonds over preserves. Place remaining cake slices on top and repeat layers, saving ¼ cup of cherries and almonds for garnish. Whip the cream, sweetening with sugar and flavoring with vanilla. Cover top of trifle. Decorate with cherries and almonds. Refrigerate. Flavor improves if made day before serving. Serves 8.

BANANA PUDDING

Comfort food for children and adults

12 ounces (or more) vanilla wafers
5 or 6 bananas, sliced
3 eggs, separated
1 cup sugar
3 tablespoons flour
Dash of salt
1 12-ounce can evaporated milk
1 teaspoon vanilla
2 tablespoons sugar
½ teaspoon cream of tartar

Line bottom and sides of a lightly buttered 2-quart baking dish with vanilla wafers. Place a layer of sliced bananas over wafers. Beat egg yolks with mixer until thick and lemon-colored. Gradually mix in 1 cup sugar, the flour, and the salt. Add milk slowly, beating well. Place mixture in top of a double boiler and cook over simmering water until thick. Remove from heat, add vanilla, and cool. Pour half of mixture over bananas. Layer again with wafers, banana slices, and custard. Beat egg whites until soft peaks form; gradually add 2 tablespoons sugar and cream of tartar. Beat until stiff peaks form; spread over pudding. Bake at 350° for 10 minutes or until golden. May be served warm, but chilling improves flavor. Serves 8.

CHOCOLATE PÂTÉ

Serve at parties with Pecan Lace Cookies or any crisp sugar cookie

1½ cups light cream
4 squares (1 ounce each)
** semisweet chocolate, coarsely**
** chopped**
4 ounces white chocolate,
** coarsely chopped**
4 eggs, slightly beaten
2 tablespoons brandy
1 3½-ounce package almond
** paste**
Whole almonds, sliced for
** garnish**

Preheat oven to 350°. Heat cream, semisweet chocolate, and white chocolate over low heat, stirring constantly, until chocolates are melted and mixture is smooth; cool slightly and gradually stir eggs and brandy into chocolate mixture. Pour into an 8½ x 4½ x 2½ inch loaf pan that has been lined with foil with a 2-inch overhang. Place pan in a pan of very hot water (1 inch deep) in oven. Bake until knife inserted half-way between edge and center comes out clean, 40 to 50 minutes. When done remove pan from water. While pâté is baking, roll out almond paste that has been placed between 2 sheets of wax paper to an 8 x 4 inch rectangle. Remove wax paper from almond paste when pâté is done and place it over the pâté immediately after taking it from the oven. Cool for 1 hour. Cover and refrigerate at least 8 hours but no more than 24 hours. Prepare chocolate glaze. Remove pâté from pan by inverting it onto serving plate. Carefully remove foil. Spread glaze evenly over sides and top of pâté. Decorate with almond slices in a flower design.

GLAZE

1 cup semisweet chocolate chips	Place chocolate, butter, and syrup in a saucepan
¼ cup butter	over low heat, stirring constantly until chocolate is
2 tablespoons corn syrup	melted. Cool.

This pâté is wonderful to serve at parties with lace, pecan, or sugar cookies (see cookie chapter). Guests slice a small amount of pâté to spread on the cookie. Serves 25 to 35 people when served in this manner.

ANN FOURNET'S CHOCOLATE TERRINE

Chocolate topped with raspberry purée, swimming in custard sauce

3 cups heavy cream
½ cup butter
20 ounces semisweet chocolate, melted
4 extra large egg yolks
1 cup almonds, chopped

Heat cream to a simmer; add butter (cut into small pieces) and melt. Add melted chocolate and stir until smooth. Stir in egg yolks, one at a time; add chopped almonds. Pour into a greased 1½-quart mold or springform pan. If using springform pan, be certain to tape seams. Place in large, shallow pan of hot water and bake at 350° for 1½ hours. Cool. Chill. When ready to serve, cut into squares. Spoon 4 tablespoons Crème Anglais onto individual dessert plates. Place chocolate squares in sauce; top with spoonsful of raspberry purée. Serves 12.

Raspberry purée: Thaw 2 packages raspberries in light syrup. Drain. Blend in blender or processor, then strain. Refrigerate until ready to serve.

CRÈME ANGLAISE

6 large egg yolks
⅔ cup sugar
4 tablespoons flour
2 cups milk
1 teaspoon vanilla
1 teaspoon almond extract

Mix egg yolks with ⅓ cup sugar and 4 tablespoons flour. Bring milk and remaining sugar to a boil. Add a small amount of milk mixture to yolk mixture. Then add yolk mixture to remaining milk mixture. Cook, stirring constantly over low heat until the mixture thickens. Add extracts. Chill.

WHITE CHOCOLATE COEUR A LA CRÈME

Garnished with strawberries and raspberry aspic and sauce, it is perfect for a wedding reception

1 cup cottage cheese
1 cup cream cheese, room temperature
½ cup sour cream
6 ounces white chocolate, shaved or chopped into small pieces
½ cup heavy cream, whipped
1 cup confectioners' sugar
½ teaspoon vanilla extract
1 recipe raspberry aspic (recipe below)
1 quart strawberries, whole with stems on
1 recipe raspberry sauce (recipe below)

Line a heart-shaped coeur à la crème mold with cheesecloth that has been rinsed in cold water. Wring out and place in mold, allowing excess cheesecloth to hang over the edge. Mix cottage cheese, softened cream cheese, and sour cream with an electric mixer. Melt white chocolate by placing in a bowl that has been warmed in hot water. (It may not be all melted, but if it is in small enough pieces, the mixer will finish blending it.) Beat with an electric mixer until blended; add to cream mixture. Whip the heavy cream and fold it into the cheese and chocolate mixture. Add confectioners' sugar and vanilla and spoon into the mold. Fold cheesecoth over the top; cover with plastic wrap. Chill thoroughly. It will keep in the refrigerator for 3 days. It may also be frozen for a week. To serve, open cheesecloth, invert the mold on a plate, and carefully remove the cheesecloth. Serve it with chopped raspberry aspic and lightly sweetened whole fresh strawberries attractively placed around the heart-shaped mold. Spoon raspberry sauce over strawberries and a little on the coeur à la crème, if desired.

RASPBERRY ASPIC

1 tablespoon unflavored gelatin
⅓ cup cold water
2 to 3 tablespoons sugar
⅓ cup framboise (raspberry liqueur)
1 10-ounce package frozen raspberries (to equal ⅔ cup)

Soak gelatin in cold water in a saucepan. Place over low heat and simmer to dissolve. Add sugar, stirring just long enough for it to dissolve. Remove from heat and stir in framboise. Place raspberries in the blender and liquefy. Strain out seeds, measure ⅔ cup, and add to aspic. Pour aspic into a square cake pan, cover, and refrigerate. When ready to serve, turn out on a plate and chop into small squares. Makes a little over 1 cup. Recipe may be doubled, if more aspic is desired.

RASPBERRY SAUCE

1 10-ounce package raspberries,
    defrosted
¼ cup sugar
2 tablespoons framboise

Purée raspberries and strain out seeds. Combine with sugar and framboise. Drizzle over the strawberries and the coeur à la crème, if desired. This recipe serves 8. It may be served with thin crisp cookies for a buffet. In this manner it will serve 35.

Jo created this recipe especially for her daughter Emily's wedding reception.

POTS DE CRÈME

An elegant chocolate mousse made quickly in a blender

6 ounces semisweet chocolate bits
¼ cup scalded milk
3 tablespoons brewed coffee,
    double strength
2 eggs
2 tablespoons Grand Marnier
½ cup heavy cream, whipped
6 candied violets (optional)

Combine chocolate bits, scalded milk, and hot coffee in blender. Blend for 1 minute. Add eggs and Grand Marnier to the mixture and blend 2 more minutes. Pour mousse into 6 pots de crème; place the tops on them and chill in the refrigerator several hours. The pots de crème may be made several days in advance. To serve, whip the cream and place a teaspoon or two on the pots de crème. Garnish with a candied violet, if desired. The little pots de crème also make an elegant presentation with a small amount of Grand Marnier floating on the top of each without the whipped cream or candied violet. Serves 6.

MOTHER'S LEMON PUDDING

An easy-to-make recipe from Mary Leigh's mother

2 tablespoons butter
2 cups sugar
4 tablespoons flour
4 egg yolks, slightly beaten
2 cups milk
6 tablespoons lemon juice
5 teaspoons lemon rind
4 egg whites, beaten

Cream butter and sugar. Blend in flour, egg yolks, milk, lemon juice, and rind. Add beaten egg whites last, folding them into mixture. Bake in a square dish for 25 to 30 minutes at 350°. Serves 8.

Lemon Pudding is delicious served plain but even better topped with Fresh Blueberry Sauce (see index for recipe).

CHERRY PUDDING

From The Burn, a Natchez mansion with overnight accommodations

1¾ cups sugar
2 cups flour
1½ teaspoons baking soda
½ teaspoon baking powder
¼ teaspoon salt
2 eggs
3 tablespoons melted butter
1 (16-ounce) can pitted cherries
   and juice
1½ cups toasted chopped pecans

Mix dry ingredients. Stir in eggs, butter, cherries, juice, and pecans. Bake in buttered rectangular pan for 50 to 60 minutes at 350°. Serve warm with warm sauce. Serves about 12.

SAUCE

¾ stick butter
½ pint whipping cream
1 teaspoon vanilla
1 teaspoon almond extract

Mix together and heat. Serve over pudding.

The Burn, built in 1832, is a white-columned home with priceless antiques. During the Civil War it was used as headquarters by federal troops and later became a Union hospital.

Slice ¼ inch off of the top of an Angel Food Cake. Pull out the middle of the cake, leaving a shell approximately ¼ inch on bottom and sides. Tear the insides of the cake into small pieces and mix it with a good pudding or custard. Fill cake and place the top back on. Ice with whipped cream.

Fruit Desserts

The dining room at Hope Farm, home of the late Mr. and
Mrs. J. Balfour Miller in Natchez, Mississippi. Mrs. Miller
was instrumental in founding the annual Natchez
Pilgrimage.

Compote of Blackberries

1 quart of blackberries,
 freshly picked
½ cup of sugar
Juice of ½ lemon

Select fine berries, but not too ripe; wash them in cold water and drain through a sieve. Boil the sugar in the lemon juice and a small amount of water and add the berries; let them boil up once very gently. Pour them into a compote, pour the jelly over and serve with thick cream. A dainty and delightful dessert.

*F*ruit has flourished in the mild climate and fertile soil of the South since before the arrival of the earliest settlers. Every season brings its joys: spring berries, summer peaches and melons, fall apples, and winter oranges. With the quantity of rural roadside stands and urban farmers' markets, finding fresh produce at peak flavor is seldom a problem. This bounty from Mother Nature makes fruit desserts popular grand finales in most homes.

Some fruits have thrived in the South since before recorded history. Strawberries grew so thickly in Virginia when European settlers arrived that one Englishman is known to have complained that he could hardly walk without stepping on them. Indians were fond of the heart-shaped berries and held annual strawberry harvest celebrations. Blueberries and blackberries also grow well in Southern soil and their season is awaited with anticipation.

Brought to America by the Spaniards in the 1600s, peaches grow abundantly throughout the lower South, and have inspired a host of desserts. Oranges are another Spanish contribution, brought by de Soto and Ponce de Leon. Oranges are used to make ambrosia — considered the quintessential Southern dessert.

Plump, green watermelons, whose seeds were brought from Africa by the slaves, are another popular fruit with Southerners, who like to cool off with a chilled slice on a hot day.

Apples grow best in the cooler climate of Virginia and West Virginia. They are less perishable than most fruits and were dried and stored in cellars for winter pie making during earlier times.

With typical resourcefulness, the first Southerners made do with the foods at hand, creating recipes on the spot for such delicacies as stewed fruit with dumplings, fritters, crisps, and roly-polys. Their legacy became the inspiration for our fruit desserts today.

AMBROSIA

An early marriage of coconut and tropical fruit

8 oranges
3 bananas
8 slices canned pineapple, juice reserved
3½-ounce can angel flake coconut
⅔ cup sugar
⅔ cup sherry
Maraschino cherries

Peel oranges and remove all white membrane; cut into sections. Slice bananas. Cut pineapple slices into chunks. Place a layer of orange slices in the bottom of a crystal or glass bowl. Spoon a layer of sugar and splash a few spoonsful of sherry over the oranges. Add a layer of bananas, then a layer of sugar and sherry. Next, add a layer of pineapple. Sprinkle with sugar and sherry. Last, add a layer of coconut, topped with sugar and sherry. Repeat process until all ingredients are used. Pour pineapple juice from the can over all. Chill for at least 3 hours. Decorate the top with maraschino cherries and a final sprinkling of coconut. Serves 8 to 10.

ORANGES ALASKA

Divinity Meringue tops an orange shell filled with fruit and ice cream

3 large navel oranges or 6 small oranges
1 banana
¼ cup sugar
6 rounded tablespoons vanilla ice cream

Cut 3 large oranges in half or remove about one-third of the tops from 6 small oranges. Carefully remove pulp, gently scraping out the white pith from shells. Dice pulp, removing seeds and membrane. Mix with diced peeled bananas. (Oranges may be prepared the day before and stored covered in the refrigerator.) Sprinkle fruit with sugar, cover, and let stand in refrigerator for several hours if necessary. When ready to serve, make meringue. Place 1 rounded tablespoon vanilla ice cream in each shell. Fill with fruit and cover with meringue. Place under broiler until meringue is browned. Serve immediately. Serves 6.

DIVINITY MERINGUE

3 extra-large egg whites
1 teaspoon white vinegar
¼ cup white karo
¼ cup confectioners' sugar

Beat egg whites until frothy, and add vinegar. Beat until meringue makes soft peaks. Add karo a little at a time, beating constantly. Repeat with confectioners' sugar, beating until meringue stands in peaks.

PINEAPPLE CUBES AND BLUEBERRIES WITH RUM LIME SAUCE

Beautiful for a buffet supper

1 pineapple
1 cup blueberries

Cut pineapple in half lengthwise, stem included. Cut around shells and remove pineapple meat. Cut into cubes. Mix with blueberries.

RUM LIME SAUCE

¾ cup sugar
⅓ cup water
1 teaspoon grated lime rind
4 tablespoons lime juice
¼ cup rum

Mix sugar and water in a saucepan. Bring to a boil. Reduce heat and simmer 5 minutes. Add lime rind. Cool to room temperature. Add lime juice and rum. Pour sauce over pineapple and blueberries. Toss. Chill for several hours. Serve in pineapple shells. Let guests serve themselves. Serves 6.

OLD-FASHIONED APPLE FRITTERS

Substitute bananas, peaches, or berries

1 cup sifted pastry flour
1 level teaspoon baking powder
1 level teaspoon confectioners' sugar
¼ teaspoon salt
1 egg, slightly beaten
¼ cup milk
2 apples, pared and cut into small pieces
Hot fat for frying

Sift together, three times, the flour, baking powder, sugar, and salt. Add the milk to the beaten egg and stir in the sifted ingredients. Then stir in the bits of apple. Drop the batter into the fat by spoonsful and let fry until delicately browned. Drain on soft paper. Serve with confectioners' sugar, Jelly Sauce, or Vanilla Sauce. May also be served in a bowl with thick cream. Makes 12 to 15, depending on size.

Jelly Sauce: Melt jelly together with a small amount of water. Brandy, fruit brandy, or wine may be substituted for water.

VANILLA SAUCE

½ cup sugar
1 tablespoon cornstarch
1 cup boiling water
2 tablespoons butter
1 teaspoon vanilla extract
⅛ teaspoon salt

Mix sugar and cornstarch together in a saucepan. Stir in boiling water. Simmer for 5 minutes. Stir in butter and vanilla. Add salt. Serve warm. Makes 1¼ cups.

APPLE CHEESE DUMPLINGS IN CINNAMON SYRUP

A dessert as old as the South with a delicious new taste

8 ounces cream cheese, room
  temperature
½ cup butter, room temperature
1½ cups flour
¼ teaspoon salt
4 ounces sharp cheddar cheese,
  grated
1 teaspoon cayenne pepper
¼ cup butter
1 teaspoon cinnamon
1 teaspoon nutmeg
1 teaspoon allspice
½ cup dark brown sugar
6 medium apples (Winesap,
  Granny Smith, or any tart
  apple)
Apricot preserves
Whipped cream, ice cream, or
  hard sauce

Combine first 4 ingredients in a mixer. Blend well. With fork or hands blend in grated cheddar cheese and add cayenne pepper, distributing evenly. Roll into a ball. Place in plastic wrap and chill at least 4 hours or overnight. Roll out pastry to ¼ inch and cut into 6 squares. Make a paste of the butter, spices, and brown sugar. Peel and core the apples, and place on pastry squares. Fill the core of the apple with the apricot preserves. Spread the spice paste over each apple. Fold opposite corners of the pastry together. Pinch edges to seal apple. Place in a buttered pan with sides and bake in a preheated 375° oven for 30 minutes. Serve warm with whipped cream, ice cream, or hard sauce. Serves 6.

Who in the South does not remember eating apples wrapped in warm baked pie crust at the end of a Sunday meal? In this old family recipe the spices and juice from the butter and preserves cook together to form a syrup and the cheese and cayenne pepper add the perfect touch.

ARKANSAS FRUIT AND RICE FRITTERS

Pieces of fresh fruit are tucked into the fritters

¼ cup rice, uncooked
1 egg, slightly beaten
½ cup milk
1½ cups sifted pastry flour
½ teaspoon salt
1 level teaspoon baking powder
Slices of cooked peach or apple
  or uncooked berries
Hot fat for frying
Sugar

Cook the rice in boiling salted water until it is tender and the water is absorbed or drained off; add the egg and milk; then the flour, salt, and baking powder, sifted together three times. Blend well. Take up by tablespoonsful, press the fruit into the center of the mixture, on the spoon, and with a teaspoon scrape the whole into the hot fat. Fry to an amber color. Serve with sprinkled sugar. Makes 12 to 15, depending on size.

1890 WITCH APPLES

From a turn-of-the-century Georgia cookbook

8 large apples
8 marshmallows
16 sugar cubes
8 tablespoons brandy
16 maraschino cherries
1 cup heavy cream, whipped

Preheat oven to 375°. Wash, remove core to ½ inch of bottoms of apples, then cut a strip from the hollowed ends. Place hollowed apples in a baking pan with ¾ cup boiling water. Cover and bake 40 to 60 minutes or until tender but not long enough to burst skins. The old book cautions that it is better to prepare half a dozen extra for emergencies. When cooked insert a marshmallow into the core space, place a cube or 2 of sugar on the top (dip quickly in some brandy), and a few maraschino cherries. When ready to serve, warm 8 tablespoons brandy and spoon over sugar cubes and marshmallows. Light just as the table is reached. The brandy will burn with a ghostly flame and melt the sugar and marshmallows. Whipped cream served in a bowl is a good addition to the dessert. Serves 8.

CHERRIES JUBILEE

Dazzle your guests with New Orleans glamor

⅓ cup sugar
2 tablespoons cornstarch
1 pound can dark, sweet, pitted
   cherries
⅓ cup brandy
Vanilla ice cream

Blend sugar and cornstarch in a saucepan. Drain cherries, reserving syrup. Slowly add syrup to dry ingredients, stirring well. Cook over medium heat, stirring constantly, until mixture is lightly thickened and smooth. Add cherries and remove from heat. Pour mixture into the top pan of a chafing dish, making certain the bottom pan is filled with hot water. Heat brandy until warm in a small pan. Ignite brandy with a long, wooden match, and pour over cherry mixture. Stir sauce until flame dies down. Place a scoop of vanilla ice cream in each of six bowls. Spoon sauce over ice cream and serve immediately. Serves 6.

Add a dash of almond extract to canned peach-pie and cherry-pie fillings.

WATERMELON BASKET

Serves also as a table decoration

1 watermelon
1 cantaloupe
1 honeydew melon
Fresh pineapple
Fresh blueberries
Small bunches of seedless grapes
1 quart strawberries
Fresh cherries with stems
Any other fresh fruit in season

Pin a tape measure around the top third of the watermelon, horizontally. If necessary, slice a small piece of rind from the botton to steady it. With a pencil lightly draw around the tape measure. Find the halfway mark and measure ¾ inch on each side (this is for the handle). The handle should be about 1½ inches wide. Stretch the tape measure across the top of the melon and pin again. Mark the handle where you will cut. Cut handle out first and then basket. If you would like the basket scalloped, simply draw in the scallops along the penciled line. Cut and remove watermelon meat. Fill cavity with the fruit of your choice. It is best to use fresh fruit in season instead of canned. One of the prettiest combinations is watermelon, cantaloupe, honeydew (cut into bite-sized pieces), blueberries, and strawberries.

SAUCE FOR FRUIT

2 cups sugar
2 cups water
½ teaspoon dried mint
½ teaspoon anise seeds

Combine ingredients in a saucepan and boil for 15 minutes. Pour over fruit and chill.

GINGERED BLUEBERRY COMPOTE

An elegant dish for the diet conscious

2 cups fresh blueberries
1 cup fresh orange juice
1 tablespoon fresh lemon juice
¼ cup confectioners' sugar
2 tablespoons minced preserved gingerroot
Fresh mint leaves

Wash blueberries; mix with orange juice, lemon juice, confectioners' sugar, and minced gingerroot. Chill several hours. Serve in sherbet or large wine glasses. Garnish with fresh mint leaves. Serves 6.

For more zip in a fruit cup, add a few drops of vanilla.

CHAMPAGNE FRUIT CUP

Equally good without sherbet as a champagne cocktail

1 cup strawberries
1 cup peaches, peeled and sliced
1 cup pineapple chunks
½ cup cognac
12 scoops orange sherbet
1 bottle champagne
12 fresh strawberries, with stems

Combine strawberries, peaches, and pineapple; pour cognac over fruit and stir gently. Refrigerate at least 1 hour. Divide fruit between 12 champagne glasses; add a scoop of sherbet, and fill with champagne. Garnish with whole strawberry. Serves 12.

The fruit cocktail has long been a favorite Southern dessert and has many variations. Fresh fruit served around sherbet or ice cream without the spirits is also a popular summer dessert, as well as a refreshing appetizer.

BLACKBERRY ROLY-POLY WITH FRESH FRUIT SAUCE

A roly-poly is seen often in old Southern cookbooks

1 quart blackberries
½ cup water
1¼ cups sugar
3 cups sifted flour
3 level teaspoons baking powder
½ teaspoon salt
½ cup shortening
1 egg yolk, beaten
Milk or water as needed (about 10 tablespoons)
1 egg white, slightly beaten
Sugar

In a heavy saucepan with high sides, cook berries with water for about 15 minutes or until soft and mushy. Press the mixture through a sieve to remove seeds. To the pulp add sugar and let simmer until well reduced. Keep half the mixture hot for a sauce and cool the rest. Sift together, three times, the flour, baking powder, and salt; work in the shortening, then mix to a dough with milk or water added to the beaten egg yolk. Knead slightly and roll into a sheet ¼ inch thick; cut into 8 or 10 rectangles; spread these with the cold blackberry mixture and roll over and over in a jelly roll fashion. Brush the top of each with the egg white, slightly beaten, and dredge with sugar. Bake at 350° for about 30 minutes or until lightly brown. Serve hot with the following blackberry sauce. If desired, top with a small amount of whipped cream sweetened with confectioners' sugar.

BLACKBERRY SAUCE

Remaining blackberry mixture
¼ cup blackberry wine (or to taste)

Mix together and reheat to serve. Serves 8 to 10.

PLANTATION MELON

Fruit and punch in a cantaloupe shell

1 small cantaloupe
¼ cup orange juice
¼ cup grapefruit juice
1 teaspoon lemon juice
1 teaspoon lime juice
2 teaspoons grenadine syrup
2 jiggers gin or vodka
2 or 3 pineapple chunks
1 maraschino cherry
Fig leaves and wildflowers for
   garnish

Cut the top of a small cantaloupe, leaving the meat and seeds exposed. Slice a small portion off the bottom to keep it upright. Remove and discard the seeds from the top portion. Scoop out the ripest melon meat and place it in a blender with the orange juice, grapefruit juice, lemon and lime juice, and grenadine syrup. Blend well and place in freezer until slushy. Wrap the shell in plastic wrap and refrigerate. When ready to serve add gin or vodka. Pour into the cavity of the chilled cantaloupe and place the pineapple cubes and cherry in last. Serve on pretty fig or other leaves and surround with wildflowers. Serves 1.

BLACKBERRY MOUSSE

An heirloom dessert from Mobile

1½ tablespoons gelatin
¼ cup cold water
1 cup fresh orange juice
1 tablespoon cornstarch
Grated rind of 1 orange
1½ pints fresh blackberries,
   washed and dried, or 3
   16-ounce waterpack cans,
   drained
4 egg yolks
1 cup sugar
½ teaspoon cinnamon
1½ cups heavy cream
½ cup confectioners' sugar
4 egg whites
Pinch salt
1 tablespoon sugar
Berries for garnish

In a small glass bowl soften gelatin in cold water 5 to 6 minutes. In a saucepan place 1 cup fresh orange juice, cornstarch, orange peel, and ¾ cup berries. Add softened gelatin and heat carefully, stirring until slightly thickened, about 10 minutes. Remove from heat and cool to room temperature. Beat egg yolks, adding 1 cup sugar gradually; add cinnamon. Place in top of a double boiler until mixture is too hot to touch. Stir yolk mixture into gelatin mixture and cool to room temperature. Whip cream and fold into cooled berry mixture. In a blender, purée remaining berries with ½ cup confectioners' sugar. Stir into the mixture with a knife until it streaks with a marbled effect. Beat egg whites with a pinch of salt and 1 tablespoon sugar until stiff but not dry. Fold into berry mixture and chill in a 2-quart soufflé dish or greased ring mold. Garnish with berries. Serves 8.

STRAWBERRIES A LA CRÈME

Makes a breakfast or brunch special

1 pint vanilla ice cream, softened
1 cup heavy cream, whipped
½ teaspoon almond extract
1 quart fresh strawberries, stemmed; reserve a few with stems on for garnish
½ cup confectioners' sugar
⅓ cup Grand Marnier

Whip the vanilla ice cream until creamy and fold in the whipped cream. Add the almond extract. You can freeze the dessert at this point if desired. Thaw in the refrigerator before serving. Slightly mash the strawberries sweetened with confectioners' sugar and Grand Marnier. Let stand in the refrigerator for approximately 1 hour. At serving time blend lightly and serve in chilled, stemmed glasses. Garnish with a whole strawberry. Serves 6.

BAKED BANANAS WITH LEMON SAUCE

A delicious finale to an Oriental dinner

¼ cup sugar
1 teaspoon cinnamon
6 small firm bananas, peeled
1 lemon
1 recipe pastry (see index for Plain Ice Water Pie Crust)
1 egg, slightly beaten
1 recipe Traditional Lemon Sauce

Combine sugar and cinnamon; sprinkle bananas with the sugar-cinnamon mixture and a little lemon juice. Roll pastry out on a heavily floured surface to ⅛ inch thickness; cut pastry into 6 equal portions. Gently wrap a portion around each banana. Moisten edges with water; pinch gently to seal. Place bananas, seam side down, on a well-greased jelly-roll pan. Brush with beaten egg. Bake at 475° for 8 minutes or until lightly browned. Serve topped with lemon sauce. Serves 6.

TRADITIONAL LEMON SAUCE

¾ cup sugar
1½ tablespoons cornstarch
½ cup water
2 egg yolks
1½ tablespoons butter or margarine, softened
¼ cup lemon juice

Combine sugar and cornstarch in a medium-size heavy saucepan; mix well. Add water; bring to a boil. Reduce heat; cook, stirring constantly, until it coats the back of a spoon. Beat yolks until thick and lemon-colored. Gradually stir in a tablespoon or two of the hot mixture into yolks; add to remaining hot mixture. Continue cooking over medium heat. Add butter and lemon juice; stir until well blended. Chill.

This recipe is from the files of Mrs. Richard Redmont, a well-known Southern hostess and a world traveler who had a genius for combining traditional Southern specialties with food from abroad and serving them in her gracious manner. Baked Bananas were served often in her antebellum home following an Oriental meal.

ANN RUSHING'S BAKED PEARS ON THE HALF SHELL

Three delicious fillings

3 fresh pears
Choice of fillings
½ cup water
½ cup brown sugar
1 tablespoon butter
½ teaspoon cinnamon

Halve and core pears. Fill centers with desired filling. Combine remaining ingredients. Bring to a boil and pour over pears. Bake at 350° for 45 minutes, basting frequently with syrup. Serves 6.

Raisin Filling: Combine ¼ cup raisins and 2 tablespoons chopped nuts.

Date Filling: Combine ⅓ cup snipped dates, 2 tablespoons chopped nuts, and ½ teaspoon grated orange peel.

Mincemeat Filling: Combine ½ cup prepared mincemeat with 1 tablespoon rum or brandy.

CARDAMOM BAKED HONEY PEARS

Hits the spot after a curry dinner

6 pears, unpeeled
½ cup water
½ cup honey
½ cup butter, cut into pieces
¼ cup brown sugar, packed
12 cardamom seeds
1 large lemon
3 ounces cream cheese
¼ cup pecans or walnuts
⅛ teaspoon cinnamon

Cut the pears in half vertically through the center. Carefully cut out the core, leaving the stem. Arrange cut side up in a baking dish. Mix together the water, honey, butter, and brown sugar. Pour over the pears. Slice lemon, unpeeled, into thin slices and arrange on top of the pears. Bake in a 350° oven until the pears are tender — about 30 minutes — basting occasionally. When the pears are tender, remove from the syrup onto paper towels and reserve syrup. Crush 12 cardamom seeds and divide evenly among the pear halves. Press into the pear halves with the back of a spoon. Mix the cream cheese with the nuts and cinnamon. Place a spoonful of the mixture into 6 of the pear halves and place the other pear halves on top forming a whole. To serve, place in a serving dish with some of the syrup. Serves 6.

A family recipe from the David Butlers of Jackson, Mississippi. Sharon Butler usually makes the dessert with pears that she has canned or frozen, when pears are out of season.

EOLA HOTEL'S HOT PEAR AND RASPBERRY COMPOTE

Natchez's oldest hotel, restored recently to its former grace and beauty

2 quarts pears, poached, sliced
1 quart raspberries, fresh or
    frozen
1 quart mandarin orange
    sections, drained
1 quart apricot halves, drained
1 cup port wine
4 cups fresh grated coconut or
    flaked, sweetened coconut
2 cups brown sugar
1 cup heavy cream, whipped

Poach pears by dropping halves into boiling water to cover. Reduce heat at once and simmer until barely tender. Remove them from the heat and drain immediately afterwards, so that they will not continue to cook and get mushy. Slice the pears and mix with raspberries, mandarin orange sections, drained apricot halves, and port wine. Place in an oblong shallow casserole. Mix brown sugar and coconut together. Scatter it over the fruit and port wine mixture. Bake in a preheated 400° oven 15 to 20 minutes or until lightly brown and fruit is hot. Serve warm in footed goblets. Top with whipped cream. Serves 8 if using ¾-cup servings.

BERRY PUFFS WITH FRUIT SAUCE

Feathery light, the little puffs look beautiful served in a fruit sauce

2 cups sifted flour
2 level teaspoons baking powder
½ teaspoon salt
2 level tablespoons sugar
2 eggs
½ cup butter, melted
1 cup milk
1 cup berries (blueberries,
    blackberries, raspberries)

SAUCE

1 pint berries
1 cup sugar

Sift together, three times, the flour, baking powder, salt, and sugar. Beat the eggs and stir in the butter; add the milk and stir into the dry ingredients, then stir in the cup of berries. Butter miniature muffin tins. Fill to the top and bake in a 375° oven for 30 minutes or until lightly browned. Not quite a biscuit, not quite a muffin, these little puffs from a turn-of-the-century cookbook are delicious served with the following sauce.

Slightly mash the berries and add sugar. Bring to a boil; continue boiling gently until cooked down about half. Makes 24 puffs.

Use leftover frozen fruit juices instead of water in gelatin salads or desserts.

STRAWBERRY SHORTCAKE

Closing stanza of many a Sunday dinner

2 cups flour
3 teaspoons baking powder
½ teaspoon salt
2 tablespoons sugar
⅛ teaspoon nutmeg
½ cup unsalted butter
¾ cup milk
1 tablespoon melted butter
1 tablespoon sugar
1 quart strawberries
½ cup sugar
½ pint whipping cream
4 tablespoons sugar
1 teaspoon vanilla

Mix dry ingredients. Cut in butter in a food processor until mixture is the texture of coarse meal. Add milk. Toss on floured board and roll dough until 1 inch thick. Cut into rounds with a biscuit cutter. Brush with melted butter. Sprinkle with 1 tablespoon sugar. Bake at 400° for 15 minutes or until light golden. Slice strawberries and stir in ½ cup sugar. Let sit at room temperature for 1 hour or until juicy. May refrigerate until serving time. Whip cream and season with 4 tablespoons sugar and vanilla. Split biscuits, fill with berries, and top with whipped cream. Serves 8 to 10.

PATRIOTIC ANGEL PIE

A festive red, white, and blue creation

3 egg whites
1 cup sugar
2 teaspoons white vinegar
3 egg yolks
½ cup sugar
2 tablespoons flour
1 cup milk
½ teaspoon vanilla
Dash of salt
¾ cup blueberries
¾ cup strawberries, sliced
½ pint whipping cream
4 tablespoons sugar
½ teaspoon vanilla

Beat egg whites until stiff. Slowly beat in 1 cup sugar and vinegar. Spoon into a lightly greased 9-inch pie pan, forming a shell. Make bottom ⅓ inch thick and extend sides up ½ inch above edge of pan. Bake in preheated 300° oven for 1 to 1¼ hours. Cool. Beat egg yolks well. Mix in ½ cup sugar, flour, milk, vanilla, and salt. Pour custard into top of a double boiler and cook, stirring constantly, until thick. Cool. Pour filling into crust. Chill for 30 minutes. Layer blueberries and strawberries over custard. Whip cream. Flavor with sugar and vanilla. Cover berries with whipped cream and decorate with whole strawberries and blueberries. Chill until serving time. Serves 8.

Cut biscuit dough for shortcake with a metal ice cube rack from the refrigerator tray.

GEORGIA PEACH CRÊPES WITH BUTTERED RUM SAUCE

Peaches with spice and everything nice

4 eggs
1 cup flour
2 tablespoons sugar
¼ teaspoon salt
¾ cup milk
½ cup water
1 tablespoon butter, melted
1 teaspoon vanilla
Crêpe maker

Beat eggs in electric mixer. Add dry ingredients alternately with milk and water. Mix in butter and vanilla. Cook crêpes according to manufacturer's instructions for crêpe maker. May be made 3 hours ahead and stacked between layers of wax paper to keep pliable. May be frozen by placing stacked crêpes and wax paper in plastic bag.

FILLING

¼ cup brown sugar
½ cup water
¼ teaspoon nutmeg
¼ teaspoon cinnamon
¼ teaspoon cloves
3 cups fresh or frozen peaches, sliced

Bring sugar, water, and seasonings to a boil. Add peaches. Simmer, covered, for 5 minutes or until barely tender. Drain liquid and save for another use. Place several slices in center of each crepe. Fold.

BUTTERED RUM SAUCE

1 cup brown sugar
1½ tablespoons cornstarch
1 cup water
¼ cup butter
¼ cup rum
Whipped cream (optional)

Mix brown sugar and cornstarch in a saucepan. Gradually stir in water. Bring to a boil and simmer several minutes until thickened. Slice butter and stir in one slice at a time. Add rum. Cook until well mixed and warm. Serve over filled crêpes. Top with whipped cream if desired. Makes 10 crepes.

Use brown sugar for stewing fresh fruits. Add the peel of ½ lemon, the juice of the whole lemon, and 1 cinnamon stick. Delicious with peaches, plums, cherries, apples, or similar fruit.

COUNTRY PEACH CRISP

Forms its own crust

½ cup butter or margarine
1 cup flour
2 cups sugar
½ teaspoon salt
3 teaspoons baking powder
1 cup milk
3 to 4 cups fresh peaches, peeled, sliced
1 teaspoon cinnamon

Preheat oven to 350°. Melt margarine in an 8 x 12 inch baking dish. Sift together flour, 1 cup sugar, salt, and baking powder, and blend with the milk. Pour mixture over melted butter. Spread peaches over this and sprinkle with the other 1 cup sugar mixed with cinnamon. Bake for 1 hour. Crust will form while in the oven. Serves 6.

PEACHES MELBA

A New Orleans adaptation of an Escoffier recipe

6 slices pound cake
3 cups vanilla ice cream
6 peach halves, peeled with pit removed
1 cup grenadine syrup or the following Melba Sauce
⅔ cup chopped roasted almonds

Place a slice of pound cake in the bottom of each of 6 dessert bowls. Top each with a scoop of vanilla ice cream (approximately ½ cup) and then a peach half, cut side down, on the ice cream. Pour over some of the grenadine syrup or the Melba Sauce and sprinkle with chopped roasted almonds. To toast almonds: Preheat oven to 250° or 300°. Place nuts in a greased shallow pan. Bake until golden, turning often and sprinkling often with melted butter.

MELBA SAUCE

½ cup currant jelly
1 cup strained raspberries, fresh or frozen
1 teaspoon cornstarch
⅛ teaspoon salt
½ cup sugar

Mix jelly and berries; add remaining ingredients. Place in the top of a double boiler and bring to the boiling point over direct heat. Place the top of the double boiler in the bottom of the double boiler that has boiling water coming almost to the bottom of the pan (this should not be in the water). Cook until thick and clear. Chill before using. Serves 6.

Peaches Melba was created in 1893 by Escoffier in honor of the celebrated Australian singer, Nelly Melba. The original recipe called for grenadine syrup to be poured over the peach halves. The recipe has been changed over the years and many people prefer the raspberry Melba sauce.

BAKED STUFFED PEACHES WITH CUSTARD SAUCE

A real Southern treat

8 medium-sized ripe peaches
1 tablespoon lemon juice
½ cup finely chopped candied
   ginger
½ cup finely chopped pecans
½ cup honey, divided
¼ cup cookie or cake crumbs
Custard sauce or whipped cream,
   sweetened

Dip peaches in boiling water for the count of 10. Remove and peel. Drop in water to cover with lemon juice. Leave until all are prepared. Mix chopped ginger, pecans, honey, and cookie crumbs. Cut peaches in half and remove stones. Place about 2 tablespoons of the nut mixture in each peach and put back together, fastening well with toothpicks. Place peaches in a baking pan just large enough to hold them and pour remaining honey over. Cover and bake at 350° until peaches are tender, about 30 minutes. Serve warm with custard sauce. Serves 8.

CUSTARD SAUCE

1½ tablespoons cornstarch
2 cups light cream, divided
4 egg yolks
½ cup sugar
1 teaspoon vanilla

Dissolve cornstarch in ¼ cup cream. Beat egg yolks until light, then combine with cornstarch mixture. Heat remaining cream, taking care not to boil, and add sugar. Pour 1 cup hot cream and sugar over egg mixture, stirring constantly. Return remaining hot cream to low heat, stir in egg-cream mixture, and continue to stir and cook 5 minutes until sauce is slightly thickened. Add vanilla, blend thoroughly, and cool.

GRAPE PARFAIT

For a cocktail party, serve grapes on toothpicks with sauce as a dip

1 pound green seedless grapes
1 cup white wine
1 cup sour cream
½ cup brown sugar
¼ cup slivered almonds, toasted
   in ½ stick margarine

Place grapes in a shallow bowl. Cover with wine and refrigerate for 3 hours. Drain and place in a clean bowl. Chill until serving time. Mix sour cream and brown sugar. Serve grapes in sherbet dishes. Cover with sour cream sauce. Sprinkle almonds on top. Tuck a fresh mint leaf in each dish. Serves 6.

FRESH PEACH DUMPLINGS

A delicious country dessert

2 cups flour
½ teaspoon salt
1½ teaspoons baking powder
⅓ cup shortening
⅔ cup milk
3 fresh peaches
2 tablespoons sugar
Cinnamon
Butter or margarine
2 cups sugar
2 cups boiling water
½ cup butter or margarine
¼ teaspoon almond flavoring

Sift together the flour, salt, and baking powder. Cut in the shortening and then stir in the milk. Roll dough on a floured board and cut into circles, about 6 inches in diameter. You should be able to get 6 circles without difficulty. Peel 3 fresh peaches (frozen peaches could be used) and place a peach half on each circle of dough. On each peach, place 1 teaspoon sugar, a dash of cinnamon, and a small piece of butter or margarine. Fold the dough over the peach, pinching the dough together a little. Combine the 2 cups sugar, boiling water, ½ cup butter or margarine, and almond flavoring. Put in a saucepan, bring to a boil, boil for 2 to 3 minutes, then pour around the dumplings in a baking pan and bake at 350° for 1 hour. Serves 6.

BANANAS FOSTER

Spectacular showstopper that's easy to make

2 tablespoons butter
4 tablespoons brown sugar
2 bananas, peeled, halved, and
   sliced lengthwise
¼ teaspoon cinnamon
1 ounce banana liqueur
2 ounces rum
Vanilla ice cream

Melt butter in a large skillet or chafing dish. Stir in brown sugar, slowly, and cook until bubbly. Add bananas and sauté on both sides until barely tender, basting constantly. Sprinkle bananas with cinnamon. Heat banana liqueur and rum in a small boiler. Pour over fruit and flame with a long, wooden match. Baste bananas with liquid until flames die. Scoop vanilla ice cream into two dessert dishes, spoon banana mixture over ice cream and serve at once. Serves 2.

Bananas Foster was created by Brennan's Restaurant in New Orleans and is on the menu at the popular "Breakfast at Brennan's." The dessert was named for Richard Foster, a patron of the restaurant.

Strawberries marinated in port wine for a few hours are wonderful.

BANANA SPLIT DESSERT

Makes enough to feed a crowd — halve it for your family

2 cups graham cracker crumbs
½ cup margarine, melted
3 bananas
Juice of 1 lemon
2 sticks margarine, softened
2 cups confectioners' sugar
2 eggs
1 large can crushed pineapple,
    drained
1 carton heavy cream
4 tablespoons sugar
½ teaspoon vanilla
¾ cup pecans, chopped
½ cup maraschino cherries,
    chopped
½ cup chocolate syrup

Stir margarine into graham cracker crumbs. Line bottom of a 9 x 13 x 2 inch pan with mixture and chill until needed. Halve bananas and slice lengthwise. Sprinkle with lemon juice and let sit 15 minutes. Beat 2 sticks margarine until creamy. Gradually add confectioners' sugar and eggs. Beat together for 5 minutes. Spread over graham cracker crust. Arrange bananas over filling and cover with drained pineapple. Whip cream, flavor with sugar and vanilla, and smooth over fruit. Sprinkle with pecans and cherries. Drizzle chocolate syrup over all. Refrigerate. Serves 15.

NAN MCROBERTS' FROSTY STRAWBERRY SQUARES

As refreshing as springtime

1 cup sifted all-purpose flour
⅓ cup brown sugar, packed
½ cup chopped walnuts or
    pecans
½ cup margarine
2 cups sliced fresh strawberries or
    1 package frozen strawberries
1 cup sugar
2½ teaspoons lemon juice, fresh
2 egg whites
1 cup whipping cream, whipped
Whole strawberries

Preheat oven to 350°. Combine flour, brown sugar, nuts, and margarine and spread evenly in a 13 x 9 x 2 inch pan. Bake 20 minutes, stirring occasionally, until mixture is crumbly. Remove one-third of the mixture and press the remaining crumbs evenly into the pan. Combine the strawberries, sugar, lemon juice, and egg whites. Beat at high speed approximately 10 to 15 minutes or until light and fluffy. Fold the whipped cream into the strawberry mixture. Spread over the crumb mixture. Top with the remaining crumbs and freeze 6 hours or overnight. Cut into squares of desired size and top with whole berries. Serves 12.

PARTY FRUIT PIZZA

Perfect for high school graduation parties

1 recipe sugar cookies
1 recipe almond cream
1 recipe glaze
Fresh fruit in season (or frozen or
    canned) such as: apricots;
    peach slices; cherries; seedless
    grapes; blueberries; pineapple
    slices; apples, unpeeled;
    kiwifruit; pears, unpeeled;
    strawberries; raspberries; etc.

SUGAR COOKIES

½ cup shortening
½ teaspoon salt
½ teaspoon grated lemon rind
¼ teaspoon almond extract
1 cup sugar
2 tablespoons milk
2 eggs, beaten
2 cups flour, sifted
1 teaspoon baking powder
½ teaspoon baking soda

Blend shortening, salt, lemon rind, and extract. Add sugar gradually and cream well. Add milk and eggs. Sift flour with baking powder and soda. Add to creamed mixture, blending well. Drop from teaspoon onto greased round pizza pan. Press evenly to form a crust. Sprinkle lightly with sugar and bake at 350° for 15 to 20 minutes or until lightly browned.

ALMOND CREAM

4 ounces almond paste
1 cup butter, softened
1 (8-ounce) package cream
    cheese, softened

Beat almond paste until soft. Beat in butter and cream cheese till fluffy. Spread on cooked cookie crust; pipe a little paste around outside edges for border. Cover with wax paper; set aside. Prepare small pieces of unpeeled apples, halved grapes, and other suggested fruits and place on the almond cream in an attractive pattern. Glaze. Chill until serving time. Serves 8 to 10.

GLAZE

½ cup apricot or currant jelly
1 tablespoon hot water

Soften jelly with hot water and spread over top with a table knife.

Ice Cream and Dessert Beverages

The dining room at Monticello, the home of President
Thomas Jefferson, near Charlottesville, Virginia.

Thomas Jefferson's Ice Cream

2 bottles of good cream
6 yolks of eggs
½ pound of sugar

Mix the yolks and sugar. Put the cream on a fire in a casserole, first putting in a stick of vanilla.

When near boiling, take it off and pour it gently into the mixture of eggs and sugar. Stir it well.

Put it on the fire again, stirring it thoroughly with a spoon to prevent it from sticking to the casserole.

When near boiling, take it off and strain it through a towel.

*I*ce cream is one of the South's special delights. Simmering July days and sultry August nights create a craving for the coldest food available — often a bowlful of the frosty delicacy. Not only does ice cream cool our bodies, it fills our souls with nostalgia. Many of us remember childhood afternoons spent dancing around the groaning freezer, waiting for that labored halt which meant the dasher was ready to be licked. Southerners are also fond of refreshing dessert beverages, often made with ice cream, which are served at parties throughout the year.

One of the South's earliest ice cream devotees was George Washington, who had a "cream machine for making ice" installed at Mount Vernon. During the summer of 1790, Washington spent approximately two hundred dollars on the refreshing dessert, but unfortunately, Martha neglected to leave her recipe behind.

Thomas Jefferson was the first president to bequeath a recipe to posterity — one he acquired in France while serving as ambassador, and recorded in his own hand. His historic directions for making ice cream are printed at the beginning of this section. Using the French method of initially making a custard with egg yolks, he prepared the dessert in a machine called a "sorbetière." Later, during Jefferson's presidency, a White House visitor reported that ice cream balls enclosed in warm pastry shells were presented — an ambitious dish for the time.

Dolley Madison served ice cream frequently during the 1800s when her husband, James, was president. At this time, restaurants such as New Orleans Exchange Coffee House listed it on the menu.

During the late nineteenth century, Northern businessmen made freezing ice cream easier when they began packing large blocks of winter ice in sawdust and shipping it to the sizzling South. Soon, horse-drawn ice wagons were a welcome sight on Southern streets.

Today, freezing ice cream is as traditional during a Southern summer as grilling hamburgers and chilling watermelon.

Thomas Jefferson's Cook Book
By Marie Kimball; University Press of Virginia, Charlottesville
Copyright 1976 by the Rector and Visitors of the University of Virginia

MONNY'S OLD-FASHIONED VANILLA
ICE CREAM

Old-time "boiled custard" flavor

3 cups milk
1½ cups sugar
3 tablespoons flour
⅛ teaspoon salt
4 eggs, well beaten
2 teaspoons vanilla (or more, to taste)
1 cup heavy cream
1 cup milk
1 cup evaporated milk

Scald 3 cups milk in a double boiler. Mix sugar, flour, and salt in a bowl with enough milk to make a smooth paste. Stir gradually into scalded milk. Cook and stir until thickened. Cover and cook 10 minutes. Beat eggs. Stir into milk mixture, return to double boiler, and cook 2 minutes, stirring constantly. Better if made the day before freezing. Add vanilla, cream, 1 cup milk, and evaporated milk. Freeze according to manufacturer's directions. Makes one gallon.

FAYE COLEMAN'S CHOCOLATE ICE CREAM

Smooth, creamy, melt-in-your-mouth chocolate

1½ cups sugar
2 tablespoons flour
⅛ teaspoon salt
4 tablespoons cocoa
2½ cups milk
5 eggs, beaten
1 can sweetened condensed milk
1 pint light cream
1 pint heavy cream
2 tablespoons vanilla

In a heavy boiler, combine sugar, flour, salt, and cocoa. Stir until combined thoroughly. Add 2½ cups milk, beaten eggs, condensed milk, light, and heavy creams to the above mixture. Cook on medium heat until mixture barely coats tip of spoon. Remove from burner and add vanilla. Let mixture cool. When cooled, fill freezer with mixture — if needed, finish filling freezer with whole milk (this usually is necessary). Makes 1 gallon.

BUTTERMILK ICE CREAM

Quick and easy with a tart taste

2 quarts buttermilk
1 pint light cream
1 cup sugar (or more, to taste)
1 teaspoon vanilla
¼ cup lemon juice

Combine all ingredients. Mix well. Pour into ice cream freezer and freeze until firm. Makes 1 gallon.

LEMON ICE CREAM

Refreshing as springtime

¾ cup fresh lemon juice
2 cups sugar
3 cups milk
1 cup heavy cream

Combine the lemon juice and sugar. Add milk and cream. Stir until sugar is dissolved. Freeze in an ice cream freezer according to manufacturer's directions. Makes 1½ quarts. Top with 2 tablespoons of Blueberry Sauce. For a parfait, put a spoonful of Blueberry Sauce in each parfait glass. Fill with lemon ice cream. Freeze until firm. Just before serving, top with fresh blueberries.

FRESH BLUEBERRY SAUCE

A glorious sauce with many uses

3 cups fresh blueberries, divided
1 cup sugar
1 tablespoon corn syrup
¼ cup lemon juice
1 tablespoon Grand Marnier
⅛ teaspoon nutmeg
⅛ teaspoon ground cloves
⅛ teaspoon cinnamon

Cook 1½ cups blueberries, sugar, and corn syrup in a saucepan over medium heat, crushing blueberries with the back of a spoon as you stir. Reduce heat to low and simmer until mixture thickens and coats spoon, about 15 to 20 minutes. Stir in lemon juice, liqueur, nutmeg, cloves, and cinnamon. Continue simmering until the sauce is thickened, about 10 minutes. Add the other half of berries and cook 30 seconds. Let sauce stand at room temperature for 1 hour. Cover and refrigerate. Makes slightly more than 1 pint.

Freeze tablespoons of leftover whipped cream on a cookie sheet. When frozen place in a freezer container. Use with ice cream. Whole strawberries may be frozen in the same manner.

DOTSY PEEL'S COFFEE ICE CREAM

Creamy, rich, delicious, and easy

6 eggs
3 cups sugar
2 12-ounce cans evaporated milk
   (unsweetened)
2 pints of half-and-half cream
1 cup extra strong coffee (recipe
   below)
1½ teaspoons vanilla
3 tablespoons light rum

EXTRA STRONG COFFEE

In a 3-quart saucepan beat the eggs until blended. Stir the sugar into the eggs. Add evaporated milk, half-and-half cream, and extra strong coffee. Cook over medium heat, stirring just until bubbles begin to form around the edge of the pan. Stir in the vanilla and rum. Place in an ice cream freezer and freeze according to manufacturer's directions. Makes 2 quarts.

To make 1 cup strongly brewed coffee, place ¾ cup finely ground coffee in the cone of a drip-method coffee maker lined with a paper filter. Let 1½ cups water drip through the ground coffee.

OLD-FASHIONED FIG ICE CREAM

A treasured family recipe

4 eggs
1¼ cups sugar
2 cups milk
3 tablespoons lemon juice
1 pint light cream
½ cup cream sherry
1 teaspoon vanilla
1 quart figs

Separate eggs and beat egg yolks with ⅔ cup sugar. Scald the milk and slowly add to the egg yolk and sugar mixture, stirring constantly. Cook in the top of a double boiler until bubbles begin to form around the edges. Mixture will be hot, but not boiling. Combine egg whites with remaining sugar, and beat until light and frothy. Pour cooked egg-milk mixture into egg whites, stirring constantly. Stir in the lemon juice and add the cream, sherry, and vanilla. Clean, stem, and purée the figs. Stir the puréed figs into the cream mixture, distributing evenly. Pour into a 5-quart freezer container, following the manufacturer's directions for freezing. Makes about 3 quarts.

Make a wonderful parfait by alternating layers of brownie crumbs and vanilla ice cream. Spoon chocolate sauce over.

MISSISSIPPI BLUEBERRY ICE CREAM

A luscious taste treat

4 cups fresh blueberries
3½ cups sugar, divided
3 tablespoons lemon juice
4 eggs
2 tablespoons cherry-flavored
  brandy
1 tablespoon vanilla extract
4 cups whipping cream

Combine blueberries, 1 cup sugar, and lemon juice in the container of an electric blender; process until puréed. Set aside. Beat eggs until thick and lemon-colored. Gradually add remaining 2½ cups sugar, beating constantly. Add brandy, vanilla, and puréed blueberries; continue beating until well blended. Pour mixture into freezer can of a 1-gallon hand-turned or electric freezer. Add whipping cream and freeze according to manufacturer's directions. Let ripen 2 hours before serving. Makes about 1 gallon.

This special recipe was developed by Ann Rushing, Marketing Specialist for the Mississippi Department of Agriculture and Commerce. Ann is also a columnist for the Clarion Ledger *and* Jackson Daily News. *Her "Let's Go to Market" column and television shows have been enjoyed by Mississippians for many years.*

BILL PARTLAM'S BLACKBERRY ICE CREAM

The perfect way to use fresh blackberries

4 cups fresh blackberries or 2
  packages (10 ounces) frozen
  blackberries, thawed
2 eggs
1½ cups sugar
¼ cup light corn syrup
1 cup heavy cream
1½ cups light cream
1 tablespoon lemon juice

Rinse berries; purée in blender or food processor or mash with electric mixer. Pour a few tablespoons at a time into a fine strainer and press through strainer with the back of a spoon into a bowl. Throw out the seeds. You may have to scrape the berry purée off the outside of the strainer into the bowl. Have patience; it's worth it. In another bowl, beat eggs and sugar with mixer until thick and lemon-colored. Add blackberry purée, corn syrup, heavy cream, light cream, and lemon juice; stir to blend. Pour into ice cream canister and freeze in ice cream maker according to manufacturer's directions. Harden in refrigerator, then place in freezer for 2 to 3 hours. Makes 2 quarts.

None of the blackberry ice creams in old Southern cookbooks have come close to being as delicious as Bill's. Our thanks to New Stage editors of Standing Room Only — *a cookbook for entertaining — for allowing us to use the recipe.*

WILLIAMSBURG BLACK WALNUT ICE CREAM

A favorite since colonial times

8 egg yolks
1¼ cups sugar
⅛ teaspoon of salt
2 cups milk
2 cups heavy cream
1 teaspoon black walnut
   flavoring
1¼ cups black walnuts, chopped

Beat egg yolks with sugar until creamy; add salt. Bring milk and cream almost to boiling; remove from heat and pour slowly into egg mixture, stirring constantly. Return to low heat, stirring constantly to avoid scorching, but do not boil. Add black walnut flavoring. Heat to scalding. Pour mixture into a 1-gallon freezer container, following the manufacturer's directions for freezing. When ready remove the dasher and add black walnuts, stirring to distribute evenly. Makes slightly more than 1½ quarts.

BUTTER PECAN ICE CREAM

Smooth texture with crunchy pecans

1 cup light brown sugar, firmly
   packed
½ cup water
Dash of salt
2 tablespoons butter or margarine
2 eggs, beaten
1 cup whole milk
1 teaspoon vanilla
1 cup heavy cream
½ cup chopped toasted pecans

Combine sugar, water, and salt in a saucepan. Cook over medium heat, stirring constantly, until mixture comes to a boil. Reduce heat and simmer gently 2 minutes while stirring well. Add butter. Beat eggs about 5 minutes, until thick and lemon-colored. Pour hot brown sugar mixture in a thin stream over eggs while continuing to beat. Keep beating until thick. Cool. Stir in milk, vanilla, heavy cream, and pecans. Freeze in half-gallon freezer until firm. Serves 6. Can be doubled easily.

PRALINES 'N CREAM ICE CREAM

Praline chunks in creamy, uncooked custard

8 eggs
2 cups sugar
1 can (12 ounces) evaporated milk
3 pints light cream
1½ teaspoons vanilla
⅛ teaspoon salt
8 pralines, crumbled

Beat eggs well and gradually add sugar. Slowly mix in evaporated milk, light cream, vanilla, and salt. Stir in crumbled pralines and freeze in ice cream maker. Makes 1 gallon.

DOT'S FRESH PEACH ICE CREAM

Celebrate summer with this sensational cooler

6 eggs
¾ cup sugar
1 can condensed milk
2 cartons heavy cream
1 pint light cream
2 cups milk
Pinch of salt
4 teaspoons vanilla
3 cups mashed ripe peaches
   (sweetened with 1 cup sugar)

Beat eggs; gradually add sugar. Mix in remaining ingredients (except peaches). For best results, mash peaches in a food processor. Pour mixture into ice cream freezer container and add peaches just before ice cream begins to harden. Finish freezing. Makes 1 gallon.

FRESH GARDEN MINT ICE CREAM

From Justine's restaurant in Memphis, Tennessee

1½ cups sugar
1½ cups water
1 cup finely crushed fresh
   pineapple
2 cups finely crushed fresh mint
   leaves
1 cup light corn syrup
1 cup canned unsweetened
   pineapple juice
2 cups milk
2 cups whipping cream,
   unwhipped
¼ cup crème de menthe

Combine sugar, water, and pineapple; cook and stir until mixture boils. Let boil to the soft ball stage (236°). Add the crushed mint leaves; cook about 10 minutes longer. Remove from heat; strain. Add the corn syrup and let cool. Add the remaining ingredients; freeze in hand-turned or electric ice cream freezer. Let ripen. Makes 2 quarts.

To ripen ice cream: Remove ice to below lid of can; take off lid. Remove dasher. Plug opening in lid; cover inside of lid with several thicknesses of waxed paper; replace lid. Pack more ice and salt around can. Cover freezer with heavy cloth or newspaper. Let ripen about 4 hours.

Piled high in a footed silver bowl, the combination of scoops of Fresh Garden Mint Ice Cream and almond-flavored Lotus Ice Cream are as Southern as Justine's, the stately old Memphis restaurant, in which they are served.

For a quick ice cream pie, use a cracker crumb crust and cover it with a layer of ice cream. Freeze. Top with whipped cream.

CARAMEL ICE CREAM

A delicious custard ice cream

1 pint milk
1 pint light cream
1 cup sugar
4 egg yolks
½ cup sugar
4 egg whites
1 quart heavy cream

Pour milk and light cream in a double boiler; scald over hot, not boiling, water. Melt 1 cup sugar in a cast-iron skillet, stirring constantly until caramel-colored. Stir slowly into hot milk and light cream mixture; continue cooking until sugar melts again. Beat egg yolks until thick and creamy; add ½ cup sugar and beat well. Beat egg whites until stiff and combine with yolks; pour hot milk and light cream into egg mixture, then return to double boiler. Cook, stirring occasionally, until smooth and thick. Whip the heavy cream; when custard is cool, strain, combine with whipped cream, and freeze. Makes about 2 quarts.

This recipe is from a cookbook written by a friend's father, and is used with his permission. The book, by Frank Simpson, is entitled Accent One — A Book of Recipes.

MARY COOKE'S CARAMEL TOFFEE CREATION

Vanilla ice cream and Caramel Toffee Sauce — an unforgettable combination

⅓ cup brown sugar
1½ cups flour
1 cup pecans, chopped
1 cup butter or margarine, melted
1½ cups Caramel Toffee Sauce
½ gallon vanilla ice cream,
　softened

Stir together brown sugar, flour, pecans, and melted butter or margarine. Spread mixture thinly on a greased cookie sheet and bake at 350° for approximately 20 minutes or until done. Be careful that it does not burn. Cool and crumble half of crumbs onto bottom of a glass 13 x 9 inch baking dish. Spread half of Caramel Toffee Sauce over crumbs. Fill dish with spoonsful of vanilla ice cream. Add rest of Caramel Toffee Sauce and top with remaining crumbs. Freeze. Serves 12 to 16.

CARAMEL TOFFEE SAUCE

Sinfully delicious!

2 cups light brown sugar, packed
2 cups dark brown sugar, packed
4 tablespoons butter
1 pint heavy cream
1 tablespoon vanilla

Combine the sugars, butter, and cream. Cook in the top of a double boiler over medium heat until it will coat the back of a spoon. Add vanilla. Cover and store in the refrigerator. Makes 2½ cups.

HIGH COTTON SUNDAE

White chocolate and coconut ice cream topped with white chocolate sauce and fruit

6 cups fresh or packaged grated
   coconut
2 12-ounce cans evaporated milk
1½ cups milk
6 eggs, slightly beaten
3 cups sugar
2 pints of light cream
9 ounces white chocolate
   (important to use a fine grade
   of white chocolate), finely
   shaved or broken
1½ teaspoons vanilla

In a large bowl cover the grated coconut with the evaporated milk and plain milk. Let stand 8 hours or overnight in the refrigerator. Squeeze the milk from the coconut by putting through a fine sieve or cheesecloth. You should have about 4 cups coconut milk. In a 3-quart saucepan mix slightly beaten eggs with sugar. Add coconut milk and light cream. Heat to scalding point. Remove from heat and stir in finely shaved white chocolate. Stir until chocolate is dissolved. Add vanilla. Freeze in an ice cream freezer. Makes 2 quarts.

WHITE CHOCOLATE SAUCE

1 cup heavy cream
12 ounces white chocolate
¼ cup Grand Marnier or orange
   juice (1 teaspoon orange zest
   may be substituted)

Heat cream to the scalding point. Stir in small pieces of chocolate. Add Grand Marnier, or substitutes. Serve warm or cold. May be stored covered in the refrigerator for 3 or 4 days. Makes slightly more than 1 cup.

For Sundae: Place ice cream in sherbet or large wine glasses. Top with a tablespoon of White Chocolate Sauce. Garnish with kiwi fruit, raspberries, fresh strawberries, or fresh peaches.

Note: The White Chocolate Sauce makes a beautiful dipping sauce for a tray of fresh fruit.

TROPICAL ICE DESSERT

Tastes like sherbet

1 8½-ounce can crushed
   pineapple
1½ cups mashed bananas
2 cups orange juice
2 tablespoons lemon juice
⅛ teaspoon salt
1 cup sugar

Combine all of the ingredients. Freeze in 2 freezer trays until almost solid. Remove to a mixer bowl and beat until fluffy. Return to freezer trays and freeze. Serve in sherbet glasses. Serves 12.

A favorite family recipe from Mrs. J. W. Butler of Jackson, Mississippi. It is easy to prepare and has the smooth texture of sherbet.

ORANGE ICE CREAM WITH GINGER SAUCE

Sprinkle with crystallized ginger

3 cups orange juice
1 cup sugar
1 cup whipping cream
2 cups milk
⅛ cup crystallized ginger,
  homemade or commercial

Mix orange juice and sugar until the sugar is dissolved. Add cream and milk, stirring to mix well. Freeze in an ice cream freezer according to manufacturer's directions. A little candied ginger sprinkled over the top is a delicious addition. Makes 2 quarts. Serve with Ginger Sauce (recipe below).

CRYSTALLIZED GINGER

1 pound fresh gingerroot
Water as needed
1½ cups sugar
¾ cup water

Clean and peel young gingerroot. Cut into bite-sized pieces. Cover with cold water and soak overnight. Drain. Cover once again with cold water, cooking and boiling for 5 minutes. Repeat the draining, covering with cold water, and boiling process three to five times until fruit is tender and transparent. Make a simple syrup of the sugar and ¾ cup water. Boil ginger pieces in syrup for 5 minutes, being sure that pan does not boil dry. You should have ½ cup syrup when finished. Reserve syrup to make ginger sauce. Remove ginger pieces from syrup; cool slightly. While still warm, not hot, shake in container filled with granulated sugar. Separate pieces and place on paper towels to dry thoroughly. Store in an airtight container.

GINGER SAUCE

½ cup ginger syrup
¼ cup honey
¼ cup brown sugar
3 ounces butter

Stir together and simmer for 5 minutes. Use over ice cream or cake. Will keep covered in the refrigerator for 1 week. Makes about 1 cup.

Roll scoops of ice cream in broken pecan pieces or shape ice cream into a log and roll in pecans. Freeze until hard and top with Carmel Toffee Sauce (see index).

JUSTINE'S LOTUS ICE CREAM

Almond-flavored, creamy, and delicious

2²/₃ cups light cream
1 cup sugar
¹/₃ cup lemon juice
¹/₃ cup chopped toasted almonds
1¹/₂ teaspoons grated lemon rind
¹/₂ teaspoon vanilla
¹/₈ teaspoon almond extract

Combine all ingredients in a mixing bowl, stirring until sugar is dissolved. Freeze in a hand-turned or electric ice cream freezer. Makes 1 quart.

At Justine's in Memphis, Tennessee, magnificent candelabra light the foyer and steps of a graceful curved stairway. Rooms, fourteen-feet high, that once formed the backdrop for belles and beaux at antebellum parties, glow with beauty and anticipation of the finest foods prepared only upon order. Scoops of Lotus Ice Cream and Garden Mint Ice Cream are served in the spring with fresh strawberries in stemmed glasses or perched atop a creamy cheesecake.

VIRGINIA HOT APPLE SUNDAE

As delicious as it sounds

¹/₂ cup sugar
¹/₂ cup orange juice
¹/₄ cup lemon juice
¹/₂ teaspoon ground cinnamon
3 tart apples
1 pint vanilla ice cream

Mix sugar, orange juice, lemon juice, and cinnamon together in a skillet. Stir over low heat until sugar dissolves. Bring to a boil; simmer 5 minutes. Add apples, peeled and sliced. Simmer covered for 15 more minutes. Serve over ice cream. Serves 4.

SOUTHERN FRUIT SHERBET

Delicious with almost any fruit in season

¹/₄ cup fresh orange juice
¹/₂ cup fresh lemon juice
1¹/₂ cups sugar
1 quart milk
1 cup of any of the following
   fruits: crushed strawberries,
   crushed raspberries, apricot
   pulp, mashed peaches, mashed
   bananas, finely chopped pears,
   apple sauce, blueberries

Mix the orange juice, lemon juice, and sugar. Add milk slowly while stirring. (If mixture curdles it will freeze smooth again.) Add chosen fruit. Pour into a freezer container, following the manufacturer's directions for freezing. Makes about 2 quarts.

BUTTERSCOTCH SUNDAE

Brings back fond memories of ice cream parlors on summer days

BUTTERSCOTCH SAUCE

3 cups white karo
½ cup butter, softened
1 tablespoon maple flavoring
⅓ cup walnuts or pecans,
   chopped

Heat karo syrup and blend in butter thoroughly. Stir in maple flavoring and nuts. This is better served cold over ice cream but may be served warm. Keeps well for several weeks if refrigerated. Makes slightly more than 3 cups.

For Sundae: Top a large scoop of vanilla ice cream with a tablespoon of Butterscotch Sauce. Add whipped cream and a cherry.

TRILBY'S CRÈME DE MENTHE MERINGUE DESSERT

A Gulf Coast tradition, the restaurant is located in Ocean Springs, Mississippi

4 large egg whites
¼ teaspoon cream of tartar
2 ounces green crème de menthe
1 cup sugar
¼ cup pecans, chopped
French vanilla ice cream
Whipped cream
Chopped pecans, shaved
   chocolate (optional)

Place egg whites in a warm mixing bowl. Add cream of tartar and liqueur to egg whites. Whip mixture until fluffy. Add sugar, one teaspoon at a time, and continue to whip until very stiff, but not dried out. Gently fold in chopped pecans. Line a baking sheet with parchment or brown paper. Drop large spoonsful of meringue mixture onto the baking sheet and form nests with the back of the spoon. Bake at 225° for 1 hour and 15 minutes; turn the oven off, leaving meringues to dry in oven (this can take from 1 to 4 hours, depending on humidity level). Carefully peel paper off the shells. Makes 8 to 10 shells.

To garnish: Each meringue shell is filled with a generous scoop of French vanilla ice cream, topped with Trilby's Chocolate Sauce, whipped cream, and a sprinkle of finely chopped pecans and chocolate shavings.

TRILBY'S CHOCOLATE SAUCE

½ pound butter
¾ cup cocoa
3 cups sugar
1 12-ounce can evaporated milk
1½ teaspoons vanilla

Melt butter in top of a double boiler. Add cocoa and blend well. Add sugar gradually, blend well, and cook for 15 minutes. Add milk and cook for 15 minutes longer. Remove from double boiler and cool. Add vanilla. Makes about 1 quart.

WATERMELON ICE

Serve in the watermelon shell with fresh black cherries and green grapes

½ of a large watermelon
  (approximately 9 cups)
1½ cups fresh orange juice
½ cup fresh lemon juice
1 cup sugar
2 pounds seedless green grapes
2 pounds black cherries, pitted
Fresh mint leaves

Split a large ripe watermelon in half. Scoop out the center and remove the seeds. Place the scooped fruit in a bowl and pick it into small pieces with a fork. Reserve the watermelon shell by covering and refrigerating it. Extract the juice from the melon pieces by putting them through a fine sieve or a food processor. Mix the watermelon juice (should be about 9 cups), lemon juice, orange juice, and sugar. Stir well and freeze in an ice cream freezer according to the manufacturer's directions. Meanwhile remove the watermelon shell from the refrigerator. Neatly trim around the top by scalloping the edges with a potato scoop. Fill the shell by alternating layers of watermelon ice, pitted black cherries mixed with seedless green grapes, stems removed. At this point the watermelon may be covered and placed in the freezer for a few days. (The watermelon shell and fruits freeze beautifully — be sure to have some watermelon ice on the top.) To serve remove the watermelon from the freezer about 30 minutes before serving. Stir a little to break up the watermelon ice and let the fruit peep through. Garnish heavily with more cherries, bunches of green grapes, and fresh mint. Serves 16 to 20.

To make an "ice cream watermelon," line a bowl with ½ gallon softened lime sherbet. Should be about an inch thick. Soften ½ gallon strawberry ice cream and fold in 3 ounces of chocolate chips. Pour over the lime sherbet and freeze. To serve, unmold and slice "watermelon."

LAURA'S ICE CREAM FANTASY

Perfect ending for a bridesmaid's luncheon

2 dozen lady fingers
½ gallon vanilla ice cream
¾ small can frozen orange juice
1 small package frozen sliced
   strawberries, thawed
1 9-ounce can crushed pineapple
½ cup sugar
1 teaspoon almond extract
1 teaspoon rum flavoring
½ cup chopped pecans

Line sides and bottom of a regular-sized spring-form pan with lady fingers. Set aside. Divide ice cream in half. Soften one half with orange juice until consistency to spread carefully over bottom of lined springform pan. Freeze. While first layer is freezing, combine strawberries, pineapple, and sugar. Put mixture into freezer only until mushy. When the first layer is frozen, spread fruit mixture on top of it and return to freezer. When both layers are frozen, soften the second half of ice cream and flavor with almond extract and rum flavoring. Add pecans. Place on top of fruit layer. Return to freezer until ready to serve. Serves 10.

HEAVENLY SURPRISE DESSERT

Coffee ice cream and Bourbon Caramel Sauce buried under a cloud of whipped cream

1 quart coffee ice cream
8 amaretto (almond flavored)
   cookies
1 recipe Bourbon Caramel Sauce
   (see below)
1 pint heavy cream, whipped
Maraschino cherries for garnish

For each serving, place an amaretto cookie or almond-flavored sugar cookie in the bottom of a sherbet dish. Place a scoop of coffee ice cream over it and spoon the Bourbon Caramel Sauce over all. Cover with whipped cream and garnish with a cherry. Serves 8.

BOURBON CARAMEL SAUCE

1 cup light cream
½ cup butter
1 cup brown sugar, packed
⅓ cup chopped nuts, toasted
¼ cup bourbon

Warm the cream and cream together the butter and sugar. Gradually stir the warmed cream into the butter and sugar mixture. Stir over low heat until the mixture boils. Remove from the heat and stir in the nuts and bourbon. This is also delicious over baked custard or bread pudding. The sauce may be kept in the refrigerator for several days and reheated slightly before serving. Makes about 2½ cups.

PARADISE BANANA SPLIT

A sumptuous banana split from Florida

4 large ripe bananas, unpeeled
2 tablespoons fresh lime juice
2 tablespoons light rum
8 fresh pineapple spears
1 quart coffee ice cream
¼ cup Coffee Syrup (see below)

Cut about ¼ inch off each end of the bananas and make a lengthwise slit in each. Without tearing the skin, cut the meat of each banana crosswise into chunks about 1 inch thick. Remove and mix with lime juice and rum. Place 2 pineapple spears on each banana skin, top with small scoops of ice cream, and arrange banana chunks around them. Pour over the lime-juice mixture and the coffee syrup. Serve and savor! Serves 4.

COFFEE SYRUP

1 cup strong brewed coffee
¾ cup sugar

Make 1 cup strongly brewed coffee by placing ¾ cup finely ground coffee in the cone of a drip-method coffee maker lined with a paper filter. Let 1½ cups water drip through the ground coffee. In a small saucepan, combine the coffee and sugar. Cook over medium heat, stirring constantly with a wooden spoon, until the sugar dissolves. Bring the syrup to a simmer and continue cooking for 5 to 8 minutes or until it starts to thicken, without stirring. Remove the pan from the heat and cool the syrup for about 30 minutes, or until it reaches room temperature. Store the syrup in an airtight container in the refrigerator for up to 1 month. Makes about 1 cup.

BROWN VELVET AND ALMOND ICE CREAM

Freeze in dessert cups

⅔ cup chocolate syrup
½ teaspoon vanilla
½ teaspoon almond extract
⅔ cup sweetened condensed milk
2 cups heavy cream
⅓ cup slivered almonds, toasted

Beat syrup, flavorings, milk, and cream until fluffy. Pour into mixer bowl and chill thoroughly in the refrigerator. Beat with mixer until flakes are formed. Add the nuts. Place in 2 ice trays or aluminium foil cups. Freeze. If desired, you may reserve a few of the almonds to sprinkle on the top and decorate with a cherry. Serves 12.

BUTTERSCOTCH BOMBE

Serve with Praline Sauce

1 cup gingersnaps, finely crushed
3 tablespoons butter, melted
1 quart vanilla ice cream, softened
¾ cup chocolate-covered toffee bars, crushed (commercial or homemade; see index for English Toffee recipe)

Combine gingersnaps and butter. Press into a 5-cup mold; freeze. Combine ice cream and toffee; spoon into mold, smoothing top. Cover and freeze until firm. To serve, invert onto chilled plate. Rub mold with hot, damp towel and lift off mold. Cut into wedges and serve with praline sauce.

PRALINE SAUCE

½ cup packed brown sugar
½ cup light cream
¼ cup butter
¼ cup chopped toasted almonds
1 teaspoon vanilla

In a small pan, combine brown sugar, cream, and butter; bring to a boil, stirring constantly. Remove from heat; stir in almonds and vanilla. Serves 6 to 8.

WINDY'S WHISKEY ICE CREAM

Pretty presentation from Mary Leigh's Atlanta cousin

3 dozen almond macaroons
3 jiggers bourbon
½ gallon almond toffee ice cream or ½ gallon vanilla ice cream mixed with English Toffee (see index for recipe)
1½ cartons (cups) heavy cream

Marinate whole almond macaroons in 1 or 2 jiggers of bourbon for one hour. Save 4 cookies to garnish the top. Line a large silver bowl or small punch bowl with the marinated macaroons. Scoop ice cream on top of macaroons. Whip cream, adding another jigger of bourbon. Top ice cream completely with whipped cream. Crumble the remaining macaroons on top. Cover and place in freezer until ready to serve. Remove 15 to 30 minutes before serving. Serves 10 or more. You may serve scoops of Windy's Whiskey Ice Cream in punch cups or dessert dishes at the table and pass to your guests.

Save leftover cake crumbs for parfaits or other frozen desserts. Use as toppings or fillings.

CRÈME DE MENTHE PARFAIT

A gala color and taste combination

**1 15-ounce can crushed pineapple
in its own juice, undrained**
1 cup sugar
½ cup white corn syrup
1 cup water
**1 tablespoon green crème de
menthe**
1 quart vanilla ice cream

Boil the crushed pineapple and juice, sugar, corn syrup, and water together until pineapple is clear and syrup is thick enough to coat the back of a spoon, about half an hour. Add crème de menthe. Cool and store covered in the refrigerator at this point if desired. Makes 1½ cups. To serve, alternate vanilla ice cream and crème de menthe syrup in a parfait glass or large wine glass. Garnish each dish with a sprig of mint. Or during the holiday season, top with a maraschino cherry. Serves 6 to 8.

COFFEE BISCUIT TORTONI

Cool and refreshing after a hearty Italian dinner

2 dozen almond macaroons
¾ cup sugar
**¾ cup extra strong coffee (instant
may be used)**
3 eggs, separated
2 tablespoons sugar
1 pint whipping cream, whipped
Maraschino cherries

Line fluted paper baking cups with crumbled macaroons and place in muffin tins. In a saucepan, make syrup of ¾ cup sugar and the coffee and pour over egg yolks that have been beaten together until smooth. Pour in a small amount of the syrup at a time to prevent eggs from cooking and becoming stringy. Cool. Beat egg whites until stiff, adding the 2 tablespoons of sugar. Fold into coffee mixture, then fold in the whipped cream. Pour into baking cups, cover with extra crumbs from the macaroons, and garnish with a cherry. Place in the freezer and freeze until hard. To serve place on dessert plates with a paper doily under the baking cups. For buffet service, place the Biscuit Tortoni on a large tray with three small Gouda cheeses. Leave the red covering on the cheese intact and slice, retaining the round shapes. Arrange Biscuit Tortoni around the cheeses, placing them attractively. If you serve a wine with dinner, place a slice of apple and a slice of pear in the wine glass at the beginning of the meal. When dessert is served the pear and apple slices are removed and eaten along with the Tortoni and cheese. Serves 12.

POOGAN'S ICE CREAM A L'ORANGE

From Poogan's Porch in Charleston, South Carolina

1 stick butter
2 teaspoons sugar
Juice of 1 orange
Juice of 1 lemon
1 tablespoon grated orange rind
1 tablespoon grated lemon rind
1 tablespoon chopped pecans
2 tablespoons Grand Marnier
1 tablespoon Kahlua
Vanilla ice cream
6 fresh peach halves

Combine butter, sugar, juice of orange and lemon, grated fruit rinds, and pecans. Sauté the mixture until it begins to bubble. Add Grand Marnier and Kahlua. To complete this quick but delicious dessert, place 1 large scoop of vanilla ice cream in a brandy snifter or oversized glass. Top the ice cream with a peach half, pit side down, and spoon 2 tablespoons of the orange sauce over all. Serves 6.

SAVANNAH ICE CREAM CAKE

Dainty and colorful

1 pint strawberry ice cream
1 pint chocolate ice cream
1 pint orange ice cream
3 cake layers (see index for Coconut Cake recipe)
½ pint heavy cream
¼ cup confectioners' sugar
½ teaspoon vanilla
½ cup Chocolate Glaze (see index for Double-Frosted Angel Food Cake)

Line 3 layer-cake pans with foil. Spread each with one flavor of softened ice cream. Cover with foil and freeze. When frozen, remove ice cream from pans. Put together in alternate layers with cake. Cover with heavy cream that has been whipped with confectioners' sugar added slowly until soft peaks form. Add vanilla. Drizzle Chocolate Glaze around the outside edge of cake so that a little of the glaze falls down the sides. Serve at once or keep cake and ice cream frozen until just before serving and then ice with whipped cream icing and Chocolate Glaze. Serves 12 to 14.

For vanilla ice cream: serve in a peach half and splash with a few teaspoons of blackberry brandy.

FROZEN FRESH PEACH MOUSSE

Garnish with country fresh peaches

3 cups sliced ripe peaches
¾ cup sugar, divided
2 tablespoons Kirsch
6 egg yolks
½ teaspoon almond extract
1½ cups heavy cream

Purée 1 cup sliced peaches in a blender or food processor. Combine remaining 2 cups with ¼ cup sugar and Kirsch. Chill until serving time. Beat egg yolks and remaining sugar in mixer at high speed until yolks are fluffy — about 3 to 4 minutes. Add almond extract. In a separate bowl whip the cream and fold with peach purée into the egg-yolk mixture. Turn the mixture into ice tray and freeze until semihard. Cover with wax paper and complete freezing. To serve scoop mousse onto serving dishes. Spoon sliced peaches on top. Serves 4 to 6.

PATSY ROSE'S CHOCOLATE SAUCE

Heavenly over vanilla ice cream

1 6-ounce package semisweet
  chocolate pieces
¼ cup butter
1 cup confectioners' sugar, sifted
⅛ teaspoon salt
½ cup light corn syrup
¼ cup hot water
3 tablespoons crème de cacao
1 teaspoon vanilla

Melt chocolate and butter in a double boiler over low heat. Beat in remaining ingredients with a mixer over simmering heat. Serve warm or cold. Refrigerate the remainder. Makes 2 cups.

ATLANTA COFFEE ICE CREAM PUNCH

Refreshing picker-upper for a hot-weather party

1 gallon strong coffee, cooled
1 quart milk
1 cup sugar
½ gallon chocolate ice cream
1 pint heavy cream
3 teaspoons vanilla
3 tablespoons sugar
Grated semisweet chocolate

Mix coffee, milk, and 1 cup sugar the day before your party. Refrigerate. At party time, place ice cream in punch bowl and pour coffee mixture over it. Whip cream and flavor with vanilla and 3 tablespoons sugar. Float on top of punch. Sprinkle chocolate over all. The chocolate may be grated the day before, wrapped in wax paper, and refrigerated. Serves 20.

COTILLION PUNCH

Zesty thirst-quencher for festive occasions

½ gallon pineapple sherbet
2 (32-ounce) bottles cranberry
   juice, chilled
2 (32-ounce) bottles ginger ale,
   chilled

Soften sherbet and mash until slightly mushy. Place in punch bowl. Pour in chilled juice and ginger ale. Serves 50.

HOPE FARM EGGNOG

Heirloom recipe from a Natchez mansion

18 egg yolks
2 cups sugar
1 fifth bourbon whiskey
2 quarts heavy cream
18 egg whites, beaten well
Nutmeg

Beat egg yolks. Add sugar gradually, beating well. Slowly add whiskey and unbeaten heavy cream. Gently fold in egg whites. Serve in a punch bowl; sprinkle nutmeg on top. Serves 20. For the calorie conscious: Substitute 2 quarts light cream for the heavy cream. Use only 9 egg whites.

This recipe belonged to the late Mrs. J. Balfour Miller, who founded the Natchez Pilgrimage. Every Christmas morning, Mr. and Mrs. Miller, who had no children, invited their friends with their children and grandchildren for eggnog at Hope Farm, their antebellum home.

COLONIAL SYLLABUB

An old Southern holiday beverage or dessert

1 pint heavy cream, whipped
¾ cup confectioners' sugar
½ cup white wine
4 tablespoons sherry wine
1 teaspoon lemon juice
Few grains of salt
Nutmeg

Whip cream until stiff, gradually adding sugar. Mix in wines and seasonings. Serve at once in cups; sprinkle with nutmeg. This dessert does not hold well. Serves 8.

Syllabub was a popular dessert beverage in the colonial South, particularly in Virginia and Maryland. The easiest method for preparing the foaming concoction was to take a bowl of wine to the barn and draw milk from the cow straight into the bowl, making a bubbly punch.

Pies and Cobblers

The kitchen at My Old Kentucky Home, Bardstown, Kentucky. The house was built by Senator John Rowan and later occupied by John Rowan, Jr., cousin of Stephen Collins Foster. While visiting there, Collins was inspired to write "My Old Kentucky Home."

The Sisters' Shaker Lemon Pie

2 large lemons, thinly sliced
¾ cup sugar
¼ teaspoon salt
4 eggs, beaten
Pastry for 1 double pie crust, unbaked

Mix lemon slices with sugar and salt and let stand until soft. Stir beaten eggs into lemon mixture. Pour into pie shell and top with remaining crust. Crimp edges together with a fork and make small slashes in the top with a knife. Bake at 350° for 30 to 40 minutes until done.

When the first English settlers sailed for Virginia, they packed their pie recipes along with their luggage. Southerners have cherished the tradition ever since. Originally they followed the British rule of using two crusts, but soon eliminated the upper crust in favor of open pastry shells called "coffins." A cornucopia of ingredients awaited their pie-making skills: pumpkins, sweet potatoes, berries, and pecans. They quickly learned to dry fruit and store nuts in order to enjoy pies during the cold winters.

When fruit and nuts were unavailable, they turned to custards, especially chess pie which is still revered as a true Southern classic. The rich, sugary dessert inspired innumerable variations, depending on what the cook had in the pantry — Lemon Chess, Chocolate Chess, Japanese Fruit, and Jeff Davis, seasoned with cinnamon and nutmeg.

By 1830, pie making was so widely practiced in the South that a special piece of furniture called a "pie safe" became a fixture in many kitchens. A wooden cabinet with tin doors decorated with perforated holes, the pie safe protected its contents from insects, the hot sun, and greedy fingers.

Over the years, additions were made to the repertoire of Southern pie bakers. Meringue as a topping came into being in the late nineteenth century and is used today, especially on lemon, coconut, and chocolate cream pies. Another nineteenth century innovation was the use of crumb crusts: graham cracker, vanilla wafer, and chocolate cookie.

Modern refrigeration was the biggest boon to pie making. How easy to thicken your pie in the refrigerator, confident that the filling will hold and any mistakes will be camouflaged by a cloud of whipped cream. Although methods may be modernized, the tradition of baking pies will always be an integral part of Southern cuisine.

JONELLE PRIMOS' PIE CRUST

Press into pie plate with your fingers

1½ cups flour
1½ teaspoons sugar
½ teaspoon salt
½ cup cooking oil
2 tablespoons cold milk

Sift together the flour, sugar, and salt. Mix oil with the milk and stir liquids into dry ingredients. Press into 9-inch pie pan with fingers. For a baked shell, prick with a fork and bake 10 to 12 minutes at 425° to 450° or until crust is golden brown. Makes 1 9-inch crust.

PLAIN ICE WATER PIE CRUST

Makes one double-crusted pie or two shells

2 cups flour
½ teaspoon salt
1½ teaspoons baking powder
⅔ cup shortening
4-6 tablespoons ice water

Sift dry ingredients into a bowl. Place in food processor with shortening and 4 tablespoons ice water. Blend until moistened but do not over-process. Add more water if necessary to make dough hold together. Divide the dough into two equal portions. Roll out one portion on floured board until desired size and place in 9-inch pie plate. Add filling. Roll out remaining portion. Prick with a fork in several places or make gashes with a sharp knife. Place on top of filling, positioning edges to meet those of lower crust. Press edges with a fork. Bake according to recipe for filling.

CREAM CHEESE PASTRY

Easy and especially good for making tarts

½ cup butter or margarine, room
  temperature
1 3-ounce package cream cheese,
  room temperature
1 cup flour, sifted

Cream butter and cream cheese together until smooth. Add flour, mixing well. Shape dough into a ball; chill 8 hours. Roll dough ⅛ inch thick and bake for 12 to 15 minutes or until pastry is golden brown. Makes 1 9-inch pastry shell.

Shortening should be cut into the pastry with a pastry blender or a knife.

ALMOND PIE CRUST

Makes 1 9-inch pie crust

1¾ cups blanched toasted
  almonds
3 tablespoons unsalted butter,
  melted
2 tablespoons white corn syrup

Coarsely chop almonds and stir in the melted butter. Add corn syrup. Spoon into a 9-inch buttered pie plate. Press onto bottom and up sides of plate.

COOKIE CRUMB CRUST

Makes 1 9-inch pie crust

1½ cups crumbs (vanilla wafers,
  graham crackers, or chocolate
  wafers)
½ cup nuts (optional)
¼ cup sugar
⅓ cup butter, melted

Mix ingredients thoroughly. Press the mixture firmly against the sides and bottom of a pie pan. Bake 5 minutes at 400° and cool.

NUT SHELL

2 9-inch crusts

2 cups pecans
½ teaspoon instant coffee
⅔ cup light brown sugar
½ teaspoon cinnamon
¼ cup melted butter

Chop pecans very fine. Mix all ingredients and press mixture into a pan. Bake at 350° for 12 to 15 minutes.

NO FAIL MERINGUE

The secret is in the cornstarch

1 tablespoon cornstarch
½ cup boiling water
3 egg whites, room temperature
¼ cup sugar
1 teaspoon vanilla
⅛ teaspoon salt

Blend cornstarch and water in a saucepan, stirring until it gets clear and thick. Cool. Beat egg whites until foamy. Gradually add sugar, vanilla, salt and cooled cornstarch mixture. Beat until stiff. Spread over the pie and bake at 425° for 4 to 4½ minutes. Makes enough meringue for 1 pie.

SOUTHERN DIVINITY MERINGUE

High, fluffy, not too sweet

3 egg whites, room temperature
1 teaspoon vinegar
¼ cup white karo
¼ cup confectioners' sugar

Beat egg whites until frothy; add vinegar. Beat until meringue makes soft peaks. Add karo a little at a time, beating constantly. Repeat with confectioners' sugar, adding a little at a time and beating until meringue holds its shape. Spread over the pie and bake at 425° in a preheated oven for 4 to 4½ minutes. Makes enough meringue for 1 pie.

EGG WASH FOR GLAZING PASTRY

1 egg yolk
½ cup evaporated milk or sweet cream

Beat the yolk of egg, add the milk or cream to it, and brush over the surface of pastry or rolls, applying it with a soft pastry brush. Mixture will keep in the refrigerator for a week. Makes a little over ½ cup.

WILMA BENNETT'S CHESS PIE

A family recipe from Tennessee

8 tablespoons butter
1½ cups sugar
3 whole eggs, slightly beaten
1 teaspoon cornmeal
1 teaspoon vinegar
1 teaspoon vanilla
1 9-inch pie shell, unbaked

Cream the butter and sugar together. Add slightly beaten eggs. Stir in the cornmeal, vinegar, and vanilla. Pour into a 9-inch unbaked pie shell and bake in a 325° oven for 45 to 50 minutes. A knife inserted in the pie will come out clean when it is ready. Serves 8.

"Chess" pie is the oldest of the Southern pies. The sugary pies didn't have to be kept in the ice house like custard pies made with cream. They were the chest or keeping pies of plantation days. It is uncertain where the pies got their name. Many feel that "chess" is chest with the "t" dropped as so often happens with soft Southern accents. Others feel that "chess" is a corruption of cheese. The English call their lemon curd pies, lemon cheese. Their pies closely resemble our chess pie and, over such a long period of time, could have resulted in the name "chess." Our favorite story is the one about the plantation cook. The sugary pie was given its name when a plantation cook was complimented by a guest on her pie. She replied, "Why thank you, it was jes' pie."

LOUREA SMITH'S EASY BUTTERMILK COCONUT PIE

Tastes like a giant, moist macaroon

5 eggs
1¾ cups sugar
2 tablespoons butter, melted
1 cup buttermilk
1 cup coconut
1 teaspoon vanilla
¼ teaspoon almond extract
1 9-inch pie crust, unbaked

Beat eggs with sugar. Add melted butter. Beat well. Stir in buttermilk, coconut, and extracts. Pour into the unbaked pie crust and bake for 45 minutes in a 350° oven. (It may take up to 1 hour.) Pie should have a fairly firm crust on it. Cool before cutting. Makes 1 9-inch pie. Serves 8.

BANANA CREAM PIE

A rich flavor that children and adults love

½ cup sugar
2 tablespoons cornstarch
3 tablespoons flour
⅛ teaspoon salt
2 cups milk
4 egg yolks, slightly beaten
1 tablespoon butter
½ teaspoon vanilla
2 large bananas
1 9-inch pie shell, baked
4 egg whites
¼ cup sugar

Combine sugar, cornstarch, flour, and salt in top of double boiler. Add milk slowly, mixing thoroughly. Cook over boiling water until thickened, stirring constantly. Stir some of mixture into egg yolks, then pour back into hot mixture, while beating vigorously with a wire whisk. Cook 1 more minute, stirring constantly. Add butter and vanilla. Cook 1 minute, stirring constantly. Peel and slice bananas into pie shell. Cool filling slightly, then pour over bananas. Beat egg whites. When soft peaks form, add sugar gradually. Top pie with meringue. Brown in the broiler. Cool. Refrigerate. Serves 6 to 8.

BETTY'S CHOCOLATE CHESS PIE

Makes two pies — freeze one, serve the other

2¼ cups sugar
5¼ tablespoons cocoa
3 eggs
1½ sticks butter, melted
1½ teaspoons vanilla
9 ounces evaporated milk
2 8-inch pie shells, unbaked

Sift together sugar and cocoa. Slowly beat in remaining ingredients. Pour into unbaked pie shells. Bake at 325° for 60 minutes. Makes 2 8-inch pies. Even better when served with a bowlful of sweetened whipped cream flavored with cointreau.

BURTON'S PINEAPPLE CHEESE PIE

Unusual ingredients make a delicious pie

2 cups crushed pineapple,
  undrained
1 cup sugar
2 tablespoons cornstarch
2 9-inch pie shells

Heat pineapple. Add sugar and cornstarch, stirring constantly until thickened. Cool. Spread pineapple mixture over bottom of 2 9-inch pie shells about ¼ inch deep. Carefully spread cheese filling over the pineapple. Cook on the middle oven shelf at 350° until the pie begins to brown (start in cold oven), about 15 minutes. Cover with an inverted pie pan and reduce heat to 300°. Bake for another 45 minutes. Let cool before cutting. Serves 16.

CHEESE FILLING

4 tablespoons butter or margarine
¾ cup sugar
6 ounces American cheese, grated
1 tablespoon flour
¼ teaspoon salt
4 eggs
3 cups milk
1 teaspoon vanilla

Cream butter, sugar, cheese, flour, and salt. Add eggs, one at a time; cream well. Add milk and vanilla.

Burton's Restaurant, from 1932-55, was considered to be one of downtown Jackson, Mississippi's best restaurants. It was located on Capitol Street between the Heidelberg Hotel and the Paramount Theater. All of these establishments are closed but memories still linger for many.

OLD-FASHIONED MUSCADINE PIE

The purple hulls are pretty in a lattice crust

2 cups muscadines
⅛ teaspoon salt
2 tablespoons butter
1 cup sugar
2 tablespoons flour
1 egg, slightly beaten
¼ teaspoon almond extract
1 8-inch pie crust with lattice top,
  unbaked

Separate hulls from pulp. Drop hulls into an enamel saucepan, cover, and steam for 2 to 3 minutes. In another enamel pan heat the pulp and pour through a sieve to remove seeds. Add to the hulls. Add salt. Cream butter, add sugar, flour, and beaten egg. Add almond extract. Pour over grapes and then into an uncooked pie shell. Place pastry in lattice fashion over top. Bake for 1 hour at 300°. Make several pies while grapes are in season and store in the freezer. Concord grapes may be substituted for muscadines. Serves 6.

KENTUCKY TAVERN PIE

A ring of kiwi and orange slices on a cloud of whipped cream

¾ cup sugar
½ cup flour
1¼ cups water
3 egg yolks
½ cup fresh orange juice
1 tablespoon orange rind, grated
2 tablespoons lemon juice
1 9-inch pie shell or graham
   cracker crust
½ pint heavy cream, whipped
¼ cup confectioners' sugar
1 kiwi fruit
1 orange, sectioned with white
   membrane removed
¾ cup grated coconut or moist,
   sweetened packaged coconut

Combine sugar and flour in the top of a double boiler. Stir in water, breaking up any lumps. When the mixture is smooth cook over direct heat for 5 minutes. Add a little of the mixture to slightly beaten egg yolks then add the egg yolks back to mixture. Cook 5 minutes longer over rapidly boiling water, stirring constantly. Remove from heat; add fruit juices and rind. Turn into a baked pie shell or a graham cracker crust and cool. When cool, whip cream and add confectioners' sugar to it slowly. Spread over the top of pie. Place peeled and sliced kiwi fruit and prepared orange sections in a circle on top of whipped cream; sprinkle with moist, sweetened coconut. Serves 6 to 8.

MY COUSIN ELLEN'S ORANGE CHIFFON PIE

A Florida treat with a lively, citrus flavor

1 envelope unflavored gelatin
1 cup sugar
Dash of salt
¾ cup milk
3 egg yolks, slightly beaten
¾ teaspoon grated orange rind
¾ cup prepared frozen orange
   juice
½ teaspoon grated lemon rind
¼ cup lemon juice
1 cup heavy cream, whipped
1 9-inch pastry shell, baked

Mix gelatin, sugar, and salt in saucepan, stir in milk and egg yolks. Cook and stir over medium heat until mixture thickens. Remove from heat; add juices and peels; chill until partially set. Fold in whipped cream and chill until mixture mounds. Scoop into pastry shell. Chill until serving time. Serves 8.

To protect a baked crust from overbrowning when heating a filling in it, put the pie, still in its pan, into an extra pan to protect it from too much heat.

KEY LIME PIE

It's easy to make this tasty, tangy treat

4 eggs, separated
1 14-ounce can sweetened
 condensed milk
½ cup lime juice
1 prepared graham cracker crust
¼ teaspoon cream of tartar
4 tablespoons sugar

Beat egg yolks until light, mix in condensed milk, and slowly add lime juice. Beat mixture briefly until thick and pour into graham cracker crust. Beat egg whites; add cream of tartar; gradually beat in sugar. When mixture holds stiff peaks, smooth it over pie. Bake at 350° for approximately 15 minutes until meringue is golden brown. Chill at least 3 hours before serving. Serves 6 to 8.

Key Lime Pie became popular in the Florida Keys when sweetened condensed milk was introduced in 1856. Cows were scarce in the area, so residents were delighted with the milk and combined it with the tart limes to create a pie. True key limes are grown only in the Keys, so Persian limes, available at most food stores, may be used in this recipe.

JUDY BLACKBURN'S JAPANESE FRUIT PIE

Tastes like chess pie with crunchy pecans and fruit

1 stick butter, softened
1 cup sugar
2 eggs
1 tablespoon vinegar
½ cup pecans, chopped
½ cup golden raisins
½ cup coconut
1 8-inch pie shell, unbaked

Cream butter and sugar thoroughly. Add eggs one at a time; mix in vinegar. Stir in pecans, raisins, and coconut. Pour into unbaked pie shell and bake at 300° for 40-50 minutes. Serves 6 to 8.

Judy Blackburn hails from Jackson, Mississippi.

LEMON CHESS PIE

A jelly-like appearance with a crunchy crust

5 eggs
2 cups sugar
½ cup lemon juice
1 teaspoon cornmeal
1 teaspoon flour
⅛ teaspoon salt
1 9-inch pie shell, unbaked

Lightly beat eggs and mix in the sugar. Add the lemon juice, cornmeal, flour, and salt. Mix well and pour into the pie shell. Bake at 350° for 40 minutes or until brown and a knife inserted near the center comes out clean. Serves 8.

GEORGIANNE'S PEACHES 'N CREAM PIE

Summertime is peach time in the Deep South

1 cup sour cream
²/₃ cup sugar
2 tablespoons flour
¹/₈ teaspoon salt
¹/₂ teaspoon cinnamon
1 teaspoon vanilla
1 egg
2¹/₃ cups peaches, diced
1 8-inch pie shell, unbaked

Cream the sour cream and sugar and beat in the flour, salt, cinnamon, vanilla, and egg. Stir peaches into mixture; pour into unbaked pie shell; bake at 375° for 35 minutes.

TOPPING

¹/₃ cup brown sugar
¹/₄ cup flour
¹/₄ teaspoon cinnamon
¹/₄ cup butter, cut into slivers

Mix ingredients together. Sprinkle over pie and bake 25 more minutes or until firm. Serves 6.

TRANSPARENT PIES IN A STACK

A conversation starter that will feed up to 25 or 30 people

3 cups sugar
2 cups butter
9 eggs, separated
1 pint heavy cream
1 pint of tart jelly (currant,
   muscadine, raspberry)
4 teaspoons vanilla
1 cup light brown sugar
5 9-inch pie shells with flat rims
   (do not flute), unbaked

Cream sugar with butter and egg yolks. Beat in cream, jelly, and vanilla. Whip egg whites and gradually add brown sugar until egg whites make soft rounded peaks. Fold egg-whites mixture into the creamed mixture. Spoon equal amounts into each of the 5 unbaked shells. Filling in each pie should be thin, much less than the normal pie. Bake 10 minutes at 425°, then at 350° for about 30 minutes, or until fillings are set. Do not stack them until an hour or more before serving, as the fillings could soak into the crust above. After stacking sprinkle with confectioners' sugar if desired, or place a paper lace doily on the top pie and sprinkle confectioners' sugar over it. This will make a lacy pattern on the pie. Makes 25 to 30 thin slices.

Sunday dinners in the South very often included many uncles, aunts, cousins, grandparents, and sometimes second cousins and great aunts and uncles. This was a popular pie for such an occasion.

MOTHER'S PEAR MINCEMEAT PIE

A Christmas tradition at Jo's house

3 cups prepared mincemeat
1 egg
⅓ cup milk
1 tablespoon flour
1 tart apple, peeled and finely
    diced
½ cup pecans or walnuts,
    chopped
2 to 3 tablespoons brandy
Pastry for double-crusted 9-inch
    pie

Place mincemeat in a bowl. Beat egg slightly and add milk and flour. Mix with the apple and nuts. Add to the mincemeat mixture. Add the brandy, mixing well. Pour into an unbaked 9-inch pie shell. Cover with a top crust or a lattice crust and bake at 450° in a preheated oven for 10 minutes. Reduce heat to 350° and bake for 30 more minutes. Serves 8.

DEEP SOUTH SWEET POTATO PIE

Serve plain or the old-fashioned way — spread with a tart jelly and covered with meringue

1½ cups sweet potatoes, boiled
    and mashed (canned may be
    used)
4 eggs
⅓ cup sugar
2 tablespoons honey
¾ teaspoon cinnamon
¼ teaspoon nutmeg
⅛ teaspoon ground ginger
1 cup light cream
⅛ teaspoon salt
1 teaspoon vanilla flavoring
1 9-inch pie shell, unbaked

Mash the boiled sweet potatoes with a mixer until smooth. Beat 4 eggs very lightly and add to the sweet potatoes. Stir in the sugar and beat all together. Add honey, cinnamon, and nutmeg with the ground ginger, cream, salt, and vanilla flavoring, mixing to blend. Pour the mixture into an unbaked pie shell and bake in a preheated 450° oven for 10 minutes. Reduce the temperature to 350° and bake for 30 minutes longer, or until a knife inserted near the pie's center comes out clean. At this point the pie may be cooled and served with dollops of whipped cream or plain with a cold glass of sweet milk. Pie may also be served spread with ½ cup melted tart jelly over the baked pie, then spread with a meringue and browned. Serves 6 to 8.

    This is the sweet potato pie recipe that was selected to represent the best in Mississippi cuisine at the 1967 Mississippi Marketing Council at Anuga, Cologne, Germany, and the United States Trade Center in London, England. It was kitchen tested by Bobby Ginn, who was then chef at the old Heidelberg Hotel in Jackson.

LOUREA'S SWEET POTATO PIE

Similar to a chess pie, sweet and utterly delicious

1 cup sweet potatoes, mashed
5 eggs
3 cups sugar
4 tablespoons flour
¾ cup butter or margarine,
  melted
1 14-ounce can sweetened
  condensed milk
½ teaspoon vanilla flavor
½ teaspoon nutmeg
1 9-inch pie shell, unbaked

You may use canned sweet potatoes, drained to equal 1 cup, but pared and cooked sweet potatoes freshly dug are traditional. Boil 2 or 3 sweet potatoes in salted water until tender. Peel and mash with slightly beaten eggs, sugar, flour, melted butter, condensed milk, vanilla, and nutmeg. Pour into prepared pie crust and bake at 400° for 15 minutes, then reduce heat to 300° and cook 1 hour or until a knife inserted in the center comes out clean. Pie freezes well. Serves 8.

GREAT PUMPKIN PIE

Best when a whole pumpkin is used

1 whole pumpkin or 1 18-ounce
  can to equal 1¾ cups
¾ cup raisins, preferably white
½ teaspoon salt
1¾ cups half-and-half cream
3 eggs
⅔ cup dark brown sugar, packed
2 tablespoons molasses
2 teaspoons cinnamon
¼ teaspoon cloves
½ teaspoon ginger
½ teaspoon nutmeg
¾ cup chopped toasted pecans
1 9-inch pie shell, unbaked

If using whole pumpkin, scoop out the inside. (Save seeds for toasting another time.) Cut pumpkin into large chunks, peel off outer skin, and dice. Place in unseasoned water and cook until very tender. Mash with an electric mixer or food processor. In a saucepan, with enough water to cover them, boil raisins for 2 minutes. Drain and set aside. Blend the remaining ingredients, except pecans. Add raisins and stir in pecans. Fill uncooked pie shell and bake at 425° for 45-50 minutes or until a knife comes out clean. Both the filling and cooked pumpkin will freeze. Pumpkin pie may be served plain, with dollops of whipped cream, or is delicious with Ginger Sauce (see index for Orange Ice Cream with Ginger Sauce). Serves 6 to 8.

The first pumpkin pie wasn't a pie at all: it was a whole pumpkin with the top sliced out, filled with milk, spices, and honey and baked in hot ashes! The North American Indians sliced pumpkins into long slices and roasted them over the open fire. It wasn't long before Early American housewives learned to split open the pumpkins, remove the seeds, put the halves back together and roast the whole pumpkins in the hearth ovens. Soon the Southern colonists were creating our favorites of today with the pumpkin pulp.

MY GRANDMOTHER'S FROZEN LEMON PIE

From Mary Leigh's grandmother — a fabulous cook

3 egg yolks
¾ cup sugar
4 tablespoons lemon juice
3 teaspoons grated lemon rind
3 egg whites
½ pint heavy cream
8-inch vanilla wafer crust

Stir together egg yolks, sugar, lemon juice, and rind. Cook in a double boiler over simmering water until thick. Cool thoroughly. Whip egg whites; add custard. Whip cream and add mixture. Pour into vanilla wafer crust and freeze until serving time. This dessert is even better when topped with Blueberry Sauce (see index for recipe). Serves 6 to 8.

TILLIE'S LEMON PIE

Old-fashioned, country-kitchen flavor

1 cup sugar
¼ cup cornstarch
⅛ teaspoon salt
3 eggs, separated
1 cup hot water
1 tablespoon butter, melted
1 teaspoon grated lemon rind
⅓ cup lemon juice
1 9-inch pie shell, baked
3 tablespoons sugar

Mix sugar, cornstarch, and salt in the top of a double boiler. Gradually stir in egg yolks, then slowly add hot water and melted butter. Cook over boiling water, stirring constantly with a spoon or wire whisk until thick. Remove from heat. Stir in lemon rind and juice. Pour into baked pastry shell. Beat egg whites until stiff but not dry; add sugar gradually. Continue beating until stiff peaks form. Mound over pie filling. Bake in 375° oven for 15 minutes or until brown. Serves 6 to 8.

MY GRANDMOTHER'S DEEP-DISH APPLE PIE

Apples, cinnamon, and brown sugar — perfect for fall

5-6 cups apples, pared and cut
   into small pieces
¾ cup light brown sugar
2 tablespoons flour
¼ teaspoon cinnamon
1 tablespoon lemon juice
1 tablespoon or more butter
1 pie crust, unbaked

Toss apple pieces, brown sugar, flour, cinnamon, and lemon juice in a bowl until apple pieces are well coated. Place them in a deep pie plate or casserole. Dot with butter. Top with a pie crust, bringing edges over sides of dish and pressing them with a fork. Prick crust in several places with a fork. Bake at 350° for 30-40 minutes or until done. Serve plain or with cream or hard sauce. Serves 6 to 8.

COLONIAL CRANBERRY PIE

Hot or cold this pie is as delicious as it is beautiful

3 eggs
1 cup dark corn syrup
⅔ cup sugar
4 tablespoons butter
1½ cups fresh cranberries,
   coarsely chopped
¾ cup pecan or walnut halves
1 9-inch pie shell, unbaked

Beat the eggs just until blended. Stir in corn syrup, sugar, and butter. Sprinkle the cranberries into the pie shell. Place pecans over cranberries in an attractive pattern. Pour syrup over nuts and berries. Bake for 50 to 55 minutes in a preheated 325° oven until a knife inserted halfway between the center and the edge of the pie comes out clean. If the pie seems to be browning too quickly, cover it with a foil pie plate. Cool before serving. Serves 6 to 8.

MISSISSIPPI MUD PIE

An ice cream, whipped cream, coffee, and chocolate delight

1 quart coffee ice cream
1 Nut Shell Pie Crust (see index
   for recipe), cooled
1 cup Chocolate Sauce (see recipe
   below)
½ pint heavy cream
¼ cup confectioners' sugar
1 tablespoon dark crème de cacao
   (optional)
¼ cup chopped pecans
Shaved semisweet chocolate for
   garnish

Slightly soften the coffee ice cream. Pile it into the cooled nut crust and smooth the top. Cover with foil and place in the freezer until ice cream is firm. Remove from the freezer and top with the Chocolate Sauce. Smooth out and return to freezer for 8 hours. To serve, whip the cream adding confectioners' sugar a little at a time. Add crème de cacao. Smooth over pie. Sprinkle chopped pecans and shaved chocolate over the whipped cream. If the sauce drips a little don't worry — this is why we call it mud pie. It is the color of mud and wonderfully messy eating. Serves 8.

CHOCOLATE SAUCE

4 1-ounce (4 squares)
   unsweetened chocolate
⅔ cup strong coffee
1 cup sugar

Melt chocolate and coffee in a saucepan (see instructions in Dotsy Peel's Coffee Ice Cream recipe for making strong coffee). Cook, stirring constantly, over low heat until chocolate melts and mixture is smooth. Stir in sugar and cook, stirring constantly, until sugar dissolves. Cool and refrigerate. Will keep at least a week. Makes 1½ cups sauce.

"No soil on earth is so dear to our eyes
As the soil we first stirred in terrestrial pies."
Poem was taken from a turn-of-the-century Central Presbyterian Church cookbook from Jackson, Mississippi. The author is unknown.

AUNT CARO'S CHOCOLATE PIE

A sought-after "secret recipe"

3 cups sugar
¾ cup flour
5 tablespoons cocoa
8 egg yolks, slightly beaten
1 12-ounce can evaporated milk
1 cup water
3 tablespoons butter
2 teaspoons vanilla
2 9-inch pie shells, baked and
   cooled
8 egg whites
⅛ teaspoon salt
1 cup sugar

Mix the dry ingredients. Add slightly beaten egg yolks to milk and water; add to dry ingredients. Cook slowly over low heat, stirring constantly until thickened. Add butter and vanilla; mix well. Pour into cooled pie shells. Make meringue by beating egg whites until foamy; add salt. Add sugar one tablespoon at a time while beating. Beat until stiff peaks form, but not dry. Spread on filled pie shells, sealing edges carefully. Bake in a preheated 325° oven for 15 minutes or until lightly browned. Serves 6 to 8.

Aunt Caro was Post Mistress in a small town in Mississippi for forty years. Every special occasion called for one of her chocolate meringue pies. When people begged for the recipe she would just smile and bake them a pie — still not revealing the recipe. Virginia Carlton asked for the recipe when she was a young bride marrying into the Carlton family. Aunt Caro gave it to her but made her promise not to reveal the secret until her death.

MOM'S APPLE PIE

Jo's children's favorite pie

3 cups tart apples
¼ cup sugar
2 tablespoons flour
1 tablespoon lemon juice
¼ teaspoon cinnamon
¼ teaspoon nutmeg
2 tablespoons butter, melted
½ cup brown sugar, packed
Pastry for double-crusted 9-inch
   pie

Peel and slice the apples thinly. Combine the sugar, flour, lemon juice, cinnamon, nutmeg, melted butter, and brown sugar. Stir into the apples, coating them well. Pour into unbaked pie shell. Top with remaining pastry. Cut slits in the top of the pastry and brush with a beaten egg mixed with a teaspoon of water. Bake in a preheated 400° oven for 45 minutes. Serves 6.

When placing dough into a pie pan, roll it onto your rolling pin. Unroll it onto the pan.

CROSS CREEK'S BLACK BOTTOM PIE

The Yearling *was written at Cross Creek, located in the Florida Everglades*

**14 crisp ginger cookies, crumbled
  fine**
5 tablespoons butter, melted

BASIC FILLING

1 tablespoon gelatin
4 tablespoons cold water
1¾ cups milk
½ cup sugar
1 tablespoon cornstarch
⅛ teaspoon salt
4 egg yolks, beaten

CHOCOLATE LAYER

2 squares chocolate, melted
1 teaspoon vanilla

RUM LAYER

4 egg whites
⅛ teaspoon cream of tartar
½ cup sugar
1 tablespoon rum

TOPPING

1 cup heavy cream
**2 tablespoons confectioners'
  sugar**
Chocolate, grated

Mix the crumbs and butter together and line a pie plate with the mixture. Bake at 250° for 10 minutes. Cool.

Soak gelatin in cold water. Scald milk and add sugar mixed with cornstarch, salt, and beaten yolks. Cook in a double boiler, stirring constantly until it coats the back of a spoon. Stir in dissolved gelatin. Divide custard in half. To one half, add melted chocolate and vanilla. Turn while hot into cooled crust, dipping carefully so as not to ruin crust. Cool remaining half of custard. Beat whites and cream of tartar, adding sugar slowly. Blend with cooled custard; add rum. Spread carefully over chocolate layer. Chill thoroughly, even overnight. When ready to serve, whip cream with the confectioners' sugar. Pile on top of pie; sprinkle with grated chocolate. Serves 6 to 8.

Mary Leigh's brother, Roy Hendee, found this recipe in Highland School Parent Teacher Association Cook Book, *published in 1950. It was submitted by Mrs. B. G. Rawlins. A chocolate wafer crust may be substituted, if desired.*

For baking unfilled pie shells, prick all over with tines of fork or weight the bottom of crust with dried beans or rice. Remove the beans or rice a few minutes before baking time is over.

OSGOOD PIE

An heirloom from the Moon family in Troup, Texas

¼ cup margarine, room
   temperature
1 cup sugar
¼ teaspoon nutmeg
¼ teaspoon allspice
¼ teaspoon cinnamon
2 eggs
1 tablespoon vinegar
½ cup pecans, chopped
½ cup raisins
1 8-inch pie crust, unbaked
Whipped cream (optional)

Cream margarine and sugar; mix in spices. Beat in eggs. Add vinegar. Stir in pecans and raisins. Pour into 8-inch crust and bake at 350° for 30 minutes. May be served with whipped cream but is delicious without it. Serves 6.

Osgood Pie is sometimes called "Oh So Good" Pie.

THE HUNGRY POTTER'S SAWDUST PIE

This famous pie gets its name from the graham cracker crumbs

1½ cups sugar
1½ cups graham cracker crumbs
1½ cups shredded coconut
1½ cups nuts, walnuts or pecans,
   coarsely chopped
½ cup chocolate chips
7 egg whites, slightly beaten
1 10-inch pie shell, unbaked

Mix all of the ingredients together in the order given, by hand. A mixer would break up the pieces. This will turn into a gooey mixture. Turn it into the pie shell. Bake in a 350° oven for 35 to 40 minutes or until the center is firm. Do not cut until it is cool. Serve warm with whipped cream. Serves 8.

The Hungry Potter Restaurant is located in Marshall, Texas.

When lining a pie plate with pastry, ease it onto the pie plate. If the pastry is stretched it will shrink after baking.

KENTUCKY BLUEGRASS PIE

Turns any day into Derby Day

1 stick butter
¾ cup sugar
4 tablespoons flour
½ cup white corn syrup
4 eggs
3 tablespoons bourbon
½ cup chocolate chips
1 cup pecans, chopped
1 9-inch pie shell, unbaked

Melt butter over low heat. Combine sugar and flour in mixer bowl. Mix in butter and corn syrup. Add eggs separately, beating after each addition. Add bourbon. Stir in chocolate chips and pecans. Pour into unbaked crust and bake at 350° for 45 minutes. May be served with whipped cream, if desired. Serves 8.

BETTY EVERETT'S PECAN PIE

A Southern classic that is surprisingly easy to make

½ stick margarine, softened
½ cup sugar
4 large eggs, slightly beaten
1 cup light corn syrup
½ teaspoon vanilla
⅛ teaspoon salt
1 cup chopped pecans
1 9-inch pie shell, unbaked
¼ cup pecan halves

Cream margarine and sugar well. Add beaten eggs and blend well. Add light corn syrup, vanilla, and salt. Stir in chopped pecans and pour mixture into unbaked pie shell. Arrange pecan halves on top for decoration. Bake at 350° for 1 hour. Serves 8.

MISS LILLIAN'S PECAN PIE

Easy but unusual preparation

3 eggs
1 cup sugar, divided in half
2 tablespoons flour
1 cup dark corn syrup
1 teaspoon vanilla
⅛ teaspoon salt
1 tablespoon butter or margarine, melted
1 cup pecans, chopped
1 9-inch pie shell, unbaked

Lightly beat eggs and gradually add ½ cup sugar. Mix flour with remaining ½ cup sugar and add to egg mixture. Add syrup, vanilla, and salt. Pour melted butter over pecans which have been placed in a bowl. Stir well. Combine with syrup mixture and pour into a 9-inch unbaked crust. Bake at 350° for 45 minutes or until pie doesn't shake. Serves 8.

CHOCOLATE FUDGE PIE

Marvelous alone, superb topped with vanilla ice cream

1 stick butter
3 squares unsweetened chocolate
4 eggs
3 tablespoons white karo
1 cup sugar
Dash of salt
1 teaspoon vanilla
1 9-inch pie shell, unbaked

Melt butter and chocolate in top of a double boiler. Cool slightly. Beat eggs with mixer until thick. Mix in syrup, sugar, salt, and vanilla. Add chocolate mixture. Combine well and pour into pie shell. Bake at 350° for 25 to 30 minutes, or until filling is set but slightly soft. It will become firmer when cool. Serves 6 to 8.

SMOKY MOUNTAIN OATMEAL PIE

A delicious "poor man's" pecan pie

¾ cup granulated sugar
6 tablespoons butter, melted
¾ cup corn syrup
3 eggs, beaten
1 teaspoon vanilla
¾ cup quick rolled oats,
    uncooked (do not use instant)
⅛ teaspoon salt
1 9-inch pie shell, unbaked

Mix the sugar, melted butter, and corn syrup together. Beat in eggs, vanilla, oats, and salt. Pour into pie crust. Bake at 350° for 30 to 35 minutes. Serves 8.

BUTTERSCOTCH PIE

Rich and creamy

3 eggs, separated
1 cup dark brown sugar
3 tablespoons flour
1 cup heavy cream
3 tablespoons water
2 tablespoons butter, melted
⅛ teaspoon salt
1 teaspoon vanilla
1 9-inch pie shell, baked
¼ cup sugar

Place egg yolks in a saucepan. Add brown sugar, flour, cream, water, butter, salt, and vanilla. Stir over low heat until it just comes to a boil. It should be fairly thick at this point and will thicken more as it cools. Pour the mixture into a baked pie shell. Make the meringue by beating the 3 egg whites until stiff peaks form. Sweeten to taste with sugar and brown in a preheated 425° oven for 5 minutes. Makes 1 9-inch pie. Serves 6 to 8.

ELLEN'S CHOCOLATE ANGEL PIE

A cloud of meringue filled with chocolate and whipped cream

3 egg whites
¼ teaspoon cream of tartar
⅔ cup sugar
½ cup pecans, finely chopped
¾ teaspoon vanilla
1 4-ounce sweet bakers' chocolate
3 tablespoons water
1 tablespoon crème de cacao
2 cups heavy cream
2 tablespoons sugar
½ teaspoon vanilla
Shaved chocolate

Grease an 8-inch pie pan. Preheat oven to 300°. Beat egg whites until bubbly. Add cream of tartar. Beat until soft peaks form; gradually add sugar; continue beating until stiff peaks form. Stir in nuts and vanilla. Pour into pie pan, forming a nest. Bake 50 minutes at 300°. Cool. Melt chocolate mixed with water in a double boiler, stirring constantly. Cool. Stir in crème de cacao. Whip 1 cup cream and fold into chocolate mixture. Pour into meringue shell; chill 2 hours. Whip remaining cream, sweeten with sugar, and flavor with vanilla. Pile on top of chocolate filling. Garnish with shaved chocolate. Serves 8.

MATILDA'S WHITE CHOCOLATE PIE

A beautiful red and white creation from Atlanta

12 ounces white chocolate,
  coarsely chopped
3 tablespoons unsalted butter
⅓ cup heavy cream
3 tablespoons crème de cacao
1½ teaspoons vanilla
¼ teaspoon almond extract
1⅔ cups heavy cream
2 egg whites, room temperature
2 tablespoons sugar
1 9-inch Almond Pie Crust (see
  index for recipe)
1 cup raspberries or strawberries
½ pint whipping cream for
  garnish

In the top of a double boiler place chocolate, butter, and ⅓ cup cream. Cook over gently simmering water, stirring until smooth. Remove from heat and set in a bowl filled with ice and water. Let cool until thick and the consistency of paste. Stir occasionally. Blend in liqueur, vanilla, and almond extract. Beat 1⅔ cups cream until stiff peaks form. Gently beat in chocolate mixture. Beat egg whites until soft peaks form. Add sugar 1 tablespoon at a time, beating until stiff but not dry. Fold gently into chocolate-cream mixture. Pour into a 9-inch almond pie crust. Smooth the top. Freeze until firm, but not frozen hard, about 5 hours. When ready to serve, mound raspberries or strawberries in the center and pipe whipped cream around the outside edges. Serves 8.

WESTBROOK'S GRASSHOPPER PIE

Wonderful anytime, but especially after a seafood dinner

1 (8½-ounce) box chocolate
  wafers, crushed fine
¾ stick butter, melted

Mix crumbs and butter (reserving ¼ cup crumbs for topping). Press crumb mixture into a 9-inch pan and chill.

FILLING

6 tablespoons crème de menthe
3 tablespoons clear crème de
  cacao
36 large marshmallows
2 heaping tablespoons vanilla ice
  cream
1½ cartons heavy cream

Heat crème de menthe, crème de cacao, and marshmallows in top of double boiler until marshmallows are melted. Cool. Add ice cream to heavy cream and whip until very stiff. Gently fold in cooled marshmallow mixture until blended well. Pour into chilled pie crust and sprinkle reserved crumbs over top. Refrigerate. Better if made the day before serving. Serves 6 to 8.

RUM CREAM PIE

From Chalet Suzanne in Lake Wales, Florida

6 egg yolks
1 scant cup sugar
1 envelope gelatin
½ cup cold water
1 pint heavy cream, whipped
½ cup dark rum
1 9-inch graham cracker pie shell
Bittersweet chocolate or pistachio
  nuts, finely chopped
Whipped cream (optional)

Beat egg yolks until light and add 1 scant cup sugar. Soak gelatin in cold water. Place the gelatin and water over a low flame, bring it to a boil, and pour it over the sugar-egg mixture, stirring briskly. Whip cream until stiff, fold it into the egg mixture, and flavor with rum. Cool until the mixture begins to set and pour it into the pie shell. Chill until firm. Sprinkle the top of the pie generously with shaved bittersweet chocolate curls or finely chopped pistachio nuts, garnish with whipped cream, if desired, and serve cold. Serves 6 to 8.

The Hinshaw family has been welcoming guests to this charming inn for over fifty years. Their award-winning restaurant has been praised by food writers of national renown.

𝒫ies that are to be served chilled are better served in a crumb crust than a pastry one.

SCARLETT O'HARA'S RIBBON PIE

Perfect for St. Patrick's Day

1 envelope unflavored gelatin
¾ cup sugar
2 cups milk
4 eggs, separated
1 tablespoon cornstarch
½ cup heavy cream
1 ounce (1 square) unsweetened
   chocolate
1 ounce (1 square) semisweet
   chocolate
3 tablespoons crème de menthe
1 9-inch pie shell, baked and
   cooled
Chocolate Shamrocks for garnish
   (see below)

Mix gelatin and ½ cup sugar in the top of a double boiler. Stir in the milk gradually and set over boiling water. Cook to the scalding point. Beat yolks with cornstarch until foamy. Stir a little of the hot mixture into the yolks and the yolks back into the milk-sugar mixture. Cook over boiling water, stirring until thickened. Chill until it starts to congeal. Beat egg whites until stiff; gradually beat in remaining ¼ cup sugar. Beat cream until thick. Beat chilled custard mixture until fluffy; fold egg whites then whipped cream into the custard. Divide mixture. Melt chocolate and fold into half of the mixture. Fold crème de menthe into the other half. Pour chocolate mixture into the cooled crust first; chill for 5 minutes. Fold crème de menthe mixture onto top and spread. Chill thoroughly until firm. Decorate with Chocolate Shamrocks. Serves 6 to 8.

CHOCOLATE SHAMROCKS

6 ounces semisweet chocolate
Shamrock cookie cutters

Melt chocolate and cool slightly (this can be done in the microwave). Line a cookie sheet with aluminum foil; pour the chocolate onto the baking sheet and gently shake it until chocolate is smooth and level and is about ⅛ inch thick. Let stand until partially set. Use a cookie cutter to outline the shapes; let stand until chocolate hardens. Reposition the cutters over the outline and cut out. Lift the cutter up, and remove the shamrock by gently pressing through the cutter with a wooden utensil. (Don't use fingers, it will leave a print on the leaves.) To store, place between wax paper and keep in a cool, dry place, away from extremes in temperature.

Cut meringue cleanly by coating both sides of knife lightly with butter.

CYPRESS INN'S PEANUT BUTTER PIE

A mocha sauce is spread over a frozen peanut butter filling

2 cups creamy peanut butter
2 cups sugar
2 8-ounce packages cream cheese
2 teaspoons vanilla
1½ cups heavy cream, whipped
2 chocolate-wafer crusts
6 ounces semisweet chocolate
7 tablespoons hot coffee (brewed)

In a food processor or with a mixer cream the peanut butter, sugar, cream cheese, and vanilla. Beat cream until soft peaks form. Add whipped cream to the peanut butter mixture and blend. Spoon into the 2 chocolate-wafer crusts. Place in the freezer uncovered until set, about 30 to 45 minutes. Melt chocolate with the coffee and spread on top of filling. Place uncovered in freezer until set, about 15 minutes. May be covered after this and frozen for a longer period of time. One pie serves 6 to 8. Two will serve 12 to 16.

Cypress Inn Restaurant overlooks the Black Warrior River in Tuscaloosa, Alabama.

MISSISSIPPI FIRST FROST PIE

Refreshing as an autumn morning

2 cups sifted all-purpose flour
½ teaspoon salt
2 teaspoons sugar
11 tablespoons unsalted butter,
  cut into chips
1 whole egg, beaten with ice
  water to equal 5½ tablespoons

Mix flour, salt, and sugar on a clean counter top. With your fingertips mix in the cold butter chips until they are the size of peas. With your finger make a trench down the middle of the flour mixture. Add about 2 tablespoons of the egg-water mixture and fluff in with your extended fingertips, intermeshing at the tips. Continue in this manner until the liquid is incorporated. Form the pastry into a rough ball. Press small portions of it with the heel of your hand, gently smearing it across the counter. When this process is completed, using all the dough in small portions reform the ball and repeat this step. When done reform the ball, wrap in plastic wrap, and refrigerate a minimum of 1 hour before using. Reserve one-third of the pastry in the refrigerator. Roll the remaining two-thirds and line an 8-inch pie pan. Trim to the edge and leave plain. Roll the scraps and reserved pastry and cut into triangular pieces about 2½ inches on a side. Continue until you have about 18 triangles. Place 6 of these around the edge of the pan and press to seal onto the pastry lining the pan. Roll small cylinders of aluminum foil to place under the triangle points so the triangles will resemble flower petals. Repeat using 6 more triangles. Drape the remaining 6 triangles over a foil-wrapped rolling pin on a cookie sheet. One side of the triangles should be parallel to the long axis of the rolling pin. Return all pastry to the refrigerator while you prepare the filling.

PIE FILLING

1 cup drained, finely chopped watermelon rind preserves
1 cup pecans
Reserved preserve syrup mixed with white karo to equal 1½ cups
¼ cup sugar mixed with 1 tablespoon flour
4 eggs, beaten
Pinch of salt
½ teaspoon ground ginger
1 tablespoon bourbon
2 tablespoons melted butter

Preheat oven to 350°. Mix the chopped watermelon rind preserves, pecans, syrups, and sugar-flour mixture. Add 4 beaten eggs, salt, flavorings, and melted butter. Pour into uncooked pie shell. Bake the pie and pastry triangles until done, approximately 1 hour for the pie. Cover the pie edges with foil strips if it browns before the filling is firm. Remove from oven. Remove foil supports and cool.

WHITE CHOCOLATE GANACHE

8 ounces white chocolate
¾ cup heavy cream
½ teaspoon ground ginger

When the pie is cool chop white chocolate finely. Scald ¾ cup heavy cream. Pour hot cream over chocolate, beating with an electric beater to mix. Add ginger. Cool the mixture over ice while beating. Beat to the texture of softly whipped cream. Spread on top of the pie. Place cooked pastry triangles around to make another circle of petals. Keep in a cool place before serving.

This recipe, which was created by Barbara Kroeze, was selected by a panel of judges, headed by Craig Claiborne, to receive the dessert award at the 1988 March of Dimes Gala in Jackson, Mississippi.

TEXAS CREAM PIE

Cool and creamy refrigerator pie

1½ cups milk, scalded
3 egg yolks, beaten
½ cup sugar
⅛ teaspoon salt
1 tablespoon plain gelatin
¼ cup cold water
3 egg whites, stiffly beaten
1½ teaspoons vanilla
½ teaspoon nutmeg
1 9-inch pie shell, baked
½ cup heavy cream
4 tablespoons sugar
Semisweet chocolate, grated

Cook milk, egg yolks, sugar, and salt in the top of a double boiler over hot water, stirring constantly, until the mixture coats the back of a spoon. Add gelatin dissolved in cold water and cool. Fold in beaten egg whites and add vanilla and nutmeg. Pour into baked pie shell and chill. Whip cream and flavor with sugar. Smooth on top of pie and decorate with grated chocolate. Serves 8.

GRANDMOTHER'S PEACH COBBLER

Melts in your mouth

1 cup flour
⅛ teaspoon salt
½ cup shortening
3 tablespoons ice water
½ cup butter
4 cups peaches (about 9
    medium), peeled and sliced
1½ cups water
1½ cups sugar
2 tablespoons flour
⅛ teaspoon cinnamon
⅛ teaspoon almond extract
Beaten egg white
Sugar
Cream

Combine first 3 ingredients with a fork or pastry blender to make pastry. Add ice water. Form dough. Wrap in wax paper and chill for 8 hours. When ready to make the cobbler, roll out pastry and cut into strips. Reserve enough strips to make a lattice top on cobbler. Place remaining strips on a cookie sheet and bake at 450° for 10 minutes or until crisp. To make the filling, mix butter, peaches, and water in a saucepan. Bring to a boil. Blend sugar, flour, and cinnamon, stirring into boiling mixture until dissolved. Remove from heat and add almond extract. Grease an 8½ x 9½ inch baking dish. Place half the peach mixture in dish; top with cooked pastry strips. Add remaining peach mixture and place uncooked pastry strips over top in lattice fashion. Brush with beaten egg white and sprinkle with a little sugar. Bake at 375° for 35 to 40 minutes. Serve warm with cream. Serves 8.

DEEP-DISH BLACKBERRY COBBLER

Juicy and crusty

1 cup flour
⅛ teaspoon salt
½ cup shortening
3 tablespoons ice water
6 cups blackberries, divided
1 cup sugar
2 tablespoons cornstarch
6 tablespoons butter
Beaten egg white
Sugar

Combine first 3 ingredients with a fork or a pastry blender to make pastry. Add ice water. Form dough. Wrap in wax paper and chill for 8 hours. When ready to make the cobbler, roll out pastry and cut half of the dough into strips. Reserve the other half of dough for the top crust. Place remaining strips on a cookie sheet and bake at 450° for 10 minutes or until crisp. Cover 4 cups blackberries with water, barely covering. Cook over medium heat until berries are tender. Mash berries through sieve. Add sugar, cornstarch, butter, and remaining 2 cups blackberries. Bring to a boil. Stir and remove from heat. Grease an 8½ x 9½ inch baking dish. Place half of the blackberry mixture in dish; top with cooked pastry strips. Add remaining blackberry mixture and place uncooked pastry over the top. Brush with beaten egg white and sprinkle with a little sugar. Bake at 375° for 35 minutes or until brown. Serve warm as is or splash with blackberry brandy and top with whipped cream sweetened with confectioners' sugar. Serves 8.

HOT CARAMEL DUMPLINGS

An old recipe — quick, easy, and inexpensive

2 tablespoons butter
1½ cups dark brown sugar, firmly
   packed
1½ cups boiling water
⅛ teaspoon salt
1¼ cups flour
1½ teaspoons baking powder
⅓ cup sugar
⅛ teaspoon salt
2 tablespoons butter
½ cup milk
½ teaspoon vanilla

To make sauce, place butter, brown sugar, boiling water, and salt in a heavy saucepan with a tight-fitting lid. Boil gently while preparing dumpling dough. To make the dough, sift together flour, baking powder, sugar, and salt. Cut in the butter; add milk, then vanilla. Mix thoroughly. Drop rounded teaspoonsful into the boiling caramel sauce. Cover tightly. Boil gently over low heat for 20 minutes without removing cover. Serve immediately. Serves 6.

CHOCOLATE PECAN PIE

From the Grand Hotel in Point Clear, Alabama

½ cup plus 2 tablespoons brown
  sugar
¾ cup granulated sugar
2 tablespoons cake flour
⅛ teaspoon salt
1 ounce butter, melted
4 ounces semisweet chocolate,
  melted
4 eggs
1 cup pecans, chopped
1 deep 9-inch pie shell

Combine dry ingredients, stirring well to eliminate lumps. Add melted butter and chocolate slowly and blend thoroughly with mixer. Beat in eggs. Let stand at least 3 hours before baking (after resting, it may separate). Stir the mixture. Place the pecan pieces in the unbaked pie shell. Fill with the chocolate mixture and bake at 325° for about 50 to 55 minutes or until firm. If the pie starts to crack, lower the temperature until finished baking. Serves 8.

Marriott's Grand Hotel, one of the South's most famous resorts, is located on Mobile Bay.

MAMA SEBREN'S EGG CUSTARD PIE

Family recipe from Maggie McKee of Florence, Mississippi

3 eggs, separated
1 whole egg
⅔ cup sugar
2 cups milk
1 teaspoon vanilla
⅛ teaspoon salt
1 9-inch pie shell, unbaked
Nutmeg
6 tablespoons sugar
¼ teaspoon cream of tartar

Beat egg yolks and whole egg slightly. Don't overbeat. Mix in ⅔ cup sugar, the milk, vanilla, and salt. Pour into unbaked pie shell and sprinkle nutmeg over top. Bake at 350° for 30 to 40 minutes, or until you can insert a knife and it will come out clean. Meanwhile, make meringue. Beat 3 egg whites until foamy; add 6 tablespoons sugar and cream of tartar. Spread over pie and brown at 400° for 7 or 8 minutes, watching carefully. Serves 8.

You may make baskets for tarts by forming handles with strips of dough molded over custard cups. When baked, sink the handles into the filling just before serving.

AFTERNOON TEA TARTS

Stack pastry rounds with your favorite fruit pie filling

12 Cheese Pastry Rounds (4 each
  of 3-inch, 2-inch, and 1½-inch)
12 Nut Pastry Rounds, cut as
  above
12 Cinnamon Sugar Pastry
  Rounds, cut as above
1 recipe apple or pear pie filling
1 recipe blueberry or blackberry
  pie filling
1 recipe cherry or cranberry pie
  filling

Prepare pastry rounds (recipes below). Serve rounds on a large platter with bowls of 3 assorted pie fillings and whipped cream. For each tart, stack 3 pastry rounds in ascending order (largest round on the bottom) with pie fillings between each round. Top with whipped cream. Makes 12 three-layered tarts.

CHEESE PASTRY ROUNDS

1 cup self-rising flour
½ cup cheddar cheese, grated
⅓ cup shortening
3 tablespoons hot water

Mix flour and cheese. Cut in shortening. Sprinkle with hot water. Stir with a fork until dough forms a ball. Let stand 20 to 30 minutes. Roll as for pie crust. Cut in circles using about 3-inch, 2-inch, and 1½-inch cutters. Cut 4 rounds of each size. Place on baking sheet. Bake at 450° for 8 to 10 minutes.

NUT PASTRY ROUNDS

1 cup self-rising flour
¼ cup walnuts or pecans, finely
  chopped
⅓ cup shortening
3 tablespoons hot water

Mix flour and nuts. Cut in shortening. Sprinkle with hot water. Stir with a fork until dough forms a ball. Let stand 20 to 30 minutes. Roll as for pie crust. Cut in circles as above and place on a baking sheet. Bake at 450° for 8 to 10 minutes.

CINNAMON SUGAR PASTRY ROUNDS

⅓ cup shortening
1 cup self-rising flour
3 tablespoons hot water
1 egg white, slightly beaten
Cinnamon
Sugar

Cut shortening into the flour. Sprinkle with hot water. Stir with a fork until dough forms a ball. Let stand 20 to 30 minutes. Roll as for pie crust. Cut in circles as above. Place on a baking sheet. Brush with an egg white, slightly beaten; sprinkle with cinnamon and sugar. Bake at 450° for 8 to 10 minutes.

EMPANADITAS

Miniature Mexican dessert turnovers

Pastry for Plain Ice Water Pie
  Crust, chilled (see index)
Sweet Potato-Pineapple Filling
  (see below)
Cheese-Raisin Filling (see below)
¼ cup butter, melted
1 cup sugar
1 tablespoon cinnamon

Roll chilled pie crust dough ⅛ inch thick and cut into 3-inch circles. Spoon one of the fillings on one side of each circle. Dampen edges of dough, fold over, and press edges together with a fork. Brush with melted butter. Bake in a preheated 400° oven for 20 minutes or until brown. Roll in a mixture of sugar and cinnamon. Makes about 3 dozen Empanaditas.

SWEET POTATO-PINEAPPLE FILLING

1 cup sweet potatoes, cooked
½ cup chopped blanched
  almonds
1 cup (9-ounce can) crushed
  pineapple, drained
¼ teaspoon salt
1½ tablespoons sugar

Mash sweet potatoes with a mixer until smooth. Add blanched chopped almonds, drained pineapple, salt, and sugar. Mix well. Chill until ready to use. Makes about 2¼ cups.

CHEESE RAISIN FILLING

1 cup country-style cottage cheese
1 egg, well beaten
½ cup sugar
¼ teaspoon cinnamon
¼ teaspoon salt
½ cup golden raisins

Mash cottage cheese with a fork or the back of a spoon; blend in the well-beaten egg, sugar, cinnamon, and salt. Stir in the golden raisins. Chill until ready to use. Makes about 1½ cups.

Index

A primitive grist mill near Chattanooga, Tennessee.